Re-reading Popular Culture

In memory of my father, Wim Hermes (1924–2000)

Re-reading Popular Culture

Joke Hermes

Blackwell
Publishing

BLACKWELL PUBLISHING
350 Main Street, Malden, MA 02148-5020, USA
9600 Garsington Road, Oxford OX4 2DQ, UK
550 Swanston Street, Carlton, Victoria 3053, Australia

First published 2005 by Blackwell Publishing Ltd

1   2005

Library of Congress Cataloging-in-Publication Data

Hermes, Joke.
  Re-reading popular culture / Joke Hermes.
    p. cm.
  Includes bibliographical references and index.
  ISBN-13: 978-1-4051-2244-3 (hard cover : alk. paper)
  ISBN-10: 1-4051-2244-7 (hard cover : alk. paper)
  ISBN-13: 978-1-4051-2245-0 (pbk. : alk. paper)
  ISBN-10: 1-4051-2245-5 (pbk. : alk. paper)
  1. Popular culture.   2. Arts, Modern—21st century.   3. Arts, Modern—20th century.
I. Title. '

  CB428.H48 2005
  306—dc22

                                                              2005008924

A catalogue record for this title is available from the British Library.

Set in 10.5 / 13pt Dante
by Graphicraft Limited, Hong Kong
Printed and bound in Great Britain
by TJ International Ltd, Padstow, Cornwall

The publisher's policy is to use permanent paper from mills that operate a sustainable forestry policy, and which has been manufactured from pulp processed using acid-free and elementary chlorine-free practices. Furthermore, the publisher ensures that the text paper and cover board used have met acceptable environmental accreditation standards.

For further information on
Blackwell Publishing, visit our website:
www.blackwellpublishing.com

contents

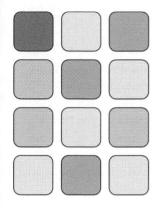

preface and acknowledgments

To defend popular culture is a patently ridiculous project. Those who love it do not need to hear it defended, while those who are not enamored of popular television, detective novels, or sports are unlikely to be convinced (or for that matter reached by this book). The ridiculousness of defending popular culture extends to the identity that you acquire when doing so. To defend popular culture to those who cannot see its merits as a domain that is of interest in and of itself is to label oneself as someone who celebrates popular pleasures, and who is "against" high culture. To celebrate popular culture is not to understand that the world has changed, and that the "old" division between the popular and the arts hardly exists any longer. To defend popular culture is to misunderstand its mind-boggling power to influence us, and it is to confess to a total lack of common sense when it comes to understanding where critical priorities should lie: with politics, power, and how and by whom the world (including the media) is run. To defend popular culture, then, is a way of saying that you are a naïve idiot on several counts – and that hardly presents a coherent picture. To complicate matters further, most writing about popular culture is read as defending it.

It is high time to challenge such a state of affairs. This book does not so much intend to defend popular culture as to take it seriously. But it does not want to do so in an uncritical manner. By my standards, a critical, serious look at popular culture takes into account its qualities and its limitations; by knowing that those of us who like it are not getting what they want, but what they can choose from. Although such choices have an effect in shaping what will be on offer, I readily grant the argument that, as consumers, readers have little control over popular culture. But as viewers and readers we do have a say in how popular culture may have meaning for us. We use popular culture for a variety of means, which includes worthy goals as much as mindless relaxation or routine filling of time. Popular entertainment offers many an opportunity for incidental learning that may make us more receptive to the world around us or have us reflect on our priorities in life.

In popular culture, as in the arts generally, we tend to follow patterns in choosing certain programs, book genres, or artists over others. I do not much care whether this goes under the name of taste or peer group pressure. Taking popular culture seriously means that I do care about how such favorites keep us enthralled and engage our fantasies about who we want to be and how we would like to live our lives. In short, popular culture is connected to who we think we are, to how we understand our responsibilities and rights, how we hold out hope for the future, or how we are critical of the state of things in the environments in which we move and of which we feel we are part.

Popular culture, then, can disclose to those who are interested what collective fantasies we hold, what scenarios and criticisms circulate. Key to understanding popular culture and to assessing its uses is the very massiveness that so often counts against it. Readers and viewers know that there are like-minded others "out there" – as well as others who are critical or misunderstand the appeal of a certain genre or medium entirely. Popular culture is not the stuff of lowest common denominators; it is the stuff of citizenship and connection. It could and should lead to widespread discussion, but it does not often do so because we are not used to understanding popular culture as a resource, as offering tools and content for public discussion. It is still mostly seen as an object of scorn, concern, or bewilderment. It can only offer tools if we learn to re-read it – in so doing, looking beyond its mixed reputation, the money that is made by successful artists or television producers, and the sometimes gross imagery or offensive language – in search of the fantasies and feelings that connect us (with varied intensity) to others. Whether this is called "community" or "affinity" or "cultural citizenship" is immaterial. The point is that we can make much better use of popular culture.

This may sound suspiciously like (a new form of) celebrating popular culture, but wait and read the case studies brought together here. My informants, all of whom I want to thank here for their time and willingness to put their views and experiences into words, are not always appreciative of popular culture. They may use it as a counterweight to daily burdens and irritations, and from time to time they may feel empowered by it – but disappointment is as important a factor. Insofar as this book is about the merits of taking popular culture seriously, it suggests that we do so at the level of hidden public and semi-public agendas, at the meta-level of citizenship. Of course, it is my deep wish that we will one day use popular culture more in public debate as a shared source of references and knowledges. But that requires an altogether much higher level of popular cultural literacy, which, as the final chapter will make clear, requires a major shift in how popular culture is still talked about.

Preface and acknowledgments

I hope that this book presents a level-headed approach to and inventory of what popular culture might have to offer in terms of cultural citizenship. The level-headedness came late, and the book took a long time to mature. There are, as a consequence, many people I need to thank. Any misconceptions and mistakes are, of course, my own.

There are formal thanks to be offered. The broad argument of this book emerged while I was conducting separate research projects. This means that chapters were published as journal articles first, and then revised and revisited here to show how popular culture is instrumental in organizing a sense of belonging and reflection on how we belong. I want to thank the editors and publishers of the *International Journal of Cultural Studies*, *Television and New Media*, *Etnofoor*, and my co-editors of the *European Journal of Cultural Studies* for permission to reuse material, as well as the editors of *International Media Research: A Survey* (John Corner, Philip Schlesinger, and Roger Silverstone) for inviting me to write a chapter on gender and media that, in retrospect, was the start of this book. Most of all, I need to thank Jayne Fargnoli, at Blackwell, the funniest and most elegant e-mailer in my computer's address book, whose enthusiastic endorsement of the project was the last push needed to finish it.

Thanks are also due to a great number of friends and colleagues. Mariette van Staveren, Stefan Dudink, Mieke Aerts, and Myriam Everard offered inspiring discussions of the personal and the political and commented on the earliest chapters of the book. My former colleagues and students at the Department of Communication of the University of Amsterdam, among whom I would especially like to thank Liesbet van Zoonen, Irene Costera Meijer, Kees Brants, and Joost de Bruin, discussed cultural citizenship and popular culture with much enthusiasm. My current colleagues and friends at the Department of Media Studies at the same university, Jaap Kooijman, Maarten Reesink, Vincent Crone, and Rob Leurs, read draft versions of chapters, offered comments and suggestions, and restored my confidence with such varied means as their good company, food and wine, and a number of cooperative projects. I would also like to thank Chris Straayer, Anna McCarthy, Toby Miller, John Hartley, Nick Stevenson, and Gareth Stanton for overseas inspiration and intellectual friendship.

My bimonthly meetings outside the walls of academia with Irene Costera Meijer, Garjan Sterk, and Marianne van den Boomen – where we discuss popular culture, philosophy, and ourselves over dinner – continue to be defining moments of intellectual friendship and of what feminism is all about, from heated discussion to unconditional support. Likewise, I am happy to share a long history with Alkeline van Lenning, Evelien Tonkens, and Monique Volman that dates from editing what was then the Dutch *Journal of Women's Studies* (*Tijdschrift voor Vrouwenstudies*), and to review work, careers, and life in general on a regular basis. I still love being an editor, all the more so for editing the *European Journal of Cultural Studies* with Pertti Alasuutari and Ann Gray. Unlikely trio that we are in some ways, we have built what is to me a precious friendship within a working relationship that extends to our partners and families. When he asked us to start the *Journal*, Pertti did not know that Ann and I negotiated the North Sea on a regular basis to spend time with one another, or that we would consider editorial weekend meetings perfect occasions for good shopping. Without Ann and without Pieter Hilhorst, my partner, I do not know how I would have managed to enjoy life and finish this book. Their support, encouragement, careful reading, and great company has meant that I have been able to do both. It has meant more to me than I can say. Thank you both.

Last but not least, all my family is present in this book. We all enjoy watching television; we exchange books and talk about them. I would not have known of the pleasures of watching football and male gossip without Pieter; and much of my enthusiasm for popular culture comes from sharing it with my mother and sister, Phiet de Haas-Spoel and Hetty Hermes. My father's mystification as to how I can love wholeheartedly what he saw as an area to be approached with caution, and a good measure of nostalgia, has always inspired me never to take my own pleasure in and reference for popular culture for granted. Although I miss him, I do have my wonderful children Sacha and Noah to share an entirely new world of heroines, heroes, and bad guys and girls. Fortunately, they also like to read and be read to, sometimes from the same books that my father read to me, and they laugh at his jokes, which I can't tell half as well. I dedicate this book to him.

Earlier versions of chapters were published as:

- "Burnt orange. Television, gender and ethnicity," *Television and New Media*, 6(1), 2005, 49–70
- "Cultural citizenship and crime fiction. Politics and the interpretive community," *European Journal of Cultural Studies*, 3(2), 2000, 215–32 (with Cindy Stello)
- "Of irritation, texts and men. Feminist audience studies and cultural citizenship," *International Journal of Cultural Studies*, 3(3), 2000, 351–67
- "Television and its viewers in post-feminist dialogue. Internet-mediated response to *Ally McBeal* and *Sex and the City*," *Etnofoor*, 15(1/2), 2002, 194–211
- "Gender and media studies. No woman, no cry," in John Corner, Philip Schlesinger and Roger Silverstone (eds.), *International Media Research: A Critical Survey*. London: Routledge, 1997, 65–95

I thank Sage and Routledge for granting me permission to reuse this material.

Joke Hermes

Preface and acknowledgments

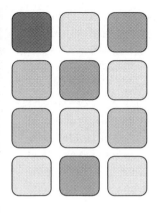

introduction: popular culture/cultural citizenship

For most of us, popular cultural texts (television series, thrillers, magazines, pop music) are far more real than national politics. In everyday life, our allegiances and feelings of belonging often relate more easily and directly to (global) popular culture than to issues of national or local governance. On a daily basis, we discuss new, exciting series with friends; when the national football team scores, we cheer together with numerous others who we will never get to know; and we worry over suitable television for our children. We do all this in the secure knowledge that others like us exist and that they share a sense of elation, outrage, happiness, or concern; that they are familiar with the arguments we want to use and the examples we refer to. Popular culture offers us imagined community (Anderson 1983) or, perhaps more accurately, a shared (historical) imaginary (Elsaesser 2000). Popular cultural texts help us to know who we are, and include us in communities of like-minded viewers and readers. While, formerly, the nation might have been thought to have primarily organized our sense of belonging, our rights, and our duties (civic and political citizenship, and – at a more practical level – social citizenship), it is now facing serious competition from international media conglomerates as well as from fan cultures (cf., Turner 1994, p. 154) that invite us into new types of collectivities that stretch far beyond national borders and produce small self-enclosed enclaves within the nation.

Popular culture is seldom given the credit it is due; nor are the types of community building that directly result from using it recognized for their cohesive social force. This book intends to remedy that situation. While this chapter offers a theoretical grounding for its claim that popular culture produces cultural citizenship, and explains what that is, the rest of the book is based on the experiences of popular culture's users. Football, police series, thriller and detective novels, *Sex and the City*, *Ally McBeal*, children's television, and digital games will provide the background against which the merits of popular culture will be sketched and theorized. The case study chapters (1–6) can be read separately; chapter 7 returns to the theoretical discussion that has started here.

In somewhat more detail, the itinerary of this chapter flows from a meta-narrative of what I understand to be the uses and qualities of popular culture. While unfolding the general argument of the book, various ways of thinking about popular culture will be reviewed, ranging from popular culture as abstract arena of struggle over meanings, and resistance to class or gender dominance, to concrete everyday practices in which belonging, community, and identity are at stake. These practices can be sports or television fandom, the reading of literary bestsellers, or web discussion. My perspective is shaped by early cultural studies discussions of culture as lived, and as shaped in power relations (Hall, Critcher, Jefferson, Clarke & Roberts 1978; Hall 1980); and by the influential work of John Fiske and John Hartley (Fiske & Hartley 1978; Fiske 1987), who gave short shrift to any notion of popular culture as "low" culture and regarded it as an important domain of pleasure and meaning-making in its own right (cf., Storey 1997). Building on to the tradition started by these authors, and combining their insights with ethnographically inspired research that developed out of the tradition started by David Morley (1980, 1986), work on television audiences by Ien Ang (1985) – specifically, on watching *Dallas* – and by Janice Radway (1984), on the reading of romances, I will argue the case of popular culture while weighing its uses and resistive force against its disciplinary and exclusionary effects.

If popular culture truly has the power to make people bond and feel that they belong – and whether and how it does is what this book is about – it makes sense, first of all, to give credit to Fiske and Hartley's notion that popular culture may be understood as democracy at work. But it also means that we should review whether popular culture is truly democratic in its effects: What kind of citizenship is (cultural) citizenship? And how does it exclude as well as include? In cultural studies discussions, Fiske and Hartley's (late 1970s/early 1980s) idealism has given way to discussion of the disciplinary and exclusive forces that are also at work when we enjoy popular texts. The sections of this chapter that are called "Freedom and stricture" and "The politics of self-formation," which are based on later work by John Hartley and on the work of Toby Miller, both outline and help to define "cultural citizenship" for the purpose of re-reading popular culture: What makes it valuable and what might we want to be critical of?

From a discussion of cultural citizenship and the forces of freedom and discipline, the chapter moves to the more concrete issues at stake in the book. Via what John Mepham (1990) has termed "usable stories," and similar suggestions by Stuart Hall and John Ellis that we look at what popular culture allows us to do across genres, I will turn to the analytic method used in this book and the image of popular culture that I would like readers to keep in the back of their minds. It ends with an overview of the case studies that will be discussed in the chapters to come.

The citizenship qualities of popular culture

Popular culture has been celebrated as a domain of resistance against dominant power relations. In turn, such views have been criticized for their naïve notion of power and politics (Curran 1990). Both arguments have merits, though I sympathize more with the former (positive) view of popular culture than with the latter negative view. Criticism of popular culture even from a radical political point of view is easily coopted for elitist and conservative purposes, and therefore needs to be wielded with much care. It requires a balancing act to both do justice to the pleasures and uses of the popular and reflect on it critically – which is what I intend to do in this book. The citizenship qualities that I suspect popular culture possesses appear to offer a means of walking this tightrope. Three features of popular culture stand out in this regard.

First of all, as argued above, popular culture makes us welcome and offers belonging. Its economic and celebratory logic (depending on its corporate-capitalist origins, or its user or reader provenance), after all, make it imperative that ever more buyers or like-minded fans are found. Even if conditions are set for entrance – a fee, purchase price, authentic interest, or the right subcultural credentials – they often make participation all the more attractive. A second aspect is the fascination that we have with popular fiction, pop music, dedicated websites for TV series, much loved media stars, or computer games, because they allow us to fantasize about the ideals and hopes that we have for society, as well as to ponder what we fear. Utopian wishes mix with feelings of foreboding about how our culture and society will develop, with the pleasure of sharing, and with a range of (often visceral) thoughts, emotions, and deliberations inspired by what we read, watch, and listen to. Thirdly, popular culture links the domains of the public and the private and blurs their borderline more than any other institution or practice, for more people – regardless of their age, gender, or ethnicity. In that sense, it is the most democratic of domains in our society, regardless of the commercial and governmental interests and investments that co-shape its form and contents. It offers room for implicit and explicit social criticism, both of a conservative and populist nature and of a more left-wing critical signature.

Democracy is deliberation by many on the best life possible for all. By minimizing the number of rules that are set for such deliberation, and maximizing the number of people who are invited to participate, we will obtain the best possible result: an ongoing and unruly process that we learn from, that entertains us, and that provides ways and means to act in the real world. For better or for worse, that realm is popular culture rather than centralized governmental politics. "Popular" by my definition denotes "of and for the people." "Culture" is both how we understand the world, as where and how we live our lives, and the production of artifacts that amuse or move us, that have us thinking about who we are and how "being" is done. In (popular) culture, the world, history, relationships between people, and so on are represented to us by means of codes and conventions all of which have their own historical lineage, and that we interpret using the particular cultural knowledges that result from our biographies. Given the enormous range of codes and conventions that are possible, the tension produced by the contradictory forces of history, and the inherent drive in all art and culture to find new forms of expression, popular culture is a domain in which we may practice the reinvention of who we are.

Cultural citizenship, rather than citizenship generally, is the term that will be used in this book to analyze the democratic potential of popular culture, even though it lacks formal structures of guaranteeing rights or enforcing duties and obligations. Citizenship has been discussed and fought over since the French revolution in 1789. It is the most concrete form that emancipation has taken in Western society. Most authors writing about cultural citizenship follow Marshall's (1994 [1964]) reconstruction of civic rights as the first stage of citizenship, to be followed by political rights (the vote), and the social rights fought over during the twentieth century. This is citizenship defined as the rights and obligations that individuals have in relation to the nation-state. Social movements claiming cultural rights for particular groups mark a new era of citizenship discussion (cf., Rosaldo 1999). Such identity politics are not the focus of this book, however. I am interested here in how cultural citizenship as a term can also be used in relation to less formal everyday practices of identity construction, representation, and ideology, and implicit moral obligations and rights.

In media and cultural studies, cultural citizenship has also been used by writers others than myself, as a theoretical means of bringing together social power relations, the role of governments, and regulation on the one hand, and cultural representation and meaning-making on the other. The combination is never entirely stable. After all, what is involved are the wayward and ephemeral qualities of cultural texts and artifacts, that may well work against forms of regulation. Relying on earlier political philosophical discussions, concrete questions have been posed as to what binds us, under conditions of globalization and multiculturalism that are more likely to drive us apart. Jostein Gripsrud (1999) edited *Television and Common Knowledge*, which focuses on citizenship and news genres (once understood to be the tool of democratic control for citizens) in television. Nick Stevenson (2001, 2003) and Bryan Turner (1993, 1994, 2001), to name but two prolific writers, have written and edited books and articles that translate political science discussions to the realm of media and cultural theory. Recurrent themes concern globalization (the end of the nation-state) (Turner 1994, p. 158), individualization (as a consequence of postmodernity), and the threat implied by these historical forces for the deep quality of citizenship (idem), conceptualized as the willingness to take responsibility for others (cf., Stevenson 2003, p. 31). In general, these studies deal in very general terms with "culture," or turn, traditionally, to news media (Gripsrud 1999). An interesting addition to this perspective is provided by Liesbet van Zoonen in her *Entertaining the Citizen* (2004). Most useful for my purposes is the work of John Hartley and Toby Miller, to be discussed in the next section, which pays explicit attention to (popular) culture and its modes of expression; the forces that shape it, and the uses to which it is put.

Freedom and stricture

Toby Miller (1993, 1998) understands (cultural) citizenship as the disciplining of subjects in the cultural realm in capitalist social formations. He sums up his *The Well-Tempered Self* by stating that "culture is a significant area in the daily organisation of fealty to the cultural-capitalist state" (1993, p. 218). Postmodern technologies of the self, which are also the subject area of his *Technologies of Truth* (1998), work particularly well in the twin domains of culture and citizenship. The "well-tempered self" is a reference to J. S. Bach's musical score, *Das wohltemperierte Klavier*: "which uses all the major and minor keys of the clavichord . . . and is regarded as an exemplary exercise in freedom and stricture" (1993, p. ix). Working his way through a wealth of material – philosophical, political, and cultural – Miller lays bare for contemporary society how people become subjects; how they are continually, in Foucault's words, invited and incited to recognize their moral obligations. To be human is to be subjected to continuous training and reforming; to be invited to find both individuality and a social sense of self, to be a never-accomplished project.

There is no way in which Miller's dazzling array of examples and references can be summarized here. However, I take from his book the notion that citizenship is a realm of subjection, and hence a realm of both disciplining and seduction. These are key terms in understanding the debate about what popular culture may "do to us" (rather than we with it); but they are also key analytical instruments to analyze viewer and reader discourse. However aware we are, in ironical or postmodern mode, that we are fooled, tied down, and regulated by the different types of invitation that come our way to be included and to be belong – to be a selfless, responsible citizen, to be a happy consumer – we also take them up, enjoy them, and live them. Miller concludes that: "the civic cultural subject – the citizen – is produced as a polite and obedient servant of etiquette, within limited definitions of acceptable behaviour" (1993, p. 223). One of the questions to be answered, then, concerns what self-imposed rules (in addition to those of industry and government) govern the communities (and the sense of community) that are built in and through popular culture. As will become clear, I wish to describe such (self-) disciplining without according it special weight either negatively or positively. Discipline – like hypocrisy, for instance – has its values as a "daily vice," much along the lines of Shklar's discussion of hypocrisy, jealousy, and other little-regarded forms of behavior and states of mind (Shklar 1984). It is the underlying system of marking some areas or some people out for extreme disciplining or exclusion on historically explainable, but ultimately arbitrary, grounds such as race or gender that needs to be challenged.

Balancing the costs and gains of popular culture has not traditionally been core business for literary and media critics, who have kept discussion of popular culture on a deliberately somber and pessimistic note. Hartley (1996, 1999) uses John Frow's term "the knowledge class" to describe and explain how critics have mostly been in the business of guarding their terrain and exclusive knowledge against the lack of taste and insight of the multitudes. It may sound rather obvious to suggest that it depends on the vantage point taken whether popular culture can be understood as cultural citizenship; that is, as an arena in which not only meaning is struggled over, but identity, subjection and subjectivity, community, and inclusion and exclusion as well. But it needs to be kept in mind that "the knowledge class" has preferred to understand drama, literature, and indeed popular culture, as areas of determination (in that they reflect deeper structures or truths) rather than as areas of production. This is not without its consequences for those who like to use popular culture. As Miller puts it: "Struggles enacted between total determinacy and total indeterminacy across the body of literary theory encapsulate the critical question here: whether symptomatic textual criticism subjectifies people undertaking it in terms of their relationship to various forms of knowledge; or whether it is amenable to a politics of identity, a politics of self-formation that abjures the subjection of others" (1993, pp. 62–3). Needless to say, popular culture has mostly been understood in determinist and negative terms. How, in terms of the project of this book, can we then re-read popular culture as a politics of self-formation? What tools are available in existing media and cultural theory? What opposition might be expected? What forces are present in the realm of popular culture itself? What identities do we (as the writer and as the readers who are reading this) forge for ourselves?

The politics of self-formation

Hartley poses this very question in *The Uses of Television* (1999), in a more pragmatic fashion, by reconstructing the history of television criticism. Early television criticism mixed the literary competencies and outlook of its practitioners with strong pedagogical zeal, which meant that viewers, television's end-users, were not included in debate. Television was damned even before it functioned as a mass medium: "Ever since Matthew Arnold theorized a political connection between culture and modernity (1869), the belief among 'university men' and schools inspectors was that culture would tame the Englishman's propensity to use his freedom to riot" (1999, p. 69). Culture was defined in the interwar period, as opposed to "what is proposed by the majority": "It follows that the critical onslaught which television has faced throughout its existence has its roots not in the medium itself but in a pre-existing discourse of anxiety about popularization and modernity; a quite straightforward fear of and hostility to the democratization of taste" (Hartley 1999, p. 66).

Like Miller, Hartley uses a Foucauldian framework to address the triangle of popular culture, intellectual reflection, and citizenship. According to Hartley, Miller's *The Well-Tempered Self* suggests in the nooks and crannies of its closed argumentation a call to arms: to reject temperance and to resist being disciplined by the corporate-capitalist state, in favor of parodic politics and incivility (1996, p. 62). Hartley summarizes as follows in his *Popular Reality*: "In other words, Miller's analysis (against the grain of his main thesis) describes not only the formation of a 'postmodern subject', but also what I'd call a postmodern politics of reading, centred on 'the actions of living persons' in relation and reaction to popular media and powerful truth-discourses; his incivility is my media citizenship" (idem). For Hartley, media citizenship is grounded in his intent to undo the intellectual-made divide between "the knowledge class" and ordinary people. Intellectual culture and popular culture are understood as "mutual, reciprocal and interdependent sites of knowledge production" (1996, pp. 58–9): hence Hartley's use of "reading" and "readerships" to describe media audiences, as a taunt to how intellectuals like to describe themselves. "'Readerships' are the audiences, consumers, users, viewers, listeners or readers called into being by any medium, whether verbal, audio-visual or visual, journalistic or fictional; 'reading' is the discursive practice of making sense of any semiotic material whatever, and would include not only decoding but also the cultural and critical work of responding, interpreting, talking about or talking back – the whole array of sense-making practices that are proper to a given medium in its situation" (Hartley 1996, p. 58).

Moreover, for Hartley, reading is a *practice* not a subjectivity, part of the cultural repertoire of actions that people may undertake (1996, p. 66). Although Hartley has never been able to care much for audience research, the point is well taken in relation to the project of this book. As citizens, the readers quoted here do not need their deepest being explained; rather, shared cultural frameworks and how they are (continuously) built and rebuilt are at stake. Rigorous investigation of what the core values of popular culture are should, therefore, include examination of how it fascinates and binds, how it is incremental in community-building as well as in practices of exclusion. Audience ethnography would seem to be an important tool for doing so. Cultural citizenship is, after all, the consequence of actions and debates in the range of contexts that make up the (semi-) public sphere of mass media consumption. Many of those actions and debates will never be published as news or reported on by other means, and will remain invisible unless cultural scholars go to the trouble of asking people about them. To me, this point of view follows logically from Hartley's observation, in *Popular Reality*, that we should neither overestimate the public sphere of political science nor underestimate the realm of popular entertainment. I agree with Hartley that the readership of "mass communications" constructs itself as "an imagined community whose public sphere is symbolic, but much more real than the Roman Forum ever was for the general public" (1996, p. 71). Those who "lament the passing of an informed, rational public sphere and the rise of popular entertainment media" both overestimate "the extent to which the Enlightenment public sphere was achieved as an institutional and socially pervasive reality" and fail to understand "the role that the public media do play in producing and distributing knowledge, visualizing and teaching public issues in the midst of private consumption" (1996, p. 156).

In the later book *The Uses of Television* (1999), Hartley moves from media citizenship and cultural citizenship to "do-it-yourself" citizenship, expanding on the thesis put forward in *Popular Reality*. DIY citizenship moves away from the disciplining that is, according to both Miller and Hartley in earlier work, inherent in all citizenship, and the strong streak of governance that runs through it. Do-it-yourself citizenship focuses on difference rather than identity – the two incompatible axes along which television works. As Hartley puts it:

Looking at the rest of the world through television, it is inevitable that differences can both be celebrated and erased, recognised and removed, insisted upon and ignored. So there's a curious toggle switching between television as a teacher of "identity" among its audiences, and as teacher of "difference" among the same population. (1999, p. 159)

The switch follows a developmental logic: first equality along the "identity" axis; then difference, or semiotic self-determination. Cultural citizenship (as identity rights) follows upon civic rights, the vote, and social security. DIY citizenship is a full step further along the road and has to do with acceptance of difference, and what I would call respect. Given that the dynamics of development can be uneven, even if the logic remains the same, identity and difference can be issues in one and the same period.

According to Hartley, the mixture of cultural and DIY citizenship can – following his argument for a bit longer – be recognized in television's "neighbourliness": others are to be treated with civility, tolerance, and acceptance of difference. "What's regarded as dramatic, uncivil or funny in each genre is directly related to the audience's sense of virtual community, . . . based on a prior assumption of neighbourliness and civility in personal, social and domestic comportment" (1999, p. 160). Like Hartley, I believe in the value of self-determination, but perhaps a little caution is needed in pronouncing fan cultures, urban youth culture, taste constituencies, consumer-sovereignty movements, and football supporters as card-carrying members of a new democracy (examples mostly from Hartley, 1999, p. 161). I am slightly more pessimistic, and more influenced by Foucault's dictum that the exercise of all power calls forth counterforces. All politics, whether style politics or governmental policy, involve rules and so do forms of community building. Rules involve a notion of what is and what is not acceptable, what can and cannot be accepted. Rules refer to norms and of necessity lead to inclusion and exclusion. Rules underlie "neighbourliness."

The domain of cultural citizenship, then, is hardly a free state in terms of acceptable behavior (while it is in terms of thought and utopian fantasy). In the chapters to follow, there are many examples of how cultural citizenship is deeply invested in the setting up of norms and rules of appropriate demeanor. They include what I have called the racist discomfort of football fans (how to talk about ethnic difference without discriminating); the hostility of middle-brow taste to any lowering of standards (an example close to Hartley's own long struggle against the self-privileged "knowledge class"); and the pleasure that fans have in taking (former) favorites down a peg when a show starts to go "off" and loses the "edge" that it used to have. Lines are continuously drawn in areas that, at the very least, overlap with others' semiotic self-determination. As a former *Ally McBeal* fan says of the series' ultra-thin leading actress: "[C]an someone get Calista Flockheart a burger?" Cultural citizenship is not a power-free zone then; and nor are the popular commercial media outside the process of citizen formation (Hartley 1999, p. 162). When power is conceptualized as a productive force, as Foucault suggests, and not just as repression, our dealings with commercial popular culture can be understood as much more than the brainwashing and exploitation of those who did not stay in school long enough.

Defining cultural citizenship in relation to popular culture

How, more exactly, can cultural citizenship be defined for the project of re-reading popular culture? A number of elements have been discussed: the link to the other citizenships, the rights that it involves (to belong to a community, to offer one's views, to express preferences), and the responsibilities (such as respecting other people's tastes, or how they are different from one's own). In general, too, I would like to avoid making this definition overly pessimistic, as in Miller's description of cultural citizenship as a domain of fealty, or too idealistic, as in Hartley's description of DIY citizenship as semiotic self-determination. I would like to give the social and the semiotic, meaning-making aspects of cultural citizenship their due weight, and provide space in which to think about its disciplining aspects, but most of all define cultural citizenship in such a way that it can be used for analytical purposes. This suggests something along the following lines: what we do with (popular) cultural texts to understand, take up, reflect on, and reform identities that are embedded in communities of different kinds (ranging from virtual, interpretive communities to membership of sports clubs or fan groups). Implicitly part of this ongoing activity of purposeful everyday meaning-making in relation to mediated culture is the production of distinctions, norms, and rules. Cultural citizenship is thus bound up with producing the pleasure of popular culture. It offers both the ground rules of interpretation and evaluation and the space to be excited, frightened, enthralled, or subject to any of the huge range of states of mind and feeling that we connect with the use of popular media. Or, in a shorter version: *cultural citizenship can be defined as the process of bonding and community building, and reflection on that bonding, that is implied in partaking of the text-related practices of reading, consuming, celebrating, and criticizing offered in the realm of (popular) culture.*

Left out of this definition is how popular culture makes such bonding easy for a potential reader; how engaging with it rewards us at many different levels of pleasure and reflection. But then, popular culture needs to be defined in its own right as a social domain that offers a wealth of materials that rewrite and codify human experience for a multitude of user pleasures, including recognition and reflection. Popular culture extends an open invitation to belong; it tends to be inclusive; the possibility is offered of utopian and dystopian fantasies; and the distinction between the public and private is blurred, which opens up a wider range of appropriate behaviors and styles of discussion and observation for public and semi-public debate. While it allows political issues to be raised, the very strength of popular culture is that it is not a manifesto. Popular culture suggests, it implies, it ironizes. It functions much like the chorus in classical Greek drama. It makes the presence known of those who are not in positions of direct political or economic power. This suggests that popular culture is above all a counterforce, but it is more than that. It provides, within limits, an alternative sense of community, one not provided by social institutions such as political parties, trades unions, sports clubs, or the family. Such a sense of community is by no means directly a political voice, or a source of either progressive or conservative sentiments. There is a push-and-pull here between manipulation by the industry, by dominant ideology, and by regrouping on the part of those who are being manipulated. Popular culture hides rather than foregrounds itself as a domain of political and ideological struggle. It suggests itself as an area of mere entertainment, of taste and idiosyncratic preference. I believe that it is much more than that. That is why I will be looking for cultural citizenship, for traces of community and reflection, in the chapters to follow. Popular cultural texts and practices are important because they provide much of the wool from which the social tapestry is knit.

Usable stories, fictional rehearsal, and working through

Others too have sought ways of describing the everyday material effectiveness of popular culture, but tend to focus mostly on the self-reflexive values offered by strong popular texts, rather than on how it offers bonding, belonging, and reflection. In a discussion of the qualities of television and ways of approaching them, John Mepham (1990, p. 59) suggests that we focus on the provision of usable stories as a marker of quality. He defines these as stories that can be put to use in "development of individual personality" and in the "creation of social self-understanding" (1990, p. 60). Stories, he argues, "are a form of inquiry to which people can turn in their efforts to answer questions which invariably spring up through their lives. What is possible for me, who can I be, what can my life consist of, how can I bring this about? What is it like to be someone else, to be particular kinds of other people, how does it come about that people can be like that?" (idem). This is television as transmodern teacher, as Hartley would put it (1999, p. 41). It definitely touches on the core activity of cultural citizenship: a process of comparison and evaluation that is helped and inspired by popular media texts.

Related to Mepham's usable stories, and echoed in my definition of cultural citizenship and subsequent refinement of what popular culture may do for us, is Hall's notion of the "fictional rehearsal" that, for example, soap opera offers to viewers, to question how they live their lives (quoted in Miller 1993, p. 79). This mirror metaphor is perhaps a little too direct. Viewers are well aware of the gap between fiction and everyday life, as is clear, for example, from Ien Ang's work on letters that viewers sent her about the prime-time soap opera *Dallas* (Ang 1985). She uses the term emotional realism, which captures more precisely the type of rehearsal that Hall refers to, while it adds to understanding popular television's quality by clarifying how it is a means to such reflexive ends. I found the same mechanism at work in how women's magazines are read. In them too, readers found means of exercising their fantasies about problem-solving and coping scenarios for practical and emotional situations that life might land them in, which they felt empowered them (Hermes 1995).

A third example of how we can gauge what popular culture does for us is offered by John Ellis (2000), who suggests, in relation to television, that the medium helps us in "working through" the uncertainties and anxieties of our time. Popular culture is our therapist. Television news, for instance, offers potential frameworks to interpret what is happening in the world: "[Television] works over new material for its audiences as a necessary consequence of its position of witness. Television attempts definitions, tries out explanations, creates narratives, talks over, makes intelligible, tries to marginalize, harnesses speculation, tries to make fit, and, very occasionally, anathemizes" (2000, p. 79). In relation to soap opera, television's most typical form at the end of the twentieth century, Ellis again underlines the openness of television as popular culture, and how this helps us as viewers come to terms with the world. "Television drama and fiction do not tend to use self-contained narratives . . . Its more habitual forms like the soap opera and the series drama are . . . open-ended . . . [T]elevision refuses 'the advantages of certainty' in favour of the pleasure and the pain of living in the uncertain present. Television, in this sense, acts as our forum for interpretation" (2000, p. 99). Although Ellis uses psycho-therapeutical terms, his work describes what I would call the doing of cultural citizenship; its very nature of coming to terms with oneself as member of a community, situated in a wider world – which involves the always continuing activity of building such community member-ships and reflection on them.

Regarding method

What does this view of popular culture and of cultural citizenship imply ana-lytically and methodologically? Although the texts of popular culture, rich as they are, make for a fascinating and important area of study, the link to cultural citizenship directs me to audiences themselves. The value of popular culture, whatever its textual qualities, is in what audiences *do* with it. Although I will gladly work with the definitions and interpretations of the authors discussed above, the added value of this project will be in tracing how audiences take up their roles as cultural citizens by enjoying and making use of popular culture – or, of course, by denouncing, hating, and vilifying it. In this way, I hope to lay bare aspects of popular culture that are otherwise hidden or of little interest, embedded as they are in everyday audience practice, while they are crucial – for better or for worse – for social cohesion and the continuation of the social order. Both Miller and Hartley plead the cause of a radical popular citizenship, but are content to wait and see where it turns up in reported practice. The excep-tional thus becomes exemplary and burdens interpretation of everyday practice – which is hardly as radical or exciting. This book has a more mundane agenda: to do justice to ordinary, everyday life. It is inspired by a large dose of curios-ity and a little misplaced pedagogic and political-activist zeal to discuss with the citizens how they read the popular media. Given that popular culture does not insist on any kind of reflection, rigorous or otherwise, much of the cultural citizenship implied in using the media or the popular arts is hidden, routine activity. Interviews can therefore be key moments at which this citizenship potential can be realized.

Audience ethnography, broadly defined, is the method of choice, including, of course, attention to textual detail and history where needed. But what exactly is it that we will be looking for? First of all, I will describe the kind of "readership" or community that is built by dispersed audience members: What is it that binds the readers that have been interviewed; how does a particular popular field address them and what does it allow them to reflect on? Secondly, since I want to know more precisely what it is that makes popular culture worth-while, I will be looking for the claims and criticisms that are voiced in relation to the "text" or popular practice discussed. I will try to find traces of "processes of working through," or "rehearsal for real life," in how popular culture is talked about and used; whether "usable stories" are indeed offered. Thirdly, given that I am using cultural citizenship as an instrument to assess the value of popular culture in terms of the bonding and reflecting opportunities that it offers, I am also interested in the rules of inclusion and exclusion that have been developed. Examples of the latter would be knowledge of the technical rules of football; or familiarity with the individual sports histories of trainers and players (chapter 1), but also literally on what grounds one may call oneself a detective novel reader (chapter 3) or a fan of a particular television series (chapter 5). And, fourthly, I will look for elements of what Jason Mittell (2001) calls the discursive genealogy of popular texts and practices by tracing their wider historical and cultural significance, where that will be of use in understanding and interpreting them.

The case studies in the chapters to follow are all ethnographically inspired, audience-led studies of popular culture, which start from the four questions above. In answering them, the balance between paying attention to texts and to what audience members say will shift considerably. The project of re-reading popular culture, of balancing appreciation and criticism, necessitates the reconstruction of ideological and power relations that are at stake and how they figure at different levels: of the popular text itself, in audience reflection on these texts, as part of the bonding allowed by popular culture, or as the more abstract result of (re)building a shared imagination – for example, of the nation (which is not yet totally redundant) or of the fan communities that one belongs to via readership practices. This is a highly theoretical project that mostly foregoes the material consequences, however important, of how popular culture is used. It does not discuss football itself, or what fashion counsel (if any) takes place amongst viewers of popular "postfeminist" television or children's cartoons. Ethnography, as used here, is concerned with understanding and explaining how social and cultural practice gives rise to agendas, to constructions of femininity and masculinity, and to imagined identities. Moreover, these will be theorized, rather than generalized across populations or used for the description of actual practice. Popular texts and images travel globally; practices of use are copied. The more we focus on their interpretive and "invitational" logic, the less they are bound to geographical location, even if local interpretation and reconfiguration are important as part of the "open" structure of popular culture. It is for that reason that interviews with Dutch audience members are used alongside globally traveling Internet voices and published international academic criticism to further an understanding of how popular culture invites and bonds in general.

While starting from and respecting the situatedness of the production of meaning, the end result of the enterprise of this book is a theoretical understanding of how popular culture has meaning and value. It is in the conjunction of local circumstance, international media genres, and situated production of meaning that we can see unfold how popular culture mirrors widely shared underlying concerns and allows for the concretizing of these concerns in ways deemed fitting by local users. This mechanism, which is at the heart of how popular culture is always amenable to conceding its textual authority to permit specific uses, has my special interest. In the end, it is popular culture itself that I want to defend, rather than its concrete practices of use, even if such a distinction is mostly academic. Concrete practices do, of course, reflect on how we value popular culture itself. Hooliganism in relation to football, is an example, as is the invention (by marketeers) of the "literary thriller" in relation to popular reading. However, in the case of global popular culture such material practice is not isolated but is linked to local practices in other places (to copy or mull over). Audience materials therefore need to be contextualized *and* abstracted from their place of origin in a dialectical and comparative process similar to what Glaser and Strauss (1967) called "grounded theory."

Popular culture as (revolutionary) force

A last huge question remains: if, indeed, popular culture is the domain in which allegiances are built and through which we feel connected, through which in effect the social order is stabilized, it is reasonable to ask how the cultural citizenship that it produces is a social and cultural force. Does it change things in the real world or is it only a result of what happens elsewhere (in the offices of the CEOs of multinationals, or of presidents)? Following Gramsci's notion of hegemony as the negotiated result between two balanced powers (Gramsci 1972) and Foucault's definition of power working bottom-up, we need to tread carefully here. After all, if all power has its counterforce, and if all force fields produce balance as a result of the many forms of power working at the same time but in different directions, stabilizing each other as a result, the popular arts and popular news forms may not be radical forces in themselves, but still part of the ongoing balancing act that is social and cultural life. Even if it might have its revolutionary moments, popular culture only rarely produces a revolutionary impulse.

To find out how popular culture may be implicated in social change, we need to look at longer periods; to become aware of how identity constructions, representations, and ideologies are rebalanced in the popular domain. Charting such social change from a long-term perspective on popular cultural texts will only constitute a small part of this book – not because it is not important, but because such work has become part of the received knowledge in the academy, especially in television and film studies. Examples are easy to name: David Oswell's work on early television programming for children, which called into being a new type of pedagogical and marketing expertise (Oswell 2002); Ella Taylor's mapping of representations of the (work) family throughout television's history, in which it transforms from the blood-related extended family to the postindustrial nuclear family, to the self-created families of colleagues and neighbors (Taylor 1989); or studies that follow the illustrious career of James Bond and chart the changing mores of legitimate public and private sexual behavior (Bennett & Woollacott 1987; Chapman 2000). And these are only a few among many.

The image of popular culture that I want to the reader to retain after the reading of this book is of popular culture as a huge piece of fabric, pulled in different directions by the many parties involved: producers, advertisers, readers, critics, activists, and legislators. While holding onto the fabric is what binds them, it is also what they fight over. The fighting, the holding onto, and the claiming of the fabric are all of interest here. Popular culture is not a mere "web of meaning," nor is cultural citizenship a state of being. For audience members, on whom I will focus, a material claim to belong and to be recognized as a co-owner is involved. Cultural citizenship is taking responsibility for (one's piece of) popular culture. We take responsibility for popular culture by judging it, and we use it to find yardsticks to judge others by. Popular culture and cultural citizenship are often about defining what is "normal" – or, put differently, about finding out what (degrees of) difference are tolerable. How can we be a "we," a community, imagined or otherwise? In what regards do we need to be the "same"? Can we respect each other without forcing straightjackets onto each other that prescribe desired sex, sexual preferences, looks, and interpretive codes, or are such straightjackets part of the pleasure?

The authors discussed here point to the fact that the pleasures, meanings, and displeasures of popular culture are of little relevance in defining the quality, as such, of texts or artifacts – but that they are a means of reflecting on who we are. As such, they may create belonging, identity, and community. I will in addition argue that popular culture does from time to time spill over and initiate rebalancing in other domains. Questions of whether and how men can be feminists were not first asked in parliament or in the halls of academia, nor were they high on the agenda of the women's movement itself. They were voiced in the double-edged narratives of comedy. Sitcoms such as *Family Ties*

(NBC, 1982–9), and later *Roseanne* (ABC, 1989–), wondered (tongue-in-cheek and seriously) what caring masculinity could be like from different class and narrative perspectives. Middle-class Alex Keaton's hippie father had a hard time with his Reagan-admiring son (played by Michael J. Fox), while Dan had to negotiate being sexy, caring, and convincingly working-class masculine as husband to the ebullient Roseanne. Rewriting the ridiculous triple standard for women (to be assertive, beautiful, and caring beings) as a result of the popularization of feminist thought, and to develop a feminine masculinity for heterosexual women, was left to young women kicking ass in *Buffy the Vampire Slayer* (1997–2003), *Nikita* (1997–2001), *Charmed* (1998–), and *Alias* (2001–), after glossy women's magazines in the 1980s tried new definitions of the "power woman," who combines a career with a family and looking glamorous, and tried to break up feminist criticism into digestible bits (Gough-Yates 2002). Their "I am no feminist but . . ." formula may have seemed the most atrocious betrayal of feminism, but it also offered the possibility to appropriate elements for those who were not convinced by the cause.

Constructions of masculinity and femininity are examples of the major ideological quagmires that popular culture scripts solutions for, by, as it were, test-running scenarios. This may take the form of sacrificing the occasional male in recent thriller novels, since their role in relation to strong women protagonists is difficult to fathom (chapter 4). Or it may involve seeking recourse to established, but not highly regarded, forms of racist discourse to express unease over the sharp increase in black players in the Dutch national football team in the 1990s (chapter 1). Given that most popular texts are open to a wide range of interpretations, without audience research it is impossible to find out which scenarios appeal. In all of the chapters, I will use my knowledge of, respectively, football, the police series, thrillers and detective novels, Internet fandom, and children's television and games to sketch the field. But what I will mainly do is follow up on the cues given by interviewees and, whenever necessary, return to the books or programs that they mention.

The chapters to follow

Chapter 1, then, deals with football talk and the national team. The community building capacity of sport in general comes as no big surprise. What makes this case study of the construction of national identity interesting as cultural citizenship is that, in the period during which male and female football fans were interviewed, the Dutch national team had an unusually high number of

Surinamese players. As it turned out, the men in particular found it difficult to find the right words to discuss this situation of change. It upset any notion of a "natural" white national identity, which forced them to rethink identity and ethnicity, including their own – a key example of audiences and media colluding in what John Ellis would call "working through." What was remarkable about the interviews was also how women used generic space opened up by new forms of sports reporting to side with the culprits of some of the men's unease. We know that ethnicity, gender, and legitimate and illegitimate expressions of sexual desire are complexly related. This chapter shows how.

Chapter 2 returns to questions of national identity in relation to genre and gender, but now as negotiated in relation to a global popular genre, many examples of which are well known to local audiences. Of all the chapters, this is the most text-based. It offers a discursive genealogy that Mittell (2001) suggests is useful when analyzing genre in popular culture, in this case the representation of women in Dutch police series in relation to standards set internationally by Anglo-American productions. In the mid-1990s, half a decade into deregulation, it suddenly became popular to produce crime series locally. The older public broadcasting organizations started three series, while the new commercial stations started no less than six new series, aimed at different audience segments. There had only been one homemade police series, early on in 40 years of public service broadcasting. More interestingly still, a high number of women were cast in central roles in series whose narrative structure and general "look" were copied from English, American, and German examples. A more precise look at their narrative function and centrality, and at the agency of the women characters, reveals how national identity is negotiated against international "standards." The trend found is also apparent in the kind of storylines chosen by commissioning stations and the settings favored by producers. On the one hand, global popular representations rebalanced national definitions of gender; but in embedding new notions of femininity and professionalism, the national historical imaginary proved tenacious, and, alas, conservative. Although it follows a reader (myself), this chapter provides a more formal text-analysis based contribution to understanding the citizenship quality of popular culture.

Chapter 3 is based on a series of interviews about reading thriller and detective novels. Initially, it was meant to investigate the popularization of feminist thought, for which, surely, the detective novel, with its various feminist and lesbian subgenres, would provide fertile ground. It is, as so often in reception studies, a tale of miscalculation. In my experience, audiences draw up their own agendas and hardly feel that they need to please the researcher. Like chapter 1, this is a highly concrete study of how popular culture is used for cultural citizenship means. The interpretive community of detective novel readers was such a well-established one that rules of use and interpretation were easy to find, if not always easy to understand. Although a seemingly open cultural form, class and middle-brow taste turned out to be important constituents of who could be included. Feminism, to my mortification and in flagrant denial of the political potential of so many of the books published, was redefined in a most conservative manner. Ironically, what this chapter also shows is how interviewing readers itself construes their cultural citizenship, and brings the hidden qualities of much-loved cultural forms to the fore.

Chapter 4 concentrates on one of the group interviews that were part of the thriller and detective novel investigation. It did not go very well: my research assistant for the project felt excluded and the ambience was somewhat grim. I decided to follow up on the interview, read the books that were mentioned, and compare them with books that were mentioned in the other 15 or so inter-views. A symptomatic reading of the books and the transcript of the maligned interview suggested that the bone of contention was related to unease over con-temporary constructions of masculinity. In the chapter, I will suggest that the novels that the three readers (two women and one man) mentioned all deal with an unresolved ideological area – which is the question of men's usefulness, and indeed attraction, for emancipated women who are so obviously capable of living their lives, solving crimes, and bringing criminals to justice. The chapter does more. It also focuses on the role of the researcher/author. Of course, we like to understand ourselves to be mere translators or facilitators of nascent knowledges that are already out there. But we do have our own subjectivity to deal with, and our offer of translation may not always be welcome. I conclude that we also have to remain focused on the game rather than on its players. Although this one interview was not a great social success, it did open my eyes to how constructions of masculinity are an important area of discussion throughout contemporary popular culture, also being evident in the football chapter and in postfeminist television, the subject of chapter 5.

Having taken such a close look at how I, as interviewer, intrude upon people's pleasures and ask them to account for their thoughts and ideas, it will perhaps not come as a surprise that chapter 5 chases the dream of any inter-viewer in cultural research: the self-transcribed audience. By chance, I was directed to a website on which audiences can cast votes and debate the loss of merit of their favorite shows. It is called "Jump the Shark" (the name is a story in its own right). Following, and later analyzing, such disembodied material remains curious. Nowhere, however, does it become more clear that cultural citizenship is about testing the quality of popular texts (their usefulness, and the sheer escapist pleasure that they offer), and about defining what is and what is not "normal" (and therefore acceptable). Inclusion and exclusion are the name of the game for those participating in web discussions of popular series.

Chapter 6 turns to an overly discussed area in popular culture: children and the media. Children themselves explain about favorite series and games; and how we may be wrong in thinking that "the right kind" of public service television will turn them into model citizens, while commercial television is no less than the beginning of the end of society as we know it. Citizenship in this chapter is of a traditionally defined kind. In the children and media discussion, it is always about awareness of the needs of others and taking responsibility for them, as opposed to egocentrism, materialism, and aggression. The first, according to culture-pessimists such as Neil Postman, is bred by reading (books, that is); the second is obviously the consequence of the demise of our culture under the onslaught of audiovisual media. Needless to say, I disagree and see much potential in such favorites with children as the *Pokémon* or *Totally Spies!* cartoons. Both the standards set by the children themselves and by cultural critics such as myself suggest a wealth of cultural citizenship possibilities of a positive and progressive kind. Perhaps, in children's fascination with computer games, the fascinations that we have ourselves with the borders of respect and responsibility become unpleasantly visible. These fascinations might well obscure what Hartley calls the underlying "neighbourliness" that allows us to enjoy gruesome actions and detailed murder scenarios. I hold that it is very much there. But then I did not agree with the thriller and detective novel readers of chapter 3 and 4 either so, as far as I am concerned, children's favorites might be one more strike against the middle-brow culture with which I was raised.

Having run through the case studies, and having studied the many ways in which cultural citizenship is part of how popular culture is used, it is time to go back to the academic debate. Chapter 7 has two sections that mirror the domains in which popular culture is discussed. Modern and postmodern arguments will help to reflect on the thesis of this book, which is that popular culture is a domain in which we may practice the reinvention of who we are; and that cultural citizenship is the way in which we do that.

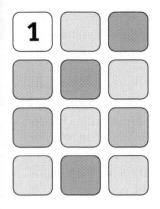

ethnicity, football, and the nation

Viewing statistics show that soccer (known locally as *voetbal*, or football) made for the best-watched programs on Dutch television during the last two decades of the last century. Televised games played by the national soccer team are major events, in particular when the team comes near the finals in a European or World Championship. In such cases, practices of television viewing run over into public social life and carnival-esque outbursts of sports loving and nationalist joy, as happens all over the world with big sports events (cf., Giulianotti 1999, p. 61). Popular culture becomes the fullest possible expression of nationhood.

This chapter is based on over two dozen interviews with football fans, held in the late 1990s, about their views and thoughts regarding the Dutch national team.[1] They were all sports lovers, and they were slightly depressed football-wise. The national team had been playing poorly, and our center forward was involved in two nasty incidents in which a man died and a woman was raped. A lot of (re)thinking had to be done. This was definitely a fortuitous moment to see whether and how sports fandom as a key popular cultural practice could be understood as cultural citizenship. Our interviewees came from all walks of live: they were predominantly male and white, but a quarter were women and some of the men were nonwhite – class backgrounds were mixed. What connected our informants was their love of football as a game. As will become clear below, many claims and criticisms were voiced in the interviews, both directly in relation to football practice (the enormous commercialization of the player market was a sore point with many) and individual players, but also in relation to what exactly constituted Dutchness. Ethnic difference was an issue now that the national team was doing less well, even though it had included nonwhite players for a much longer period of time. How ethnic distinctions were used, and by whom, is one of the themes in the second part of the chapter.

But first, in order to make the interview material intelligible and ground the argument for understanding popular sports culture in relation to cultural citizenship, some historical context is offered. Central to this tale is the importance of the Surinamese-Dutch to the success of the Dutch national team. From the early 1680s onward, Surinam was a Dutch colony in the Caribbean region, on the northeastern coast of South America. Folklore has it that it was exchanged for New Amsterdam, currently known as New York, and it remained part of the Dutch kingdom until it sought and achieved independence in 1975. Large numbers of Surinamese – who, after all, hold legal Dutch passports – migrated to the Netherlands. They still constitute the largest community of nonwhite Dutch.

The football history of the 1980s is caught up in a heady national delight in multiculturalism, inspired by the Surinamese-Dutch among the football stars. On a rising tide of football success, the nation reinvented itself along multicultural lines. Ruud Gullit, center forward of Surinamese-Dutch descent, was our hero. A similar phenomenon was witnessed by the French, with the success of its Algerian-French star player Zinedine Zidane in the second half of the 1990s. International football success had even wider emancipatory effects in the Netherlands. Women, as a new group of viewers, were invited to join in this formerly exclusively male domain. However, when the tide of success waned, a more worried atmosphere necessitated further reflection, especially on ethnic difference and who may represent the nation. The incidents that involved Surinamese-Dutch center forward Patrick Kluivert created an even grimmer atmosphere, as did the awkward self-presentation by Kluivert and his soccer mates, with its overtones of Surinamese nationalism.

Watching football and following sports reporting in the 1990s constitutes a domain of "working through," in John Ellis's words, of the Netherlands' colonial history as well as of notions of gender privilege. In two sections below, I will offer a (partial) discursive genealogy of sports talk and sports reporting, that focuses on football and the national team, and especially on two key characters: Ruud Gullit, born in Amsterdam in 1962, the son of a white Dutch mother and a black Surinamese father, and Patrick Kluivert, also born in Amsterdam, in 1976. Newspaper reporting and sports gossip only mention his overly protective black Surinamese mother. After these two sections, the focus of the chapter shifts in the second half to analysis of the interview material, which will show how cultural citizenship is constituted in how the women appropriated a female gaze, and in how the men worried over the nation. Of importance as background to both sections is the ongoing deregulation in the 1990s both of television – witness the introduction of new formats in sports reporting along talk show lines by the new commercial stations, and of new types of sports print journalism that began to foreground the male sports body in sexualized terms.

Dutch football and the Surinamese legion

Although Surinamese players had been present in Dutch football from the mid-1950s onward (Tan 2000), ethnicity became an issue in the mid-1990s in the Netherlands, with a solid one-third of the players of the national team being nonwhite, and mostly Surinamese-Dutch. Moreover, on September 9, 1995, young Patrick Kluivert, top-scoring pride and joy of Ajax and of the Dutch national team, hits and kills a theater director, while driving way over the speed limit.[2] Before the case comes to court, Kluivert is caught speeding again in the inner city, driving a borrowed BMW. He is sentenced to 240 hours of community service[3] and his driver's license is suspended for 18 months[4] – a lenient sentence. He has just served this sentence, when a young woman comes forward (June 12, 1997)[5] and accuses Kluivert of gang-raping her with a couple of his friends at his home earlier that spring (April). The case never comes to trial because there is insufficient evidence. In a civil case, Kluivert is acquitted.[6] That there had been a "sex orgy" is not denied, either by Kluivert or his lawyers.[7] The woman, on her own admission, had been very drunk and cannot locate any corroborating witnesses or evidence that anything had been done against her wishes.

Newspaper coverage is very restrained, but does pose the question – with the World Championship in France coming up (1998) – as to whether this is a man who we would want to represent the Netherlands.[8] Everyday talk poses the same question. There is little doubt that Kluivert was involved. Even before his lawyer admits that there has been an "orgy," myths of black male sexuality are readily available and suggestive. But perhaps they are also too tainted by racism, and therefore socially unacceptable, for Kluivert's reputation to be totally ruined. Newspapers do report threats and abuse.[9] Despite the gravity of the situation, this comes as a surprise. Multiculturalism had, after all, ruled representation of major Surinamese-Dutch soccer players for a solid decade at that moment in time.

Multiculturalism in Dutch experience is easily tied to footballer Ruud Gullit, the other key figure in my reconstruction of recent Dutch soccer history. Kluivert and Gullit represent the two generations of our soccer players, in whose case ethnicity became so highly visible (1980–2000). Although there had been nonwhite players in local competitions and in the national team, discussions of ethnic difference had centered on racism on the field. With Gullit in the 1980s we had, for the first time, a highly charismatic nonwhite soccer player with star quality. Gullit embodied what Garry Whannel in *Media Sport Stars* (2001, chs 1 and 6) would call "the sportsman as moral example." One generation later, Kluivert, also Surinamese-Dutch, would prove to be the opposite. A superbly talented player, Kluivert was initially coded as young and immature via reference to his protective Surinamese mum. This shifted, as the incidents unfolded, to an overall reputation for clever and ruthless behavior, both on and off the field. But Kluivert also had a reputation as a teenage heart throb, an identity that predated the car accident and the rape accusation, and which has not entirely died down. For example, Kluivert appeared in a festive episode of a Dutch sports show (August 31, 1995) entitled *Those Two New Cows* (*Die 2 Nieuwe Koeien*, Veronica).

Those Two New Cows ran a special program to celebrate the last night that Veronica, its broadcaster, was in the public broadcasting system before going commercial. *Those Two*, as in *Them Again*, are two famous television sports journalists with a penchant for doing a "different" kind of sports show. Harry Vermeegen, one of the two presenters, continued with a television series called *The Raincoat* (Veronica, 1996–8), in which he indeed wore a raincoat and poked fun at this standard uniform of trainer-coaches. Amongst other things, Vermeegen employed a gimmick with a goldfish bowl, asking a soccer player to hold it, often for the entire length of the show. He also had a standard item called "the football wives," in which he would visit with wives of players and interview them, preferably in their kitchens. *New Cows* refers to the Dutch saying "dragging old cows out of canals," which means to keep talking about things that have already been talked to death. On August 31, 1995, Henk Spaan (co-presenter of *Those Two New Cows*) and Vermeegen invite around 30 girls to talk about their feelings for Patrick Kluivert. They claim to be doing a show on sports fandom. The girls are depicted in individual head shots against a uniform dark background, while they describe how beautiful his face is, as are his eyes, his hair, and his butt. Spaan and Vermeegen then invite them to come outside for a group photograph. While they are posing for the camera, Kluivert is shown – in slow motion – approaching the car park where the girls are, with a big grin plastered on his face. His arms are filled with dozens of roses. While the girls swoon, Kluivert starts presenting them roses and kisses each and every one of them.

Gullit

Gullit was never so much a teenage idol as a womanizer. The man has been married several times and has a number of children. As one of the interviewed women said, "Ruud Gullit and his women, well you know . . . !" (Faye). Gullit has never found it difficult to live down his reputation. Throughout his lengthy soccer career as a player and then as a trainer, he always had a good relationship with the Press, was easy-going, and appeared mostly to simply enjoy life. He started his career playing for clubs such as Haarlem and Feyenoord. Later, he played for the elite club PSV. In 1987, he was voted European Footballer of the Year and World Footballer of the Year (Tan 2000, p. 119). AC Milan acquired Gullit as well as another Surinamese player, Frank Rijkaard. Together with Marco van Basten, a white Dutch star player, they formed a formidable trio that helped AC Milan to win both the Italian national championship and the European trophy for clubs. With the national team, these three also won the 1988 European Championship in Germany.

The 1988 European Soccer Championship was an extraordinary event. Dutch fans were clad in orange, the national color, and many sported orange caps with Rasta curls attached. Gullit wigs were everywhere. The driving force of the national sentiment was an understanding of the semi-finals game played against Germany (and in Germany) as revenge for the German occupation of the Netherlands during the Second World War, and also for the lost finals match against West Germany, which had also been played in Germany, in 1974 (Giulianotti 1999, p. 13). David Winner, author of *Brilliant Orange: The Neurotic Genius of Dutch Football* (2001 [2000]), describes the event as follows:

> Dutch fans were allocated some 6000 tickets, but managed to cram into the Volkspark Stadium in huge numbers – invasion in reverse, journalists gleefully noted in Holland. They were decked in flamboyant orange and their mood was edgy and ebullient. Their banners bore explicit and bitter references to the war. "Give us back our bicycles," the crowd chanted, a reference to the Germans' mass confiscation of Dutch *fietsen* during the conflict. "Ein Reich, Ein Volk, Ein Gullit," mocked one flag in parody of the Nazis' *Fuehrer* slogan. (2001, p. 108)

They win the tournament and Gullit is at the height of his fame. He dedicates his footballer of the year awards from the year before to Nelson Mandela, who is still in prison at the time. This is the same Ruud Gullit who plays for Silvio Berlusconi's AC Milan. Berlusconi is known to have extreme right-wing sympathies, and has already made clear that he will not hesitate to use his many television stations and other media to further his own political career (indeed, at the time of writing (2003) he is the Italian Prime Minister). Confronted with working for a man who some see as a neo-fascist and a racist to boot, Gullit answers that he is just a football player, not a politician.

Ideologically, then, Gullit moves spectacularly between global politics and seemingly sincere support for the anti-apartheid movement, and later the new regime in South Africa, and astounding local naïveté. Giulianotti notes that, as a result of globalization and the international movement of players, "the political involvement of football players [these days] is much more likely to touch upon international than local issues" (1999, p. 35). Indeed, Gullit has remarked that he never felt "black" until he was in his teens (Amerongen & Leistra 1990, p. 100; Tan 2000, p. 118). As the son of a Surinamese father and a white Dutch mother, he cleverly chose to use his father's (Surinamese, non-Dutch-sounding name) when he started his football career. He had been Rudi Dil up to that time, which he felt – at 14 years old – was not a strong name for a professional footballer (Amerongen & Leistra 1990, p. 10). It rhymed with "bil," he explained, which is Dutch for "butt" (Tan 2000, pp. 113–4).

Gullit is an interestingly hybrid figure, able to pass as both black and white, as politically savvy and naïve. His name is without doubt the one that is most tied up with Surinamese emancipation and social integration. By winning the European Championship, Gullit earned himself honorary status. Ethnicity plays only a small part – and a tributary part at that – in recognizing Gullit as a worthy successor to Johan Cruyff. The conservative and populist newspaper *de Telegraaf* gives Gullit his own by-line, complete with a picture. Multiculturalism is at its height and allows only for the celebration of difference. Although colonialism was a dark page in history, today's postcolonial outcomes – new foods, different music – are enriching culture and society. Mixed marriages have increased significantly. Critical left-wing journalist and cultural critic Martin van Amerongen writes a Gullit biography, turning Gullit into a symbol of a new era (Amerongen & Leistra 1990). Gullit's nickname for the football bosses, "bobos," becomes part of everyday language. In fact, 1988 is the year that social historians mark as the beginning of Surinamese assimilation in Dutch society. In a commemorative program, *50 Years of Dutch Television: The Most Important Moments* (2001), Gullit's meeting with Nelson Mandela, first black president of South Africa and on an international goodwill tour in the Netherlands, is shown as a "most important television moment."[10] Gullit, without his Rasta dreadlocks these days, but relaxed and with his usual friendly, eager-to-please style, is a studio guest.

Despite great expectations, the 1990 World Championship in Italy is a disastrous football experience. There are rumors that there is trouble with the national coach, a man named Libregts, who is reputed to have said (when he was Gullit's coach with Feyenoord) that "those black players have no discipline" or even that they are lazy. There is more than a resonance here of racist prejudice about lazy blacks or, in the Netherlands, Surinamese. Whether or not there has been a conflict between the players and the coach is not confirmed, but another coach is brought in to take the team to Italy. In a match against Germany, Frank Rijkaard is sent off for spitting at German center forward Voeller after, according to Rijkaard, Voeller had uttered racist insults. Although Gullit and Rijkaard will notch up other successes in Italy, this championship marks a downward turn for the Dutch team. Four years later, in 1994, Gullit declines to go to America with the Dutch team. Gullit wigs are burnt – and many of his fans still have not forgiven him (Winner 2001, p. 195). Gullit never discloses his reasons. Speculation suggests an incident between Gullit and coach Advocaat. It is only much later that Gullit states that there was a difference of opinion regarding the strategy for the Dutch team.[11]

In 1995, Ruud Gullit is contracted to Chelsea as player coach. His easy smile and good humor, plus the fact that he is the first black trainer ever in the United Kingdom, who will go on to win the prestigious FA Cup, turn him into a television personality. His Press conferences go well and soon Gullit is invited to appear on a raft of quiz shows and other light entertainment programs, as well as on *Match of the Day* (BBC, 1964–). Gullit is Europeanness personified. He brings in a number of international talents, and breaks radically with the English soccer tradition. Later, he will become manager of Newcastle, another English Premier League club. English friends tell me that they adore him. According to journalist Fred Caren, Gullit is seen as a "renaissance man": a footballer with brains and principles, a rare phenomenon.[12] Today, Gullit is with his umpteenth wife, each younger than the other, and is still a media personality (so close to us, so human, so affable, and friendly) – but is he still a star? Richard Dyer has suggested in his book *Stars* (1998) (quoting Alberoni) that stars are a remarkable phenomenon: they are an elite, a privileged group who yet do not excite envy or resentment (1998, p. 7).

Discussing populism, David Lusted adds to this that the populist hero – and Ruud Gullit can certainly count as one – has to take care to always negotiate his status. He always has to show that he is one of the people, a common guy. Quoting earlier work by Richard Dyer (1992), Lusted goes on to argue that the key to understanding populism and the populist hero is to understand these figures as being linked to a utopian sensibility, through which

> [strong] feelings emerge not just at the representational level (in what people say or do) but also at the non-representational level (in more abstract qualities of movement, colour, music, shape, line, etc.). For Dyer, the meaning of the utopian sensibility lies in its feelings of abundance, energy, transparency, intensity, and community. (Lusted 1998, p. 181)

Most important in Lusted's discussion is to understand that populism can only tolerate difference within unity and community: "Step outside community and difference threatens to be deviant. The trick . . . is to be seen as one of 'them' without losing the sense of being one of 'us'" (1998, p. 184). As is clear from the *50 Years of Dutch Television* program (2001), Gullit has managed to be both a star, one of them, functioning at some distance from ordinary human beings because of his soccer talent, and to remain one of us. He expresses himself in simple, direct language; he is easily given to shows of affection and emotion. Gullit manages to use his mixed ethnic background, the sexually charged connotation, the myths that surround life in the Caribbean – easy-going, relaxed, more emotional and affective than highly rational – to build a most attractive star persona. As Dyer's discussion (1998) of the ideological functioning of stars makes clear, this is exactly the feat that stars may achieve: they may bridge contradictory discourses or ideologies and thereby become as fascinating as they do. In Gullit's case, we find a charismatic combination of the hedonistic lifestyle attributed to blacks in Dutch society, enormous energy, and team spirit, as well as soccer talent. What Gullit himself has called his "sexy" style of playing football thoroughly seduced the Dutch (and later the English). According to Winner (2001, p. 222) this is not so much because it has always been successful (apparently, according to this English commentator, we don't care so much for that), but because it is both joyous and stylishly efficient – a deadly combination.

The media love him, and Gullit has always obliged, apparently oblivious to the seamless shifts in the media interest between his appearance and his performance. He is the exception to the rule that star players do not make the greatest television (or media) material (cf., Whannel 1992, p. 122). As a star, he bridges contradictions that would seem to be unbridgeable. He is a black man representing the Netherlands, the former colonial power; who honors Mandela, but has never been accosted in a racist manner, he says; who only realized at age 14 that he was not white; who has always declined to comment on coach Libregt's outright racist remarks – a man who temporarily erases an ethnic barrier that separates Surinam from the Netherlands and amalgamates the two. Dyer's (1998) discussion of the star phenomenon suggests that stars function not only ideologically but also politically, without having to be the agent of that power. It is possible that the political significance of stars such as Ruud Gullit is all the greater for being less easily resisted (cf., Dyer 1998, pp. 7–8) – if not, in his case, for being irresistible.

When there were no "characters" for him to play, Gullit chose to star in his own "personality show," rather than appear in commercials, the choice of many a sports star to make some money, and an integral part of how the sportsperson's body has come to have symbolic as well as economic significance in what Toby Miller has called "sportsex" (2001b, p. 129). The program *Gullit* is on Dutch commercial television (first aired December 2001 – January 2002, Yorin). Although it is quite bad television, it is interesting to see how Gullit and the camera are still deeply in love. With many a joke for "the ladies," as Gullit puts it, he interviews Ruby Wax, Nelson Mandela, Victoria Beckham ("Posh Spice" and wife of footballer David Beckham), and Antonio Banderas – but mainly he puts himself on show. A 1980s and 1990s sports star moves on to go with the flow of other long-existing codes of media interest. Our shameless interest in the personal is offered a bribe, while we are allowed a close look at a body that is both renowned for its shape and fitness and, implicitly, for its sexual prowess.

Kluivert and the Cable

After Gullit, Rijkaard, and van Basten, a new generation of football players follow, more from Surinamese descent than ever before. They are heralded as new football heroes, which they never become. They are, perhaps, too tight-knit a group, a product of the Ajax (Amsterdam's first division club) youth training program. Later, they form a separate block in the national team and use the Surinamese word for a strong friendship group, Cable, to refer to themselves. They do not hesitate to tell the Press that they would prefer to play for a Surinamese national team, although they have since denied saying they would prefer to play in an all-black team, according to Winner (2001, p. 196).[13] Although they are radical postcolonialists, the Cable (Kluivert, Davids, and Seedorf) are read as a brat pack, and associated with being a gang – secret codes and social behavior included. Ideologically, this is a danger zone. As long as they perform well (with Kluivert in the first team, Ajax win the national competition, the national cup, and the European Championship for clubs in 1995), they can be individualized as honorary citizens. As soon as performances are not up to expectations, as in the case of Clarence Seedorf missing a crucial penalty (1996), they can count on heavy criticism and little understanding, least of all for their position as black players in a white country, an issue that is addressed implicitly as well as explicitly by Cable members and by sports and general journalists.

Whereas Gullit's career had its high point at the peak of multiculturalist enthusiasm in the Netherlands, the Cable manifests itself during the downward turn of this ideological moment. Moreover, it is easy enough to incorporate black men as individuals, but much harder to accept them as a group. As such, they call forth connotations of danger and violence. Interestingly, Cable members are not read by young people via older racist myths, but are considered to be cool and part of global youth culture, the badges of which they sport. For a considerable period of time, Edgar Davids – smallish, compactly built, and with long Rasta hair – plays wearing round-the-face spectacles that give him a "gangsta" look that was to achieve wide popularity. Different stories circulate about the glasses. One suggests that he has been injured and that he is wearing them to protect his eye sockets. They certainly add to his image.

The specter of the dangerous young black male – both in terms of street violence and of sexuality – is easily raised, even if it is also too socially uncouth to be used very directly. When Kluivert is charged with manslaughter (1995) and then with being party to a gang-rape of a young white woman at his house (1997), sports journalism ignores both incidents as much as they can.[14] Specialist newsmen (and women) that they are, they see Kluivert as coordinated muscle and strategic thinking, and the Netherlands' ticket to international fame. As a result, unease over the Cable, and what is called the "attitude" of the new generation of star players, is clearest when Edgar Davids, the third Cable member, who is immensely popular with young sports audiences and is known for his enormous and uninhibited aggression, insults coach Hiddink. The black players in the Dutch national team at the 1996 European Championship in the UK suspect Hiddink of favoring older white footballers. Using ghetto slang, Davids suggests that Hiddink should not stick his head up the white players' asses. Taking unprecedented heavy disciplinary action, Hiddinks sends Davids home. The championship is a total loss. Moreover, the impression is strengthened that what these young Surinamese black guys need is discipline. Although clearly part of the repertoire of racism, this is foregrounded in newspaper discussion as well. Davids later stars in a Nike television and cinema commercial. His "street cred" with global youth culture probably only increases as he challenges vested authority.

As for Kluivert: with the advent of the 1998 World Championship in France, there are news reporters and columnists who suggest that surely a convicted killer and a suspected rapist cannot represent the Netherlands as part of the national football team.[15] Rather than a star, nationalist discourse requires a hero with an unblemished record. Kluivert does not qualify for this role, but he does go to France, where he doesn't achieve much. It is questionable whether sportspeople are still widely read in terms of heroism and moral uprightness. In *Media Sport Stars* (2001, p. 72), Whannel suggests that this is actually a lost discourse, only employed – in England – by politicians who are out to suggest that the moral fiber of the nation (its capacity to take both success and failure in its stride) would improve if there were competitive team sport. This particular discourse has, according to Whannel, been supplanted by a sexualization of the sports star (2001, p. 71).

I disagree. Gullit and Kluivert are inscribed in both discourses and have continued to be so. A recent billboard campaign (winter 2001–2) for a sports magazine called *Sportweek* features a semi-naked Kluivert with his arms folded across his chest. Clad only in boxer shorts (tighter underwear, or none at all, would clearly have given rise to the wrong reading), he looks at the viewer over a caption that reads, "I will only expose myself for *Sportweek*." The double meaning in Dutch is partly sexual and partly about journalistic disclosure. *Sportweek* is a newer sports magazine that initiated a shift in the codes of representing the athletic body: apart from serious sports journalism and interviews with sportspeople, it published a swimming costume special in 1998, major sports stars being the models. *Sportweek* connects ideologies of physical fitness and no flab (cf., Bordo 1993) with the suggestion of sexual attractiveness. Color, as in ethnic difference, however, is totally absent, erased from its map of meaning.

Having Kluivert pose semi-naked is cheeky, but it is not a political or anti-racist gesture. Comparing Kluivert to Gullit, we can conclude two things. First, Gullit is certainly exceptional, especially in how he has turned from being a sporting hero and an emblem of nationalist pride (the football fans' orange caps endorsed with Rasta curls) to a star and a television personality and, who knows, an entertainer. Never mind that Gullit's career choices have thereby firmly remained within what can be recognized as legitimate cultural arenas in which nonwhites can excel. Secondly, although Kluivert was read negatively as a gang member, he also benefited from the state of confusion over racism and ethnic ideology in the late 1990s. From the late 1990s to the present time, Islam has been a much more pressing political issue. In the right-wing political debate about closing the borders and allowing as few immigrants as possible to enter, the Surinamese are silent. After all, they are Dutch nationals. Religion and women's emancipation are issues that capture the popular imagination of the moment, rather than racism, or suggestions of dangerous black male sexuality. This is an old myth, still "on call" but not highly active. Meanwhile, Kluivert has continued his career in Barcelona. He is often featured in the Spanish gossip Press with his (current) wife and children.

In recent Dutch football history, the black sports body has become more and more visible, both on television and in the printed media. When sports fans are interviewed, it is clear that ethnicity is also an issue in everyday sports talk. Via the pleasures of television sports viewing and sports talk, the next section will return to issues of televisual representation, ideology, and national identity in terms of cultural citizenship.

Ethnography

When we broached the question of the media upheaval over the black players in interviews with enthusiastic fans of the Dutch national football team in 1998, shortly before the World Championship in France, they felt uncomfortable answering.[16] They hoped for the carnival that follows international success, but were expecting defeat. While expectations had been high, the prospects for the national team were not very good. The talented young Surinamese players were not achieving much. Football fans felt let down and irritated about the "attitude" of the Cable. In addition, there was no suitable repertoire of terms available to address concerns regarding (black) ethnicity and (white and black) nationalism. While disclaimers of racist intent were often offered, racist frames of reference are much used: the superior athletic ability and elegance of the black players is mentioned, but also their lack of discipline, self-control, and team spirit. It is painful for some that the Netherlands, a nation felt to be essentially white, should be represented by nonwhites.

When men talk football

International football is Important; it involves the national honor. Too much money is circulating in the international players' market, and commercialization will ruin the game before long. If you really want to appreciate football, you need a vast amount of background knowledge. This is the gist of what the interviewed men who have been following the national team for as long as they can remember have to say. When they talk about football, they invoke different types of specialist knowledge. There is, of course, technical knowledge (the rules of the game, tactics, and strategy). There is knowledge of the curricula vitae of players and trainers – when a particular player scored in which major game, and so on – and there is the art of interpreting these facts as part of a more speculative and interpretive knowledge. Will a player do well with a particular trainer? Can the team perform under specific weather or field conditions? Will Bergkamp conquer his fear of flying? I have not heard the players' love lives and intimate relationships mentioned much, but gossip thrives in football talk under a smoke screen of technical terms and insights. Note that there is hardly a link to racist discourses, or to discourses that involve ethnicity or cultural difference.

When the national team plays, something else happens though. There is strong national(ist) feeling, involving a suddenly clear sense of "Dutchness." It is a time of partying and near-madness. The Dutch like to call it *Orange madness* (Oranjegekte, orange being the national color). It is my impression that what informants describe (dressing up in orange scarves and hats, standing on the couch, running out into the street when a goal has been scored) has elements of carnival, of an *"Umwertung aller Werte,"* which does not, as one would expect, erase difference, but that makes it possible for things to be thought, felt, and said that otherwise (quite rightly) would be proscribed by political correctness. The carnival of a national team going further and further in the competition produces a "villagey" way of relating to others, which is linked to a need to feel instant identification – us together – which the color composition of the Dutch national team apparently endangers:

Dick: I don't mind a few blacks, but so many of them. Then it's not a really Dutch national team any more. Eleven blacks, no . . . That's not a Dutch national team to me.

Paul: At the back of my mind, I don't recognize myself [in the multi-ethnic national team] because I am white, and the Dutch are originally white.

Peter: Well, I think it does make a difference, because . . . why shouldn't there be white players that are better than those black . . . , why would you turn the entire Dutch national team black? It is after all the Dutch national team and the Dutch are, of course, originally white. People of color have arrived here: that's fine by me, but you should not turn the entire Dutch national team into a black team.

Johan: I don't really care, but I do think there will be people who think why does this team only have dark guys? It is a matter of indifference to me, but I do think that there are people who will say – there are seven or eight dark boys in that team, where are the real Dutch farmers' lads, to put it like that.

A Chinese-Dutch and an Antillian respondent state that they don't mind because they look at it "football-technically" (Xang), and from the point of view of achievements:

Lionel: That's what I find important. The best guys should be there according to me. Whatever he is, I don't care.

Apart from outright denial of the importance of race and ethnicity, the interviews show the use of three discursive regimes. *Enlightened racism* is one of them. Black players are seen as the naturally (biologically) more gifted players: "They have special athletic qualities . . . they can do more than the average European player." Although, of course, "they" are less cultured, and have not learnt to play for the team rather than individually, because that is not what they learn in "their" culture: "They play from the heart" (both quotations, Jaap). "The way they play the ball, it's instinct" (Johan). Opposed to this is *multiculturalism*, which nonetheless finds it "natural" that minority groups would bond together for support (Paul). This implicitly defines the colored players as the weaker players and at the same time underscores the political fact that the black players are a minority in the team, as well as coming from a social minority group. In fact, there is a strong suggestion here of a gendered division within a one-sex category, wherein the ethnic other comes to occupy the position of the woman. The nationalist third discursive category ("This isn't a Dutch team any longer," illustrated by the above quotations) is the one that is most upsetting to the carnival-esque nation-as-village feeling: it is based on concern about the numerical balance in the national team, and it is reminiscent of the fears of my youth, about the yellow hordes coming to take over our culture and our lives.

Girls' talk: objectification of the male body

All nine of the women who we asked about enjoying football on TV, and how they had come to take up this particular pastime, said that they had fathers and brothers who were avid television sports fans. Some of them were also active on the field. Since sports programs and matches were on anyway, they had picked up the habit of watching and continued to do so as adults. Caroline likes to watch with women friends, and so does Nicky, who watches with a good friend whose mother is a real fanatic about football. The way in which the women talked about football was very different from that of the men. Although they did occasionally mention players' technical football-playing qualities, it was clear that their information, or the information that they alluded to in the interviews, stemmed from a wider variety of sources. Contrary to the men, they used newspapers less while they used television more, including the new "soapified" sports shows. *The Raincoat* was often mentioned as a funny show that gives "alternative" background information to football. Gossip magazines were also used, although they do not contain much on football players. Nicky said she far prefers *Voetbal International* (a traditional football magazine), because it has so much more background on the players. In general, the women felt freer to gossip than the men (who disguise their gossip behind a smoke screen of technical jargon) and did so with a stronger emphasis on personal lives.

Watching football together was, the women said, a sociable way of spending their time ("cosy"), to which they added, half in fun, that it was a good way to watch men: "Doesn't he have a cute butt?" (Faye). Faye later qualified that, of course, she doesn't always judge men by their looks: "Some are really sympathetic." She compared her favorite, Ajax goalkeeper Edwin van der Sar, to Patrick Kluivert, whom she really dislikes. At the time of the interview, Kluivert's lawyers had just lodged an appeal with the court for him not to have to do his alternative punishment for the car accident. Faye was convinced that van der Sar would have reacted in a totally different way. She made an almost stereotypical masculine move when she joked about looks, and then said that character, of course, is much more important. Caroline offered the same set of arguments, the other way around. At first, she denied that she was that interested in footballers' looks. She liked the game. A little later, she added that she had run into Marciano Vink (another Surinamese player) once, and that she rather fancied him. She associated judging men by their appearance with a typical girls' way of looking and confessed that, when she was younger, she did watch because there was a nice guy. This led to much talk about which footballers were "cute."

Fan involvement as citizenship

If anything, sports talk personalizes. Its very functioning requires central figures, characters, in the stories it tells, whether as part of serious journalism or light entertainment sports reporting. In personalizing, television generally condenses social relations and cultural meaning (Fiske 1987; Hermes 1999). It literally distills them, and intensifies the meaning and impact of the subjects captured by its attention. Social change thus finds its way enlarged onto the small television screen, presented in such a way that it will be able to compete with all the everyday routines and practices that surround the set, and that are a perennial threat to the attention bestowed on what television shows. The football anecdotes and interviews show the way in which television has taken up (and responded to) multiculturalism and ethnic diversity. Television found its perfect foil in Ruud Gullit, the happy black guy – always, it seems, grateful for any attention bestowed on him. Gullit made multiculturalism sexy.

The Cable turned football and multiculturalism into a different kind of story. Even though sports television is typically light entertainment programming (and has become more so since deregulation and the introduction in the Netherlands of commercial television by the late 1980s), it tends to hanker after the status of hard journalism. Kluivert, Davids, and Seedorf were shocked by the avalanche they had set in motion when they turned to the sports media in 1996 (during the European Championship in England). They aired their grievances about being paid less by Ajax than the white players and they linked this to Dutch racism. In truth, this was not a race issue but a technical one related to changed rules of football finance, and the ban on clubs making money by having other clubs buy off contracts. Sports journalism took them much more seriously than they had ever expected to be taken. After Davids' insult aimed at coach Hiddink (for which he was sent off back home), the Cable decided not to talk to the Press any more, a decision that they have mostly kept to up to the present time.

This short-lived interlude for Dutch sports journalism as hard news gathering makes all the clearer how sports television, in its usual guise, is light entertainment television, and that this is its strength. For one thing, populist light entertainment allows for both saying and not saying things that are highly sensitive (cf., Lusted 1998). Examples can be found in the Winner quote about the bicycles and Dutch resentment (as part of national and of sporting history) in the 1988 match against the Germans, but also in how issues of ethnic difference and discrimination can be addressed. Jokes will allow for breaking rules of proper conduct and for addressing discursively forbidden zones by calling forth sensitive subjects and then twisting them around. When the Cable started to make demands, rather than being grateful for any attention that was paid to them, it became impossible to use popular entertainment's half-serious, half-in-jest style of talking. No wonder the three Cable players themselves were probably most shocked by the boomerang effect that they had created, and that they have felt much safer in the realm of global commercial youth culture.

A mere analysis of televisual and other sports journalistic texts would certainly have brought out the stylistic characteristics of television versus print sports journalism. However, without an ethnographic counterpart, it would have been more difficult to, as it were, "record the temperature of social feelings around ethnicity and masculinity" (cf., Whannel 2001). The interviews make clear how social feelings about multiculturalism and ethnicity certainly do not present themselves in a clear-cut manner. By choosing to oppose the interviews with the men and the women, I have foregrounded how sentiments about ethnicity, masculinity, and national identity are cut through by gendered, sexualized perspectives. Lines of inclusion and exclusion are clearly drawn at either or not recognizing the male sports body as sexualized. Such erotic appreciation of the male body on television has only recently become possible, with the greater technological sophistication in video cameras. Earlier sports reportage was technically inhibited from using close-ups and stills. Much lower definition made a good appreciative look almost impossible. It is intriguing that technology (with all its connotations of masculinity) has opened up this new possibility for looking at and sexually appreciating the male body. It has turned sports stars into semi-sexual performers, much as Yvonne Tasker (1998) has described women's double encoding in fiction film and television (and see also Miller 2001). In ethnographic (or any type of qualitative audience) research, the mixture of discourses that are brought to bear on, in this case, football becomes clear, and allows for a different type of reconstruction of an era of sporting history and the genre of sports journalism.

That we may, in fact, be speaking about the end of an era is suggested by a recent news report about a scandal that involved the Dutch national team, playing a qualification match in Denmark.[17] Allegedly, a group of players had visited with Danish escorts. Later, this was denied. One of the escorts involved, a woman named Kyra Eggers, published a message on her web page that said that the Dutch footballers were "party poopers." Apparently, they had been invited by a sports broker to a party at the hotel where they were staying, but had left when they realized that the partying was a bit rough for their tastes. Of course, Kluivert was involved. Journalists tried to construct the incident (reported on both the front and back pages of the quality newspapers *Volkskrant* and *NRC*) as another black players versus white players story. But this would not fly. The white players who were also involved let it be known that they all felt that discipline for the team had been a bit heavy, thus taking the sting out of a history of insults addressed to the black players (that they lack discipline). Ethnic difference has lost its power in telling the story of football and of the nation. In the late 1980s, it reached a peak of multiculturalist interest, countered by the confusion that resulted from the Kluivert incidents, and disappointment over the lack of perseverance of the Cable.

Football connects and may allow for temporary outbursts of nationalism that would normally not take place. My initial project, when I started working on cultural citizenship, was to defend popular culture and show how bureaucratic democracies such as the Netherlands are dependent on a multitude of cultural forms and interpretive communities that allow us to (temporarily) own the world via fantasy constructs, via imagining what the world could be like, rather than what it *is* like, and by offering legitimate ways of venting criticism, disappointment, and so on. Cultural citizenship stands for how we bond in communities (both actual and virtual) that allow us to define, for ourselves and for others, who we are. This sense of belonging can have both appreciative and critical forms, and perhaps even a disinterested form. To call this "citizenship" is to show how the construction of identity and the formation of subjectivity take place in situated force fields, and are produced both in pleasure and in the discipline of the rules that govern the interpretive community of loving football. Moreover, cultural citizenship offers the possibility of not only reconstructing rules and allegiances that bind interpretive communities (an inward perspective), but of reconstructing the ways in which different communities are linked, or how smaller communities may function as testing laboratories or playgrounds for other, larger communities (sports lovers practicing nationalism).

However, the moral side to citizenship, by which I mean the implicit value of responsibility – the reason why many cherish the concept – seems to be precisely what is resisted in the cultural citizenship that a popular form such as watching the national team play realizes. Likewise, values such as equality are hardly cherished. It is quite clear that the popular pleasure offered here is predicated on difference (even though these differences are not necessarily aligned with social power hierarchies), on strong identities (the good versus the bad; our team against theirs), and only in the best cases insists on fair play. Many a foul is easily forgiven by the supporters. However, at the same time it is important to underscore that popular culture does recognize the existence and the rightness of a rule system – even if it is often felt that this should be dealt with in a creative way, rather than in the typical manner of the boring, rule-abiding . . . citizen. Cultural citizenship is a domain of creativity, of (safe and temporary) forms of resistance – of, in a sense, a citizenship half-time interval. At the same time, cultural citizenship, as a domain of utopia and temporary freedom, feeds allegiance to the very system that it resists. David Tetzlaff (1991) warns that these fragmented and fragmenting pleasures of the popular are exactly the way in which corporate capitalism functions effortlessly. Edgar Davids may have broken all the rules of player behavior and disappointed a great number of football lovers but – on the basis of his fabulous ball technique and "look" – he could still become a youth culture icon and hence boost shoe sales.

Insofar as a critical–political (rather than a cultural-interpretive) understanding of the pleasures of football as a television sport is possible, it is in the nexus of gender and sexuality rather than race and ethnicity. The women who we interviewed used football to turn the tables on men and male codes of talking. They appropriated sex talk and what in cinema studies would be called "the gaze." Most interestingly, they totally dissociated their sporting and erotic interest in the men from any racist discourse. In that sense, in my opinion they are way ahead of the men, who will let themselves be easily drawn into racialized types of talk that border on outright racism, however much they would like to keep their distance from such a vocabulary. For them, nationalism supports favored definitions of masculinity and sports heroism. It spells out the importance of football in capitals, which they see as being underscored by the money that changes hands between the world's big football clubs, however much they also feel that sport should not be commercialized or politicized. They appear to have a vested interest in understanding the nation as a bastion, and sport as a battlefield.

The women support the new soapified forms of sports reporting much more than the men, and are in that regard in the vanguard of televisual and media development. This means that the current commercialization of sport, and of black sportsmen in football, is also a progressive political force. Given that Patrick Kluivert is the epitome of today's footballers – media-trained to keep quiet and not say too much, or disclose much of himself – we might as well look to such unexpected (and unreliable) allies in anti-racist and feminist struggle as commercial TV and global capitalism. Kluivert does not have the Gullit charisma, except for his phenomenal talent as a football player and an impressive body.

Like Davids, his talents are best used when on display as an icon for the multicultural and nongender-exclusive joys of sport. But we also need new vocabularies to explicitize what could be called "racist discomfort," to realize the potential of football-as-cultural-citizenship. In that regard, "No comment" doesn't get us very far. Therefore, I hope that Ruud Gullit makes more bad television, even though he has taken to the world of football again, first training the Dutch national youth team, and more recently as coach with his old club Feyenoord. However, such contracts tend not to last very long.

notes

1 Only seven of the men and three of the women interviewed are quoted in this chapter.
2 In *Trouw*, April 27, 1996, p. 35.
3 In *Algemeen Dagblad*, June 24, 1996, p. 15 (source: Persdata.nl, May 20, 2000).
4 In *de Telegraaf*, May 15, 1996 (source: Telegraaf-i, May 19, 2000).
5 In *de Telegraaf*, June 12, 1997 (source: Telegraaf-i, May 19, 2000).
6 In *de Telegraaf*, April 20, 2000 (source: Telegraaf-i, May 19, 2000).
7 Joost Niemoller, "Kluivert, de film," in *Groene Amsterdammer*, July 2, 1997, pp. 18–19 (source: Persdata.nl, May 20, 2000).
8 Orkun Akinci, "Tribune," on the sports page of *NRC Handelsblad*, August 30, 1997 (source: Persdata.nl, May 20, 2000); Gerben Stolk, "Mag Kluivert nog in Oranje spelen" (Is Kluivert still allowed to play for the Orange team?), *de Telegraaf*, July 17, 1997 (source: Telegraaf-i, May 19, 2000).
9 *Algemeen Dagblad*, June 4, 1996, sports page (source: Persdata.nl, May 20, 2000).
10 Aired on October 2, 2001, by NOS, the Dutch Public Broadcasting Organization.
11 Maarten Moll, "Een jongensboek" (review of Bert Hiddema's Gullit biography, entitled *Gullit*, 1998), in *Parool*, PS 2, May 11, 1998.
12 Fred Caren, "Terug op aarde. Chelsea was Ruud Gullit op het lijf geschreven" (Back on earth. Ruud Gullit was a natural for Chelsea), in *Parool*, PS 2, May 11, 1998, pp. 2–3.
13 Patrick Kluivert, when interviewed by *Obsession*, a Surinamese magazine, did say that he would strongly prefer to play for a Surinam national team if such a team existed (September–October 1997 issue). See also the sports section of the British daily *The Express*, November 6, 1997, which published an interview with a number of black Dutch players.
14 This is especially true of quality newspapers such as *NRC*, *Volkskrant*, and *Trouw*. Populist newspapers such as *de Telegraaf* and *Algemeen Dagblad* did report on Kluivert's mishaps (see earlier footnotes).
15 See Akinci and Stolk in note 8. Roelant Oltmans (hockey coach) in Orkun Akinci on the sports page of *NRC Handelsblad*, August 30, 1997, p. 11: "I would not select

him. Obviously we don't need to discuss his football capacities, but there is more than quality . . . Football is much more than just sport, it is a social phenomenon."

16 Twenty men were interviewed (four nonwhite), nine women (one nonwhite). The interviews were conducted by Marion van Beelen, Martijn Peerenboom, Judith Verhoeff, Art van der Vorm, Iris Reynen, Marije Peddemars, Katelijn Wilhelmy, Georgette Albers, Jeroen Wolff, and Marika Zijp. All of the interviews took place in 1998.

17 *NRC Handelsblad*, "Danish press reports Dutch football team sex party," December 13, 2001, sports page (p. 12).

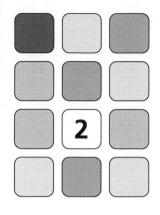

negotiating global popular culture

This chapter returns to questions of national identity in relation to genre and gender, but now as negotiated in relation to a global popular genre. It offers the discursive genealogy that Mittell (2001) suggests is useful when analyzing genre in popular culture, and focuses on the representation of women in Dutch police series, which it compares to the gender coding of internationally successful Anglo-American crime drama.[1] Genre analysis and its connotations of formal textual analysis have made it an approach that is seldom used by cultural media scholars. In Mittell's poststructuralist reformulation, however, looking for genre is understanding the nexus of cultural power relations that involve the industry, audiences, texts, and cultural practice more broadly defined. By starting from a specific media case study,[2] we may analyze how genre can become a site for debating cultural norms of, for instance, gender-appropriate behavior: appropriate, that is, in relation to historically formed national notions of identity; but also in relation to how those notions are challenged by second-wave feminism or migration and multiculturalism, and, most importantly from the perspective of this book, by the rules and conventions carried within global genres. In the Netherlands, as in other nation-states, broadcasting was important in "constructing the national family" (Morley 2000, p. 105). Its materials for doing so, however, were never exclusively Dutch. As a small country, there was always an economic interest in and a cultural taste for imported television. There is a tradition, then, of local negotiation of international genre rules, which has recently spread to television production itself. How is this process of negotiation an instance of cultural citizenship, and how does it help us to understand the uses and qualities of popular culture?

My goal is not to foreground Dutch national identity or history as such. They are here pretty much by accident, but will do well enough as an example of any of the local–national communities that negotiate the force of global popular culture.³ My intentions are more theoretically inclined. I am interested in the process of negotiation itself, of what is and what is not deemed appropriate and attractive within the generic confines of a television series produced for a specific (in this case, national) community. That is what I regard as the doing of cultural citizenship, the bonding over common identity and reflection on it, as indicated by viewer preference generally and, in this case, by my own viewer biography specifically. Following the negotiating process sedimented in a specific text (its storyline, the casting of its key actors) can make clear how popular culture is important to us, beyond the specific properties of that given text and beyond its specific national locality.

Genre analysis, in this case then, is not just the location of key textual properties, but the contextualization of entire television programs. Here, those contexts are local broadcasting history; the imagining of national identity and international (academic) discussion of changing conventions of gender representation in globally disseminated crime drama. This approach to genre analysis, allows me, in Mittell's words, to look at the workings of media as a component of social contexts and power relations, while gathering instances of "genre activity" in the interrelated sites of audience, industrial, and cultural practices (2001, p. 18). National identity is mediated in local appropriation of the format of the internationally successful crime series. More importantly, in putting pressure on local negotiations over identity construction, popular culture can be a force against complacency that favors reflection, adaptation, and inventiveness.

There are two major sections in this chapter. The first describes and analyzes local Dutch production of television crime series and its use of internationally circulating formats as a point of departure. Given the large number of women in key roles in these series, analysis of the representation of gender roles is my first port of call. A second analytical moment is the setting of the new series and their rendering of Amsterdam and Rotterdam, both big cities, as relatively safe places. This is quite an achievement – given that crime series by their very nature deal with danger, threat, and suspense – but why do they? Why are there so many women, and how does their presence and role relate to the need for safety? The second section of the chapter turns to international discussion of crime fiction. It suggests that the conservative genre contract between local viewers, producers, writers, and broadcasters springs from their deep investment in a particular version of national identity, and results in rewriting the genre of crime fiction away from its radical and feminist potential.

As a viewer, I feel lucky to belong to two interpretive communities, one global, one local, which allows me a comfortable critical distance from both. My popular cultural citizenship grants me the viewer pleasures of local and international crime series for their own benefit, while – and because – it also provides an opportunity for reflection and criticism. I can see the construction of national self-identity at work, matching itself against changing notions of gender in an arena delineated by generic rules. Adjudicating the claims of both offers me a most pleasurable means of reflecting on the parameters within which I define my own identity, as a feminist and as a Dutch national.

Dutch police series . . .

Half a decade into the deregulation of television in the mid-1990s in the Netherlands, it suddenly became popular to produce crime series locally. The older public broadcasting organizations started three series over a 4-year period. In the same time span, the new commercial stations started no less than five new series aimed at different audience segments. Prior to 1995, there had only been one homemade police series (*Maigret*, Vara, 1963–5) in 40 years of public service broadcasting. More interestingly still, a high number of women were cast in central roles in series whose narrative structure and general "look" were copied from English, American, and German examples; and whose reputation is still that they are part of a masculine genre. A more precise look at the narrative function, centrality, and agency of the women characters reveals how national identity, and its historically evolved notion of gender difference, are negotiated against international "standards." Also negotiated are the kind of storylines that were sanctioned by commissioning networks and the settings that were favored by producers. On the one hand, global popular representations rebalance national definitions of gender; but while generally accommodating to new notions of women's public role and professionalism, the national historical imaginary proved tenacious and, alas, conservative in how feminine characters were detailed.

Dutch public service television has always bought and aired all major crime series (from *The Saint*, *The Man from U.N.C.L.E.*, and *Starsky and Hutch* to *Hill Street Blues*, *Cagney and Lacey*, *Twin Peaks*, *Inspector Morse*, *Silent Witness*, and so on). Although formally set in England, North America, or occasionally exotic locations, they became part of Dutch national heritage. They also functioned, and continue to function, as specific identity markers tacked onto the image of the broadcasting organizations. The KRO (the Catholic broadcasting organization) linked its name to "English quality crime drama." They screen *Inspector Morse*, *A Touch of Frost*, *Prime Suspect*, *Silent Witness*, *Dalziel and Pascoe*, and *Second Sight*. The NCRV (the Christian broadcasting organization) forged a connection with "auteur" television producer Steve Bochco (Caldwell 1987). They aired his innovative police drama series *Hill Street Blues* (NBC, 1980–7) and later *NYPD Blue* (ABC, 1993–). *Cagney and Lacey* (CBS, 1982–8) was an obvious choice for the socialist Vara; while the quirky series *Twin Peaks*, directed by David Lynch, was bought by the then youngest public broadcaster Veronica, which left public broadcasting to become a commercial station.

Until the mid-1990s, no one felt the need to produce crime drama in the Netherlands, apart from the 1960s *Maigret* series. It was too costly, there was little experience with types of drama genre other than comedy, and there was no incentive to innovate. This changed with the deregulation of television at the end of the 1980s. More television hours needed to be filled, and under new competitive circumstances station profiles became more important than they had been in a long time. With its close associative link to BBC drama, the pinnacle of quality television, and its correlation with crime literature and the thriller, television crime drama was the ideal battleground for public broadcasting organizations, but why were commercial stations interested? They followed not the high cultural lineage but the crime series' popular links back to American action series and light drama such as *Charlie's Angels* (ABC, 1976–81). With its wide generic span, television crime drama effectively renders the high/low culture barrier obsolete. Moreover, audiences who had always greatly liked subtitled English- and German-language crime drama were exceedingly happy with Dutch-language series. It is not just language that gives these series their much-appreciated local flavor; they also, in a most interesting manner, manage to represent working women as nonthreatening to the local "housewife ideology"; and big cities as mostly friendly, manageable places.

In terms of characters, narrative, and setting, then, the new Dutch crime series share a number of startling resemblances that underline my intuition that these police and detective shows are all involved in negotiating global (Anglo-American) genre rules, against national heritage and lore. A brief overview follows, before their similarities are further discussed. Commercial television's *Baantjer* (RTL4, 1995–), based on a book series, is a straightforward city-based police procedural. It is the best-watched Dutch crime series and the ultimate in family television, airing at 8.30 p.m. on Fridays. It drew an audience of around three million viewers in 2003, which is only equaled by the widely respected 8 o'clock news (*Het Journaal*, NTS/NOS, 1959–) and by the matches of the national football team. The socialist broadcasting organization Vara had a series centered around a woman DA and a police team working on serious crimes that ran for 2 years (*Unit 13*, 1995–7). Then, over a 3-year period (1998–2001), six new police series were introduced. RTL4 commissioned *Blue Blue* (*Blauw Blauw*, 1999–), a precinct-based, nitty-gritty realist series, set in Amsterdam for an urban streetwise audience, and *Dok 12* (2001–2), which focuses on a Rotterdam harbor police team. *Dok 12* has an attractive young soap star as lesbian computer nerd on its team. It drew the young and hip viewer segment that it was intended for. The competing, smaller commercial station SBS6 entered the field in 2001 with two private eye series, *Wildschut and De Vries*, a *Moonlighting* clone, and *Luifel and Luifel*, which centers around a father policeman who has a PI son with James Bond inclinations. Not to be outdone, the public broadcasters started *Russians* (KRO, 2000–), which centered around an undercover police team, shot in somber surroundings, and *Spangen*, a Rotterdam precinct-based show with two central women characters (TROS, 2000–). *Spangen* was immediately likened to *Cagney and Lacey*, but in fact it was originally based on a German script.

. . . as imports: women's emancipation

There are surprisingly many women in these series, more than a cross-section of the international series that are now produced would suggest that are really needed. Women's emancipation is implied to be a good thing, and to add to a strong representation of policing – not so much in terms of the special qualities that women would bring to policing, but simply in terms of a socially representative police corps. The number of women characters is surprising, given that the Dutch used to define bliss in terms of domesticity and "cosiness." Children would come home from school at 3 o'clock in the afternoon to find mum waiting with tea and cookies. There is a gap between this old and regularly referred to nostalgic ideal and the gun-toting and justice-wielding gals in the police series today. What should we make of it?

Apart from the striking number of women who are prominent members of the casts in the new Dutch crime series, there is also, as in Dutch comedy and soap opera (Moran 1998; O'Donnell 1999), an unusually strong emphasis on the group of police men and women as a work family, which is underlined by the high number of family relationships within the police teams. *Blue Blue* has a brother and sister who work in the same precinct, as well as a divorced couple with a son, among its detectives. *Dok 12* has two brothers whose loyalty and competition with one another is a source of continuous dramatic tension, in much the same way as the successful love triangle in the soap opera. The meal served to the team at the end of each episode of *Baantjer* by the senior detective's wife in their big live-in kitchen has all the hallmarks of a family Sunday lunch. *Spangen's* senior woman detective has a son to whom she is mostly a cliché divorced father, but whose presence is often important to storylines. The Dutch police series take Ella Taylor's assertion that families (whether real or work families) are a key element in television fiction to extremes (Taylor 1989).

The emphasis on work families goes a long way toward explaining the presence of all those women in the new Dutch police series. They are simply necessary to complete the fictional work families; their presence doesn't seem to be an indication of a collective fantasy of the Netherlands as a fully emancipated, postfeminist country. The women station chiefs in *Blue Blue* and *Dok 12*, and the female DA in *Unit 13*, are not independent figures with unquestioned authority and control – whether over a team, in terms of their own action radius, or ambition. Unsurprisingly, in this regard, nor are they given many women's issues to raise. The popular linking of *Spangen* to *Cagney and Lacey* suggests this possibility, but not to the commissioning editors at the broadcasting organization. At first and a second glance, the high number of women in the casts, some of them in senior positions, is no more than a fortuitous congruence of an international trend and a local preference for the family. Regretfully, from my perspective as a viewer, the new series do not, as a result, allow for either a feminist perspective (that women have to fight to get to these positions), or for a postfeminist perspective (that having women at the top will put pressure on existing conventions and ways of working).

The women detectives' dual subject status as feminine (by gender) and masculine (by profession) could easily have been problematized narratively, but it is not. Professionalism is simply extended to include caring and a strong sense of responsibility toward civilians (children are returned home; bereaved family members are comforted). Likewise, it seems a sympathetic thought that one's sexuality should simply be a matter of a lifestyle choice (*Dok 12*), but it is obvious in everyday life that this is hardly social reality. Potentially progressive and feminist representations are not suppressed, but they are undercut by lack of grounding in material practice or narrative centrality. Whilst this is not "masquerade" as in Sherrie Inness's description of Emma Peel in *The Avengers*, to be discussed below, it does come close to how women characters have often been treated in international crime drama since the 1970s (with *The Avengers* an early forerunner in the 1960s) and prior to the 1990s, which gave us Jane Tennyson, Sam Ryan, and Dana Scully (to whom we will also return in this chapter).

If there is a discernible vocation in these series, it boils down to maternal instinct: the chiefs in both *Blue Blue* and *Dok 12* operate with a stern but sensitive motherly authority. Mariska, Luifel senior's partner, tends to both assume and mock a caregiver's role in relation to both father and son (*Luifel and Luifel* is, after all, a comedy/detective hybrid). The mum-and-dad framework of *Baantjer*, with De Cook as a fatherly figure and his wife as the nominal center of the work family when she serves food or drinks at the end of each episode, is a throwback to unapologetically pre-feminist ideology that measured women in terms of their motherly capacities. In *Spangen*, however, motherhood is a site of tension and trouble, which mixes interestingly with the feelings of solidarity and competition that bind the two central women characters.

Spangen – after *Baantjer*, the most-watched series – is interesting. It merits a closer look to get a more focused view of Dutch local mores and the pressures that generic drive can exert to readjust them. It makes clear that there is a tug-of-war going on over how popular culture should represent (national and other) identities. *Spangen* in particular shows some of the ideological struggle that resulted from the redefinition of women's social roles instigated by second-wave feminism, if not directly in explicitly feminist themes or narrative twists. However, the fact that women working outside the home carry a heavy burden of guilt for their refusal of a conservatively defined motherhood, as homemaker and caregiver (whether full-time or part-time), is not denied by the series or glossed over. In the first season (2000–1), the older detective of the two-woman team, played by all-round movie actress Monique van der Ven, is portrayed prim-arily as a divorced mother and, indeed, a tragic figure, who lives apart from her teenager son. In the second season, both the older and the younger woman detective start romantic relations that do not last. Here, we find a portrayal of women that feels more true to established international conventions and is, in fact, a more realistic representation of actual life in the Netherlands. In their work too, from time to time, the women have to negotiate ingrained notions about women and femininity that interfere with their professional identities.

Unlike the other series, *Spangen* does not foreground family relations as either a simile or actual fact of the police work family either. It thus brings a new ele-ment to the national understanding of gender roles and motherhood. *Spangen* has learnt from international television crime drama, and it articulates that understanding with local tradition and self-image. The all too familiar logic that brings together women and family, femininity, and intimacy is held at bay. Popular culture, in this case the local rendering of international formats, contributes to ongoing processes of national gendered self-understanding, but hardly in predictable ways.

. . . as exports: safe for tourists

In general, it is mothers, then, and one remaining father (De Cook) who are keeping the world safe in Dutch crime drama. If we continue to accept both that drama is a stage of identity (Leeuw 1995) and that realist crime drama may have an important ideological function in mapping a consensual view of the world (Davis 2001, p. 135), where does that take us in our project of finding out about how popular culture is a means of exchange in defining national identity in relation to global generic formats? Although there are some grounds for hope, local narrative conventions mostly produce an unquestioned underlying conservative gender ideology. Key settings for the series, and the filmic conventions used in shooting, provide a second area of genre investigation that underwrites the assumption that Dutch popular culture is conservative. As Shohat and Stam put it in their discussion of stereotypes, realism, and representation: ". . . the constructed coded nature of artistic discourse hardly precludes all references to a common social life. Filmic fictions inevitably bring into play real-life assumptions not only about space and time but about social and cultural relationships" (Shohat & Stam 1994, p. 179). They too, then, argue that popular fiction should be taken seriously as a forum of self-reflection, and suggest that we look for references to common social life.

When asked, viewers will explain that they like *Baantjer*, *Spangen*, and the other series because they recognize so much. Mostly, this is in reference to the settings of the new Dutch police series, which are best described as being couched in terms of tourist clichés. Like the setting of the British ITV series *Inspector Morse*, they are part of a modern-day heritage industry (Sparks 1993), but that too produces a space in which "the politics of location is inextricably interwoven with the politics of identity," as argued by Peter Billingham in his *Sensing the City through Television* (2000, p. 1). *Baantjer* and *Spangen*, the one unapologetically conservative in format, the other a little more adventurous, provide examples that allow for a new route to explore national self-understanding filtered by popular televisual conventions, a meeting place of global generic rules and imagined national uniqueness.

In *Baantjer*, the backdrop of most outdoor scenes contains canals, the characteristic curved bridges of the inner city, seventeenth- and eighteenth-century canal houses, or attractive, compact, nineteenth-century city streets. While viewers tend to see this as "recognizable and real," it is both a romanticizing and an alienating view of Amsterdam. Despite the outspoken storylines that deal with such things as murder in a gay bar, interethnic relations gone haywire, mob-related crime, and so on, the city has mostly become a sanitized space, free of social inequality, poverty, and urban problems. Even De Cook's favorite bar in the Red Light District is like a second living room rather than a border area or a danger zone. In Amsterdam, the look of the series suggests, we may safely spend our money and enjoy picturesque surroundings. *Spangen* is different. It is shot more cinematically and has a more dangerous feel. Wide-angled shots are used over wide-open spaces, which creates a sense of loneliness and alienation. In the end, *Spangen* too sells a city, and was funded by the Rotterdam Film Fund to do so. As a result, Rotterdam's harbor, and its architectural triumph of bridges and innovatory high-rise buildings, dominate the leader, and are recurring sights/sites throughout the episodes. This *mise-en-scène* does not ask the viewer to identify with the day-to-day living environments of the Rotterdam boroughs (of which Spangen is one), but with isolated characters set against a cinematic backdrop.

This is not to argue that the realism of either *Baantjer* or *Spangen* is fake. But it would be illusory to read either series for realism in the sense of authenticity. The metaphorical value of the characters and the cityscape are what I want to focus on here. As with the "safe for tourists" image presented via the settings, the metaphorical value of the women in the casts seems to be reassurance. Why would reassurance and a sense of safety be of such importance to Dutch crime drama? This goes to the heart of Dutch social relations. Answering this question illustrates how cultural citizenship is an arena in which individual viewers, viewer communities, and institutions such as broadcasting organizations all bring their own issues and preferences to bear, in the meantime finding a shared vocabulary and agenda that underwrites the existence of a sense of national identity that is continually under construction.

Safety and security

The specificity of the social relations portrayed in Dutch crime drama is best understood in contrast to British police series and the unreconstructed hierarchical class culture that they appear to spring from. Morse habitually puts down his sergeant, Lewis; John Nettles portrays a genial detective inspector in *Midsomer Murders* (ITV / A&E, 1997–), who nevertheless uses his hierarchical advantage to make fun of his sergeant. Certainly not all popular British television drama is class-biased in this sense. Other series present a rougher social realism (such as the BBC series *Between the Lines*, 1992–4), while in other genres there is a strong tendency toward anarchy, carnival, and unrefined humor. The tension span that strings together *Inspector Morse* on the one hand, and *The Benny Hill Show* (ITV/Thames, 1969–89) and *The Young Ones* (BBC, 1992–4) on the other – that is, from hierarchy to anarchy – is unknown in Dutch culture. Our comedies are a bit more refined (fortunately), while (less fortunately) our police series tend to resemble the comedies and soaps that are made here as well: police drama is a new branch on the Dutch tree of family drama. The Dutch, then, do not understand themselves via a strong sense of class. Politically, too, the pillars[4] represent a mix of class and confessional or religious interests, which was held together by a strong consultative structure amongst the elites of the pillars (Lijphart 1968). Consultation and the wish for consensus-building are key national characteristics, both politically and culturally.

Police teams are portrayed in this light. They are congenial working situations – and hardly sites of tension, whether socially or dramatically. *Spangen,* again, is interesting. In the first season, the two protagonists start out in an aunt–niece type of relationship that balances competition and solidarity. Moreover, Nicky Spoor (the younger one, played by show host Linda de Mol) is also something of a cynic. Cynicism is a most unusual form in Dutch genre drama, and is more usually to be found in high-drama production as a sign of sophistication. In day-to-day "polder model" culture, based on continuous consultation between parties, cynicism is after all a sin. Cynicism questions the very grounds of the consultation system itself, and the basis and legitimacy of each and every contribution. Cynicism has its merits within a class-based system, in the challenge that it poses to that system. In a society and a police force that only recognize hierarchy as a means of working efficiently, and as being based on skill and (prior) experience, it is no more than a spanner in the works. Neither cynics nor bad police officers, for that matter, are popular with the producers. One of *Spangen*'s text writers[5] told me that he has suggested such thematics, but they have always been killed, either by the production company or by the broadcasting organization. They are convinced that such storylines or characters will discourage viewers and reduce audience figures.

Judging by its crime drama, then, the Netherlands has managed to reinterpret the development of gender identity and issues of authority and control in global crime drama in a conservative vein, while paying lip service to the ongoing emancipation within the genre. Mum is all-important, and reigns metaphorically from the kitchen (well, literally in *Baantjer*). Within the bounds of this scenario, women may leave home, hearth, and kitchen, but will keep on drilling those around them to be properly washed and dressed, and to be well-mannered in public. At the station too, they make sure that well-manneredness is the rule, that procedures are followed, and that emotions are aired. *Plus ça change* . . . This may, of course, be indicative only of the teething troubles of a young industry embarking on new generic domains. For now, in Dutch police series, the police may be innocents, as illustrated by the high number of (young) women and the prominence of young men in love, but they are bound to grow up at some point. As producers and writers gain more experience, the police and detectives themselves may become less central to storylines than the bad guys (and girls) and the social cost of crime. Possible proof of this hypothesis lies in the fact that many of the key personnel working on the more interesting series, *Spangen*, learned the ropes while making *Baantjer*.[6]

In the interest of completeness, I need to mention that we have had "bad" cops in *Russians*, which had a link to a debacle in real-life Dutch policing, in which newly formed interregional crime squads were accused of drug-dealing on a wide scale (in the early 1990s). Newspapers reported that 15,000 kilos of cocaine had been imported with the help of corrupt civil servants, while

100,000 kilos of soft drugs had been brought onto the open market. At least 500,000 euros (then 1.2 million guilders) had been stolen.[7] A parliamentary inquiry (1990–1) uncovered this scandalous state of affairs, but the administrators and politicians in positions of responsibility managed to escape unscathed. This offered sufficient material for a *Between the Lines* type series, but – given its high-drama aspirations – *Russians* emphasized the claustrophobia, the psychological effects of general undercover work on its key characters in relation to each other, rather than the drill of policing the police case after case after case. Moran's (1998) and O'Donnell's (1999) comments on the claustrophobic character and somberness of Dutch family life in soap opera apply well to this high-drama series. Implicitly, throughout the spectrum of the new series, it is suggested that the police are our best friends. Questions of the *right* to police, which Charlotte Brunsdon (1998) suggests were key issues in British crime drama (and politics) from the mid-1980s to the mid-1990s, are not posed at all.

In conclusion, we have seen how recent, locally produced, crime drama can be understood to "mediate political discourse" (Davis 2001, p. 134), to be a product of the organization of broadcasting and its deregulation, and how it is a field of translation of the codes and conventions in global popular genres. Apparently, the simple visceral thrill of crime, the breaking of social norms, the attacks on bodily integrity, and the fatal misunderstandings of the division between public and private life translate well, as does the opportunity to follow a group of people bound by the ties of having to make do with one another as colleagues. What a television scholar would understand to be the particular markers of the quality of the original text are apparently of less consequence, whether they take the form of humor, in-depth psychological drama, or narrative and dramatic self-reflexivity and self-questioning. It is attractive to argue that Dutch crime drama has simply taken a more American, less class- and more image- and action-based, route. But that would be patently untrue. British crime drama can be as fast-paced as American crime drama and, historically, American crime drama certainly also invested in the exploration of class relations, as Paul Cobley has shown in his discussion of *Kojak* as a particular type of working-class hero (Cobley 2000, 2001), while first *Miami Vice* and later *The X-Files* offer thought-provoking representations of masculinity.

What we witness on Dutch television is the logic of affect, the sensibility of (global) popular genres at work in constructing an arena for discussion of Dutchness. The overwhelming viewer preference for the conservative series *Baantjer* suggests that many feel comfortable with its highly formulaic and traditional framework. Not unimportantly, however, *Spangen*, the most progressive and challenging of the new series, comes a strong second in the ratings for the crime series. This too deserves explanation. By my reckoning, the wide availability of international crime fiction, in the form of novels and television series, must have produced a greater literacy than is suggested by the Dutch crime series and how they are received. As part of my genealogical investigation, I will now turn to that other interpretive community to which I feel that I belong – to my own experiences and expectations as a fan of English-language thriller and detective novels and police series on television, told in dialogue with the observations of all those other fan/critics in media and cultural studies who write on this subject. What literacy is potentially available? What further challenges and pressures can global crime fiction offer to local, national self-understanding?

International crime fiction . . .

. . . and women

There is a long tradition of foregrounding women characters in crime fiction. Women figure in crime novels from the nineteenth-century American dime novel onward. They have a well-known strong presence in the so-called Golden Age of detective fiction in the inter-war period and have been present ever since (Klein 1988). Critics, such as Katherine Gregory Klein, have pointed out that they were mostly amateurs, with little formal power. The spinster-detectives of the inter-war period, of which Miss Marple is the quintessential example, managed to be masterminds without challenging propriety. As older women on their own, they could hardly be suspected of usurping male prerogative or of disruptive sexuality.

As many young teenagers still do, I read my parents' Agatha Christie novels, and their Ngaio Marsh and Dorothy L. Sayers mysteries. My mother, my sister, and I loved to watch the entirely different heroes of *The Persuaders!*, and later *Charlie's Angels* and *Starsky and Hutch*, in more or less the same period of my life. The combination of humor, murder, and puzzle-solving has always been a constant element in my media diet. Moreover, male and female lead characters in television spoke to who I wanted to be: hip, ironic, smart, and able to rest in the secure knowledge that my friends would be loyal no matter what. I don't think I ever reflected much on the misery that the storylines also imply for the victims and their families, who are affected by murder and such. As reader, you can be squarely on the side of the investigators. Identifying with male characters was not a problem either. Like most young women, I was adept at re-reading gender attributes (cf., Douglas 1995). In *The Persuaders!* (ATV/ITV, 1971) for example, Tony Curtis and Roger Moore are two playboys with time on their hands, who are roped in by an old judge to investigate crimes that the judicial system cannot handle. Although they are two middle-aged men, I easily related to their affable rapport and light-hearted camaraderie. Nor have I ever grown out of viewing a life of fun and leisure – without egotistical hedonism – as a worthwhile goal in life (after all, in each episode, *The Persuaders!* do help others) (cf., Hermes 2001). Miss Marple too, for that matter, always seems to have a lot of time to go detecting and crime-solving while "visiting" with friends.

As a political science student, I discovered feminist detectives, which I read to date. Sara Paretsky's *V. I. Warshawski* (1982–), Nevada Barr's park ranger *Anna Pigeon* (1984–), Sue Grafton's *Kinsey Malone* (1982–), Sarah Dreher's *Stoner MacTavish* (1985–90), Sandra Scoppetone's *Lauren Laurano* (1991–8), Marcia Muller's *Sharon McCone* (1977–), Linda Barnes' *Carlotta Carlysle* (1987–), and Val McDermid's *Lindsay Gordon* (1990–) or *Kate Brannigan* (1993–) are only a selection of the strong women heroines I loved as a member of their worldwide readership. One of the more likable aspects of these feminist crime novels, I suspect, is the independence of the women protagonists. They do not have to deal with the burden of family, most notably, the nuclear family (Décuré 1994). I do not know of any who are married when we are first introduced to them. They seldom have children. They may, from time to time, feel lonely but they do usually have a small number of good friends in both animal guise (dogs and cats mostly, such as Anna's cat Piedmont and V. I.'s golden retriever Peppy) and human form, including the occasional lover. Over the years, some of them do build more steady relationships, as I have done in the two decades since I was a student. What they retain and what, for me, connects them to *The Persuaders!* and *Charlie's Angels*, is their strong and self-reflexive sense of humor.

While keyed to find more of what I like, I watch all kinds of television crime fiction. Some of it is really good and enjoyable; some of it depresses me. In the academic debate that ensued over the same period, I watched the series and began to teach mass communication, and later television studies, and a picture emerged of the price that the mainstream mass media wish women to pay for holding center stage in (formerly) male genres. Women in television crime fiction have difficult lives and don't have much fun. Popular culture in the audiovisual media (aimed at larger audiences via more public technology) pulls in a different direction than in literary fiction.

In the audiovisual media, we do still find crime and humor connected, though much more flippantly than in "the old days"; that is, in my case, the 1980s and early 1990s. Janet Evanovich's crime comedy series around bounty hunter Stephanie Plum (10 novels, 1994–2004) is a case in point. Fashion, romance, and solving the crime are of equal importance. Headstrong, but with a noticeable lack of a well-defined sense of self, Stephanie is like other late 1990s popular heroines such as Bridget Jones (Helen Fielding: novels 1996 and 1999; films 2001, dir. Sharon Maguire, and 2004, dir. Beeban Kidron). In their cases, to be independent is, alas, hardly as satisfying or as worthwhile a goal as it used to be for my heroines of two decades ago. Evaluating the development of women characters in popular literature and television, I can see how feminism became a marketable commodity by the late 1970s, how it moved from small feminist publishing houses to the big publishers in the 1980s, and how feminist heroines were over time adapted for mass audiences, who were less enthralled with progressive political doctrine. What is also obvious is that books are a more open and diverse media space that allows for a much more politicized perspective, while the audiovisual media – that is, film and television – are more conservative in responding to the social change instigated by the women's movement.

Feminist detective novels present a particular version of the feminist dream. It features the woman who can take care of herself, who will kick ass, and who doesn't depend on anyone else for anything. There are no "significant others" who hold her back from serving the higher goals of justice or, more simply, from the goal of leading an independent life while Nosy Parkering away. These women don't appeal to film and television producers. The film based on Sara Paretsky's *V. I. Warshawski* novels (Jeff Kanew, dir., USA, 1991), starring Kathleen Turner as V. I., is anemic compared to the books. The self-sufficiency, humor, and strong-headedness are there, but make no sense without the oftentimes politicized plots of administrative crime in the novels. Feminism turned into mainstream nonromantic comedy is not amusing. The stark realism of *Cagney and Lacey*, *Prime Suspect* (ITV/Granada, 1991, 1992, 1993, 1995, 1996, 2003), or, more recently, *Silent Witness* (BBC, 1996–2003) is far more palatable despite a noticeable lack of humor. I watch them, but hardly identify with them.

The attraction of these strong but slightly tragic women protagonists for television producers has, I suspect, to do with the fact that all of them pay for their professional successes – won at great cost in the workplace – by having decidedly unhappy personal lives. Although we also find tragic heroes among male police officers and investigators (Morse is a good example; *Inspector Morse*, ITV, 1987–2000 – cf., Thomas 1995), as a man you have a better chance of a happy private life in television crime drama (Inspector Wexford, for instance, is a happily married man; *The Ruth Rendell Mysteries*, ITV, 1988–), as is Barnaby in *Midsomer Murders*. Scripting the lives of female detectives as beyond the bounds of "normality" is a way of making them pay for their transcendence of gender norms, while adding a challenging element to crime drama. Detective fiction fans might argue that older "noir" detectives such as Dashiell Hammett's *Sam Spade*, and others too, were typically marginal figures, who lived and worked outside the range of bourgeois society. They did manage to have fairly active, exciting sex lives (albeit by implication) (Symons 1985). Regrettably, this too is uncommon for female television police officers.

Television has yet another way of distinguishing between the genders. Contrary to my literary heroines, television's women detectives tend not to fight criminals directly hand to hand, or chase them, as *Starsky and Hutch* (ABC, 1975–9) did, nor do they lay down the law *Miami Vice*-style (NBC, 1984–9) (cf., Gamman 1988). Emma Peel in *The Avengers* (ITV, 1961–9) and *Charlie's Angels* (ABC, 1976–82) are the exceptions. Their fighting prowess was legitimated – by John Steed, in Emma's case, or by Charlie in the Angels' case – while all could be taken for models showing the latest in women's fashion (cf., Innes 1999; Gough-Yates 2001). Although I like them, it has to be said that these women go through their fictional lives with a certain naïveté. This is, ultimately, what defines them as being outside feminism, and what justifies their critical reception in international academic debate. They don't share any knowledge of a world that is unjust to women, or any other group; nor do they take pleasure in operating from an alternative sense of self, based in self-styled communities rather than given traditional forms.

Academic debate in this area stems, I am convinced, from viewer pleasures and the investments of authors. They mind, as I do, that so many interesting women are not allowed to be really strong or independent. This is pointed out in the literature over and over again. According to Sherrie Innes, for example, Mrs Peel's tough image was undermined in "a variety of ways, such as her repeated use of masquerade and disguise" (1999, p. 35). The same had happened earlier with Angie Dickinson as Pepper in *Police Woman* (NBC, 1974–8). Pepper's main use to the police force (and to us viewers, as bearers of a male gaze) was to go undercover, usually as a hooker. Masquerade, Innes suggests (1999, p. 36), is often used to reveal that a woman's attitude is only skin-deep – another disguise, if you will. Female detectives in later series too are often eye candy, or fodder for romantic scenarios: *Moonlighting* (ABC, 1985–9) and *Dempsey and Makepeace* (ITV/London Weekend Television, 1985–6) are suggested by Gamman (1988, pp. 10–11) as examples of this. In this regard, *The X-Files* (Fox, 1993–2001) is a most exceptionable series, even if, by my (conventional) standards of what constitutes a good murder case, it was not much fun. It did, uniquely, celebrate unresolved sexual tension between the male and female protagonists, with Dana Scully in the role of the skeptical and rational professional and Fox Mulder as passionate, intuitive, and – in a way – more emotional (Wilcox and Williams 1996). We will return briefly to *The X-Files* below.

Cagney and Lacey is also exceptional. As a two-woman detective team in a New York police precinct, they were not isolated from other women. Isolating the woman protagonist, according to Gamman, is a ploy to undermine her strength and the political significance of her independence. It "personalizes" her struggles as well as her victories (Gamman 1988, p. 11). Cagney and Lacey had one another. As with the male buddy couple (cf., Spangler 1992), the suggestion of homoeroticism is contained by focusing on Christine Cagney's boyfriends and Mary Beth Lacey's relationship with her husband Harve. The pleasure of this series is located, I agree with Gamman, in the female gaze that it offers and, most notably, in the series' mockery of machismo, as shown by its representation of Isbecki – a co-officer (1988, p. 25). Julie d'Acci takes this argument further and suggests that although *Cagney and Lacey* is rooted in liberal notions of social and feminist change (as simply a matter of equal roles, equal jobs, and equal representation), it "manages to keep in play alternative and even oppositional discourses. Issues such as single, working mothers, federal cutbacks in social service programs, nuclear irresponsibility and inhumane treatment of 'illegal aliens', as well as race, class and gender have also been addressed" (d'Acci 1987, p. 222). Rape and wife-battering were made matters of wide public attention. I always liked the series for its mix of real issues and cases, self-reflection and occasional humor, even if *Cagney and Lacey* could be a bit slow. Liking it was closely linked to being a fan of *Hill Street Blues* (MTM, 1980–7), which was broadcast in the same period. *Hill Street Blues* also had a number of strong roles for women, one of whom was also a lesbian. The generic adventurousness of these two series, mixing police procedural with longer storylines about emotions and relationships, was easily recognized as an exciting and revolutionary move in television history.

A decade later, *Prime Suspect* was the series that I discussed and watched with friends. British rather than American, and driven and somber rather than occasionally humorous or reflexive, *Prime Suspect* had extremely strong storylines and a wholly exceptional protagonist. Although Helen Mirren, who plays Jane Tennyson, was at the time (and still is) something of a sex symbol in the UK, we did not like her much at all. Tennyson is extremely ambitious. She cannot spare her few loved ones much time (her partner, or her parents; cf., Brunsdon 1998). She smokes and she drinks; she puts down her inferiors, much like Morse or Frost (*A Touch of Frost*, ITV, 1992–), but without the excuse of being a (gentle)man. Although a painful road to travel, hers is an example of the cost that women incur in gaining agency and control in popular fiction, and perhaps elsewhere as well. Despite her movement up the promotional ladder, Tennyson's fight is ongoing. Agency and control, then, remain a moot point for all of television's women detectives.

. . . and men

Definitions of femininity are both upheld and renegotiated in crime fiction. The same goes for masculinity. Series such as *Miami Vice*, but also *Twin Peaks* and

The X-Files, bespeak a radical undermining of the notion that the male subject or police officer is in a position of control. *Miami Vice*'s Sonny Crockett is an unhappy man in his personal life, who often doubts his abilities as a police officer. He can be read as a "feminized" male, but he can also be read as a postmodern, fragmented subject (King 1990). Special Agent Cooper cannot solve the murder of Laura Palmer in *Twin Peaks* (ABC, 1990–1) by using rationalist, deductive – that is to say, standard – police methods. Cooper turns to intuition and a sense of the paranormal, and that is how he makes "Bob" (evil *alter ego* of Laura's father) show himself. However, "Bob" cannot be brought to justice by Cooper. Insofar as the male detectives are indeed the ones to lay down the Law, as is suggested by Gamman (1988), they are less good at it than they used to be in the days of *Columbo* (NBC, 1968–78; ABC, 1989–) and *Kojak* (Universal, 1973–8).

Agent Fox Mulder of *The X-Files* is another case in point: banished to the basement, and placed under the (implicit) supervision of agent Dana Scully, his convictions and intuition are his (only) assets. Sonny Crockett, Special Agent Cooper, and Fox Mulder are attractive, though, and invite a female sexualized gaze. Sonny is usually dressed in a contrived casual style (loafers, no socks), which becomes him. Cooper's very untouchableness makes him attractive. Fox Mulder goes furthest. We often get to see his naked upper body, and sometimes the whole naked man but for a pair of briefs (first season pilot, 1993). His chest hair is a sign that this is indeed an orchestration of heterosexual desire, and that Mulder, although placed in a feminine position, is a "real" guy. The occasional hint of a flirtation with another woman clinches the argument ("War of the Coprophages," 1996).

Although series such as *Twin Peaks* and *The X-Files* are fascinating, they are not series I easily love – for one thing, because while we do get to lust over desirable males, they are also "damaged goods." These very same male police officers and detectives are no longer undisputedly in a position of power and control, and worse: nor are women allowed to take up this position (despite the price they pay in personal unhappiness). Dana Scully in *The X-Files*, though a detached and rational scientist, still has her body infested with cancer and a monstrous pregnancy, which makes it clear that roles have not simply been reversed between men and women, but that both genders have had to relinquish authority (and the notion that we have some autonomy). *The X-Files* as a whole suggests that we are at the mercy of unseen forces, including the American government, and that any position of control is illusory (Howley 2001). The same happens in other end-of-the-millennium series. Nikita, for example, in *La Femme Nikita* (Warner Bros, 1997–2001), is a formidable fighter and is both morally and intellectually independent, but often seems to be at the mercy of Section One, her elusive and corrupt bosses.

Charlotte Brunsdon points to a similar development in British police series, that – from the end of the 1980s into the early 1990s – turned to questioning the right to police, a concern voiced in news items and politics, that was taken up and developed within the genre. The crime series as genre, Brunsdon suggests,

> works over and worries at the anxieties and exclusions of contemporary citizen-ship, of being British and living here, now. This genre, I would argue, has proved so resonant with both producers and audiences because it repeatedly, even obsessively, stages the drama of the responsible citizen caught in the embrace of what increasingly seems an irresponsible state. (1998, p. 225)

As soon as *Inspector Morse*, *Prime Suspect*, and *Between the Lines* (shown all over the world) travel, how they have meaning changes. From dramatic reflection on and interpretation of local specific circumstance, they turn into metaphoric tales that more broadly define issues of gender and control. What remains, for example, is the figure of Jane Tennyson in *Prime Suspect*, who familiarizes us with the figure of a senior (white) woman giving orders (Brunsdon 1998, p. 242); what remains after seeing *Between the Lines*, about the Complaints Investigation Bureau of the Metropolitan Police, is the notion that cops may be bent, that police officers who have already been turned into human beings by *Hill Street Blues* in the early 1980s are not necessarily heroes, or even very likable.

While women have become credible police officers and detectives, the whole profession appears to have lost social status and authority internationally. Narratives show them as fallible human beings who, on occasion, are wrong, distrusted, or insecure. Even such patriarchal icons as Morse and Frost have to cope with bosses and prove their worth time and time again; on occasion, they are negligent or plain wrong. Storylines, then, have turned on the formerly untouchable protagonists. Not just soap elements but tragedy have become parts of the television crime genre. Cuklancz (2000) charted a similar evolution for representations of rape in fiction television; while the German FrauenFilmInitiative *Murderesses in Film* collection (1992) suggests that the tragic link between women and crime is nothing new, but is infused with new meaning through the advent of the women's movement.[8] Television simply has been late in catching on.

Practices of representation and the reader

The local negotiation of international genre rules is a delegated form of cul-tural citizenship, traced here at the level of programs. As a reader, one follows more idiosyncratic logics. Reflecting on my own pleasure in crime fiction, it is clear how the two reader communities to which I belong overlap but are entirely different. I am a Dutch viewer and a feminist, who understands locally made television in relation to national television history, to the internationally successful series that are part of that national history, and in relation to nationally cherished notions of good motherhood. I am also a feminist academic, involved as fan and as critic in an international community of readers and investigators of (reader) pleasures in crime drama and in strong heroines. The usable fictions that I look for, both as a local and as an international reader, have to do with reassurance (women can be strong and sexy) and anger (about continuing male prerogative and limiting definitions of gender); and with working through the pain and the exhilaration of (slowly) changing gender roles.

The tug-of-war staged in the arena of popular culture engages me as reader, as academic employee, as fan, and as mother. Like others, I use the offer of crime drama to identify with the investigator–protagonist as central figure, to connect and reflect on these roles. There is none of the emotional and relational turmoil of soap opera's many protagonists here, or the always double-edged message of comedy that undermines and restates structures of authority at the same time (Marc 1997). Part of that reflection is how, in my viewing practice, I also align myself and am in debate with national identity and its investments in national gender ideals. The very fact that others are engaged in the same process shows how reading popular culture is not just fun but important, in enabling the act of cultural citizenship. How others read crime fiction, and with what results, is the question for the next chapter.

notes

1 Original air dates of television series, the broadcasting organizations that commissioned them, and in some cases production companies have been derived from various sources and checked against at least one other source. Some errors may, however, remain. Internet sources include the following: epguides.com; www.museum.tv; timstvshowcase.com; dedicated fan sites such as corrie.net, and the sites of television broadcasting organizations in the UK, and the USA. Other sources include Bianculli (1996), Swanson and James (1996), and the Netherlands public service (www.omroep.nl) and the Dutch national television archive (beeldengeluid.nl) websites.
2 One of two approaches counselled by Mittell (2001, p. 17).
3 Jostein Gripsrud's (1995) reconstruction of the reception of the television program *Dynasty* in Norway may stand as an example that moves beyond stating the well-known cultural imperialism of American programming thesis; another example

would be Katz and Liebes's (1990) internationally comparative reception study of the soap opera *Dallas*.

4   This is a reference to "pillarization," the social system of the twentieth-century Netherlands that split up social groups across class divisions into Protestants, Catholics, liberals, and socialists.

5   Jan Harm Dekker, interviewed in May 2001.

6   Interview between Joost de Bruin and Pollo de Pimentel, consecutively the director of both series; cf., Hermes and de Bruin (2003).

7   Haenen, *NRC*, February 2001.

8   For this argument, see also Tasker (1998).

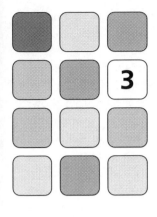

3

conservative feminism and the detective novel

This chapter is based on a series of interviews about reading English and American thriller and detective novels.[1] Initially, it meant to investigate the extent to which feminist thought has become "popularized," part of everyday popular culture use, and thus one of the elements available for use in cultural citizenship – preferably as one that strengthens women's sense of self, assertiveness, and pleasure of being in the world. The detective novel that I like so much, with its various feminist and lesbian subgenres would, I hoped, prove fertile ground.[2] However, as is often the case in reception studies, this is a tale of miscalculation. I am apparently too much a member of an international feminist readership to have gauged this properly, and too much of an optimist in how I think about feminism's reputation. The reconstruction below, of how crime fiction is read, will make this clear.

Like chapter 1, this is a highly concrete study of how popular culture is used for cultural citizenship purposes. The interpretive community of detective novel readers was well established, and rules of use and interpretation were easy to find. Readers clearly bond over how they feel the genre needs to be read and appreciated. Although it is a seemingly open cultural form, class and middle-brow taste – not a part of my identity that I cherish highly – turn out to be important constituents of who can be included in the reader community; while feminism – which I do cherish – was redefined in a conservative manner, taking for granted the political potential of so many of the books published. What this chapter also shows is how interviewing readers is itself a moment of allowing cultural citizenship to surface. It sets in motion reflection on readership, which brings hidden qualities of crime fiction to the fore, as well as how readers bond over defining these qualities rather than using them to reflect on issues outside of the pleasure of reading – although, in fairness, this too was claimed by some. Moreover, I have learnt that class, translated into middle-brow taste, is more important in the Netherlands than I thought it was. I suspect that enjoying English-language crime drama may be connected to "middle-classness" elsewhere too, whether in novels, television series, or movies.

There are sound reasons for taking the detective novel, and the feminist thriller and detective novel, as points of departure for an investigation of popular feminism. Even a cursory look at the bookshelves of a general bookstore shows that crime fiction is very popular, and that women authors are prominently marketed alongside long-standing male authors such as Jonathan Kellerman, Dick Francis, and John Grisham.[3] The novels of Elizabeth George, Patricia Cornwell, and Minette Walters have pride of place in many bookstore displays; as have books by authors who, only a short while ago, would have been considered too feminist to appeal to a mainstream audience. Val McDermid is a good example. After her feminist lesbian amateur investigator Lindsay Gordon novels (journalist and reluctant sleuth, who was also revived for a new novel recently), she started a new series around a professional heterosexual woman private eye, Kate Brannigan. Brannigan promises to do for Manchester (UK) what V. I. Warshawski did for Chicago, says the back-cover blurb, in reference to author Sara Paretsky's American success and what might be called the emerging tradition of the new women's crime novel. McDermid has also published three serial killer novels and nonfiction work.

Since Kathleen Gregory Klein's somewhat somber study of the woman detective (1988), publishers' policy has markedly changed: a more "gender-conscious" type of book is now brought out. Klein shows how in the early 1980s, despite a considerable number of female protagonists, they are usually the inferior detective, they use intuition rather than logic, and they bow to men's superior wisdom or serve a patriarchal system that tends to victimize women. In line with Klein's conclusions, it can be argued that the essays in Glenwood Irons's collection *Feminism in Women's Detective Fiction* (1995), Sally Munt's monograph *Murder by the Book?* (1994), and Anne Cranny-Francis's discussion of feminist detective fiction (1990), suggest that the female authors and portrayal of heroines in crime fiction still do not coincide with a deep change toward feminist values and norms. However, an important change *is* taking place. More self-aware and (relatively) autonomous heroines operate in crime detection, and feminist values and a sense of "sisterhood" (however old-fashioned the term) are embodied in recently published crime novels by both female and male authors (cf., Hermes 1998). Judging by the crime fiction shelves, feminism's achievements are something to be proud of.

In this chapter, interviews with 19 readers of crime readers, conducted by myself, a group of students, and an assistant, will be used.[4] We wished to know whether feminism had become part of how readers discuss and evaluate mystery novels at all, or whether crime fiction is more easily related to distinctions other than those between men and women, and interpreted by means of other discursive frameworks. "Cultural citizenship" and "interpretive community" were our key concepts to find out about (everyday) feminism and the detective novel. The interview material is introduced and analyzed in the second section. The last part of the chapter will discuss how readers' constructions of crime reading and the reader community can be understood as "cultural citizenship," and whether there is space within the rules set by this community of crime fiction reading for such a politicized knowledge as feminism.

Everyday feminism, the interpretive community, and cultural citizenship

The initial drive for this project was to document the possible existence of a more widespread "everyday feminism" amongst crime fiction audiences. In retrospect, I was hoping to find that the critical energy so lacking in what used to be the women's movement in the Netherlands (as documented in a 1996 Dutch collection entitled *Feminism Yes, Emancipation No Thanks*, by Van Lenning, Meijer, Tonkens & Volman) and perhaps also in academic feminism, had passed on into new channels. Despite its enormous achievements, by the end of the 1990s neither the movement nor the theory seemed to be going anywhere fast. The movement in the Netherlands was first institutionalized (in specialized government-subsidized bureaus for monitoring the representation of women), but now faces a slow process of dismantling. After having been a moving force of great importance behind the introduction and acceptance of postmodern philosophy and new insights in identity formation, academic feminism has also reached an impasse. Discourses of emancipation, however important in individual cases, do not have the critical or political purchase that they used to have. From the framework of fragmented identities, it is difficult, if not impossible, to go back to the older certainties of emancipation, however much power differences continue to structure both global and national and also everyday social relations. This is not to say that feminism is dead, but it may have passed out of the hands of those who, like me, consider themselves part of an erstwhile feminist "elite."

The interviews, five of which were with self-identified feminists, show feminism as relatively marginal to the pleasures of and reasons for reading. There is a domestication of feminism that is shocking not so much for its deradicalization of the issues involved (such as violence against women, or how women still and often have to fight for respect and acknowledgment in the workplace), but for its acceptance of a status quo that should, but is not highly likely to, change at short notice. One of the earlier interviews was with Diane, a 39-year-old PR manager and thriller devotee, as well as a former council member for the liberal party. We discussed a host of examples, such as Claire Rayner's Dr Barnabas series (a female pathologist) and the television series *Prime Suspect* (see chapter 2), to then move to – mostly American – thrillers featuring professional women protagonists (often lawyers or judges, or occasionally a computer programmer, who find themselves both intended victim and investigator). Excerpts from this interview follow below, to illustrate the point made above and to introduce the need to find a suitable theoretical framework for the project to accommodate the puzzling status of a formerly strongly political knowledge (feminism) in a popular cultural genre. Diane has suggested that the Barnabas series illustrates how there is never an end to fighting crime and injustice: "There is no final solution." I respond to this by asking about *Prime Suspect*'s Jane Tennyson, who does move up in rank:

> *Diane*: She does, she does, but her problems don't get any less. She gets to be a DCI in that case of the burnt boy, but she keeps having problems: they don't believe her, there's rampant sexism around her and her bosses don't support her at all. There's really no progress. Just as things are in real life. That's why I like these books. That's not cynicism; in fact, they make things prettier than they are! Those women are in good places; they do manage to overcome all sorts of exclusion mechanisms. They survive, is what it comes down to . . .

Later on, about the difference between feminist hard-boiled PI novels and more "mainstream" thrillers:

> *Diane*: Well, it's the puzzle, of course, that makes them attractive, just like real life; but those hard-boileds are a caricature . . . Those women [in mainstream thrillers] have to keep going and they have a dream, standards that should be met. They simply have to accept unfair disadvantages; you have to live with those, you're not the only one . . . It isn't a matter of rampant ambition; you just want to have a life. It's terrible not to be taken seriously, to always have to prove yourself; it's more insidious than outright hostility. But you know it's there. There may be a thousand other explanations when you ask about it, but that makes you the weak party, who needs attention, and they keep asking you to clarify, to explain what it is, then, that you want to say.

Diane considers her's a "normal wish" for more woman-friendly work environments, which takes us back to *Prime Suspect*:

Diane: You'd think they'd start listening to her, have more confidence, but no! Those who don't like her, don't like her. Or they come round to her view in the nick of time. But society is changing. Those men won't be able to escape that. That's what these books are about; that's what they're a sign of. The work environments are simply a metaphor for society. And it shows how women are not solo players, because there's no reward for that.

Thrillers, Diane and I agree, are a means of coming to terms with a changing society – of learning, within a safe space, how to cope. And if that is not what you want, you can simply sidestep their message. She does not call herself a feminist; she sees as much merit in fighting as in accepting that some things are difficult to change. She explains her dislike of the most outspokenly feminist of the detectives in terms of their unrealistic and soloist format: "That's not what women are like." In general, she will not buy a thriller written in the first person singular, which indicates precisely a hubris that she totally distrusts. Not only does she draw on a particular interpretive framework ("realism") to explain her reading of thrillers, but she contrasts thrillers with literature for offering the possibility of recognition rather than reflection. She likes them for portraying women "like her," and she sees women and men as distinct groups. Reading is a coveted means of engaging with the world outside; the books that she really likes strengthen a sense of community with others in comparable positions, which makes her feel less alone.

Although Diane does not call herself a feminist, her appreciation of detective novels is clearly informed by feminist political thought. The same held true for the interviews with other readers. However much feminism, changing gender roles, and women's position in the workplace are all of importance to the pleasure of reading detective novels in its widest sense, this everyday feminism of crime fiction cannot be described as a political knowledge or pleasure in itself. Central to understanding feminism and the detective novel must be appreciation of the cultural mediation of political knowledge, of how a popular genre may position us (speaking as fans), as members of a community of insiders, of those who understand not just the books as pleasurable texts but also their wider sociocultural significance. Such understanding need not be explicit or reflective. It may be mixed with other rewards or the mobilization of identities that would not immediately spring to my mind, but the cultural domain of the detective novel is, however indirectly, linked to questions of politics, society, and identity – not just for academics delving deep but for readers as well. This is, of course, what has been defined as "cultural citizenship" in this book.

Textual analysis claims convincingly that specific subgenres in crime fiction can be deemed feminist, and thus as much part of the popular as of political discourse. However, the accounts of the readers who we interviewed made it clear that there is no direct link between academic interpretation and accounts of everyday use. Culture is always more than "texts" defined by their (lack of) aesthetic, political, or moral merit. Culture, or production of "the cultural," involves the elaboration of forms of knowledge and articulations of social difference, according to Allor and Gagnon (1994, p. 26). This is to understand culture as a situated, historically founded practice with specific power effects, that in its production of texts (either concrete or virtual) also produces shared norms, lines of inclusion and exclusion (between those "in the know" and those who are not), and so on. Hence Allor and Gagnon's definition of cultural citizenship: "[The production of the Cultural also] involves the production of the field of *la citoyennete culturelle*, a field of distinction of the citizen as both the social subject, the sovereign subject of a nation, and as the object of new forms of political power linking the distinctive traits of the citizen with those of the cultural producer and consumer" (idem). The question then is: As what kind of cultural citizenship should reading a mass-marketed genre such as crime fiction be construed, and how (if at all) does it relate to politics or the political?

John Street has argued that popular culture does not need to be like politics, to be about politics. He understands popular genres to be political because they are part of arguing about ways of life (1997, p. 198). At its most political, the construction of crime fiction reading as a form of citizenship might, first of all, take the form of an agenda, of social issues that need to be worked through, in John Ellis's words, in order to eventually, hopefully, find a shape more suitable to the restrictions of (public) debate. The citizenship revenue of crime reading will, secondly, also be apparent in how particular social subjectivities are mobilized and achieved. As what kind of person are we constructed as crime readers? Thirdly, there is the question of the domestication of feminism: How in the accounts of readers, does this form of popular culture, used mainly for the pleasures it has to offer, allow for the enmeshment of feminist ideals and the rules of the genre? Feminist crime fiction as a set of texts offers new (professional and personal) identities for women, as well as reflection on feminist questions to do with justice, anger, retribution, fear and the overcoming of it, the finding of strength, and the turning around of identities from victims into fighters. But what do readers think?

The interpretive community

To analyze the interviews, I have leaned on earlier work in cultural studies in which "interpretive community" is a central concept. The term was introduced by Janice Radway in her work on romance reading (1984, 1985) and discussed in detail by Thomas Lindlof (1988). Radway uses it show how a particular form of cultural competence may be seen as a bond between groups of readers who will never meet physically. If crime reading can be constructed as a form of citizenship, cultural or otherwise, I will need to show, at the very least, such a bond and some degree of intersubjective agreement. In that regard, Lindlof's discussion is useful. He distinguishes three types of achievements of an interpretive community, thereby broadening literary critic Stanley Fish's (1980) original use of the term. Fish understood an interpretive community to be a discursive construct: the set of rules that governs genre and canon building and the meanings of texts. Lindlof takes this further and understands interpretive communities to also define rules of social action. He speaks of genres of content, genres of interpretation, and genres of social action.

These three genres together describe the continuum from textual rules and conventions to the social use of mediated content. A genre of content, according to Lindlof, implies a lengthy history of cultural development, in which it will diversify and change. At some point, a genre of content will have considerable social power and standing as a particular way of looking at the world (1988, pp. 94–5). The use of subgenre labels in the interviews (the women's detective novel, hard-boiled, the "noir," a classic) makes it clear that the detective novel is well established as a (historical) genre. The importance of a detective novel "ending well" (no literary open endings) can be taken as an investment in the detective novel's reconstruction of law and order at the end of the tale, even if law and order are recognized as dependent on social and political outlook: a feminist detective novel will not necessarily deliver the bad guys or girls to the police. It is enough for most readers that we know who and why.

Genres of interpretation can be assessed by finding out "how individual utterances, historically situated in a long series of usages, exhibit dimensions of intersubjective agreement" (Lindlof 1988, p. 97). At any given moment in time, readers will have their own version of what a particular genre is about. This is what Lindlof calls "the virtual text." Class position, feminist allegiances, sexual preference, ethnicity, and age might all contribute to different versions of what a genre is about and might differ from the best known virtual text: the canonical version. There were indications of the struggles going on over what detective novels, and detective novel subgenres, are about. Our key spokeswoman, Indra Anderson, who runs a thriller bookstore and who introduced us to nine of our informants, feels strongly about the differences between men's and women's genres. According to her, men's genres are childish: "I have this theory that men do not grow up in the way women do. That's why they want boys' books. Something outside the realm of life-as-they-know-it. They want adventure . . . Whereas women want ordinary, everyday reality."

Genres of social action describe not so much how detective novels as fiction are used *per se*, but how readers of detective novels may use their knowledge of particular subgenres or authors to communicate with others, and thereby build the community itself in its most concrete forms. For example, in the small group interview (there was also one interview with a larger group), Elizabeth described a holiday situation in which she found herself in the midst of a group of a particular type of middle-class Germans, by saying: "I suddenly found myself in a[n episode of] *Derrick*." The reference to the extremely long-running German police series was immediately clear to the others, who nodded "How terrible!" and grinned in recognition of her predicament.

Shared knowledge of the history of the variety of subgenres that make up "the detective novel"; the building of virtual texts – for example, a sense of what constitutes a "good" detective novel – and the ability to use one's knowledge of this form of popular culture to communicate and make contact with others, form the core properties of an interpretive community. Given the agreement amongst the varied group of interviewed readers, it is certainly legitimate to speak of an interpretive community regarding crime reading.

A "good" detective novel and the ideal reader: the ambiguous status of the detective novel

General characteristics

Readers give strikingly similar accounts of how and when they prefer to read a detective novel: in bed before they go to sleep and on vacation. The good detective novel, moreover, is easy to read, hard to put down. Suspense, recognition, and transportation into another world is what they are about. Some examples follow:

Linda E.:   Fielding's characters: they could be my friends.

Yessica: Those Judge Dee books: you read 'em, and immediately you want to drink green tea and eat rice with chopsticks.

Patricia: Poirot's perfectionism is beautiful. I have it too, but he's never ashamed of it!

Irena: I feel strengthened, empowered, after reading a detective, whether a feminist one or not. It gives me energy and strength to tackle the world again.

These quotations suggest recognition, personal empowerment, and a strength-ened sense of self and self-esteem through reading detective novels. This may not ultimately be why readers read detective novels. As in the rest of the chap-ter, I can only offer examples of how detective novel reading is discussed, of the discourses and distinctions central to the interview talk, rather than of actual social practices. Given that my search here is for the rules and structure of an interpretive community, and their link to yet another discursive construct, namely cultural citizenship, I offer the interview extracts as indicative of the reper-toires and terms that our group of readers has available and decided to use. Their veracity is of no concern here, but the type of distinction that they mobilize is – not just for detective novel reading, but possibly for cultural citizenship in a much larger sense as well.

Suspense and recognition are not the only criteria that readers bring to bear on the detective novel. Quality of writing is important as well. The question of who is a good writer needs to be discussed. Some dislike Elizabeth George, whose Inspector Lynley/Sergeant Barbara Havers novels are set in England: "You can tell she's really an American – no use pretending you're not" (Yessica). Others see her as top quality, and rising above mere popular literature. To read detect-ive novels in English (their original language) is preferred over reading bad Dutch translations. Quality of writing is also measured against literary criteria: play-ing with conventions (Yessica), construction of the narrative, and the culture criticism in which the novel engages. Do we get to know the story "behind" the people? Is the novel a miniature sociological study?

> *Henry*: I can't remember the exact title, from the 50s, something like "The man who was going to kill his wife's husband . . . ," it is a drama that unfolds. A Shakespeare, a Hamlet that takes place there. The ending is totally predictable of course, . . . but those are global themes.
>
> *Gaby*: Take Eric von Lustbader. His books do give me insight into another culture. So it works both ways, as suspense and as education.
>
> *Barbara*: What I kind of like is P. D. James . . . Most of those thriller writers . . . it's not much when it comes to their literary merits. But she's . . . She crosses from pulp into literature . . . She's a psychologist, she has a perspective on human beings totally her own . . .
> *Cindy*: And another example of a book you really liked?
> *Barbara*: Well, Barbara Vine's *House of Stairs*. [Describes plot and narrative structure.] It's almost a kind of sociological study of life in London in the 1960s and 70s.

The worst thing that an author can do is introduce too much violence, and make descriptions too gruesome or detailed – "I don't need blood splashing off the pages" (Barbara) – or, obviously, be boring. Another key element is that the story needs a solution. Open endings are not done in a detective novel. To simply have a "psychopath appear as if by magic from a top hat" (Linda B.) is no good at all. That the novel is too complicated or unrealistic are also major objections.

The cultural status of the detective novel

What is striking in the interviews is the insistence of our interviewees on "being a reader." To be a reader is to be a certain kind of person. There is the obvious connotation of being literate, and also of having cultural capital, a claim to knowledge, and a certain standing, besides simply taking pleasure in immersing oneself in worlds outside oneself. Our readers had invested in their reader identity: they described reading and talking about books, and they bought books. And they were adamant that detective novels are no longer seen as "low" culture: "Detectives today are more an art form than they have ever been. Ten or twenty years ago, they may have been looked down upon but today . . ." (Henry). Still, there was an undertow of defensiveness. The cultural standing of detective novels is an issue.

Likewise, the ideal reader is nothing less than a collector – of a particular subgenre or author – and widely read in literary genres as well. Richard is an exception when he remarks: "I've read literature all my life, and I'm totally fed up with it. Since then I started on detectives, and have been hooked for the last ten years." The interpretive community of detective novel reading is built on knowledge of well-known authors, possibly specialization in a particular area, and a sharply honed sense of when it is allowable to label detective fiction as "popular" reading, as in nonliterary, and when this should not be done. In the words of Elizabeth (after she had denied the low status of the detective novel): "Well, I agree that the public at large [would not know this]. I remember telling someone that I was reading a detective, who said: 'A detective, oh, I don't have time for those. There are so many good novels to read first.'"

The interviews, then, were ruled by a remarkable double code. Remarks about how detective novels have become a totally accepted genre to read were in obvious discord with reservations about crime fiction as popular literature. Likewise, the good detective novel does not solely offer suspense; it should also offer literary qualities or sociocultural–anthropological or historical background knowledge. The social identity of the detective novel reader, as well as some of the pleasures that the genre offers, are constructed across this divide. Barbara: "The people I exchange books with, they don't read detectives." Linda E. has a reading club and again, "the others don't really read detectives, apart from Barbara Vine and Elizabeth George. But that's because they're so very very good, really beautifully written." And Yessica, one of the women who started an Internet website called the Bookgirls, explains that there is a heavyweight and a lightweight list, and that "detectives from time to time do creep [sic] onto the lightweight list."

The cultural status of the detective novel, and by implication that of the detective novel reader, is ambiguous. As a result, as a reader who is "in the know," you can and should create a certain kind of distinction for yourself. Of course, the rules of the interpretive community were not continuously reinstated. Yessica, a very critical reader, who likes Faye Kellerman's well-told sagas and Karen Kijewski's mix of personal and professional elements in her stories, also makes an associative leap to a cat detective series by Lillian Jackson Brown, which she deems to be "cute silly little novels" with supreme disregard for the double standard that she applies when criticizing other authors for writing flat prose or "always the same thing." In a sense, then, the interpretive community of detective novel reading constructs the reader in terms of a typical middle-brow culture: relaxation and pleasure are its central goods, yet it has aspirations to be something more. The rationale behind the social subjectivities mobilized by detective novel reading is to achieve a particular type of "middle-classness."

To try to achieve "middle-classness," or a particularly liberal version thereof, by means of a popular genre, is almost to defy the purpose of the exercise before undertaking it. Popular culture, after all, is associated with easy pleasures and lower-class taste. The strict rules of what is a good detective novel and who is a model reader can perhaps be explained as protection against undesirable identification. They turn the – publicly offered – identity of "reader," "collector," or "specialist" into an obvious sign of (middle-class) distinction. All those interviewed – and especially the men (Albert and Richard) – have favorite writers, but some of the women also introduced themselves as collectors (Irena) or "series builders" (Yessica). To identify yourself as a reader or a collector is not only a mark of distinction; it is as important a source of pleasure as the personal empowerment that the books offer.

More practically, there are the rules for reading a detective novel well. For example, one should not read the last page before coming to the end of the book – and some owned up, almost guiltily, to doing so from time to time. Middle-class cultural capital would teach you to respect the structure of the text, but perhaps most of all to be able to postpone the satisfaction of your personal need to know, in order to gain the even greater satisfaction of having endured the suspense or possibly to have reconstructed the "whodunnit." Even in reading, there is something to be achieved. Some did rebel against this dictum, such as Fiona, who took pride in telling us that her grandfather had taught her that reading a detective novel is much more pleasurable when you do read the last page first (which remains an infringement of the rule, and is likely to disqualify you, going by comments of other readers, who felt that this was "not done"). On the other hand, it is acceptable to be a "lazy reader" (not keep up with the plot development) from time to time, to skip gruesome scenes or technical explanation or an overload of background.

Conservative feminism?

The middle-class connotations of detective novel reading are also apparent in relation to questions of gender roles and feminism. There is clearly a kind of political pleasure in forming and offering an opinion about these issues, and on the emergence of the feminist detective novel, about which our feminist interviewees, and quite a few of the women who would not specifically call themselves feminists, were knowledgeable – yet another way to distinguish oneself. Rather than offer what may have seemed a too easy or politically correct confirmation of the importance of the feminist detective novel, however, most, apart from Irena, are rather critical of them. Yessica feels that "McDermid's novels were too much into therapy." "Too many women in Minette Walters' novels" (Gaby). Yessica thinks that *V. I. Warshawski* (by author Sara Paretsky) is as one-dimensional as Raymond Chandler's characters.

There is, surprisingly enough, much criticism of the fact that many women's thrillers and detective novels offer a second plot line of romance, next to the theme of crime and detection. Yessica feels that it is just a trick to offer "a little romance for the ladies," and Miranda remarks that although she likes lesbian detective novels, they are too hung up on sex. Barbara simply passes over romantic scenes. Some of our respondents, such as Irena and Diane, do appreciate love and romance in a detective novel and don't mind a little sex, which is what we would have expected from the existing literature. Décuré (1994), referenced briefly in chapter 2, offers an intriguing insight into women's crime fiction in her article "Friendless orphans." The feminist private eye, in her view, is a lone operator, relieved of the burdens of care for a family. That, accordingly, opens up room for sex and romance. In fact, in more mainstream women's thrillers there is also almost always a love interest for the protagonist. The reticence of so many of our informants appears to confirm the ambiguous status of the detective novel. Linda E., in fact, appreciates eroticism in women's crime fiction and strongly criticizes male authors for totally lacking a sense of humor when it comes to sex. Eroticism, of course, does have a higher standing than romance . . .

Although the feminist thrillers and detectives could only count on mixed sympathy, feminist ideology in itself was not taboo. On the contrary: virtually all of our informants felt comfortable talking about the differences between female and male authors. They underline the qualities of female authors (and of women in general) and criticize men. Indra: "It's details that make a story real . . . Men's books don't have those common, daily details." Women characters are more intuitive and more self-reflexive (Fiona); have more personal concerns and more drama (Miranda), and contain more humor (Greg). Women authors do more in terms of character development (Yessica). However, whereas women have more emotions, men can write more technically (Barbara), have more analytical insight, and can write more complicated plot lines (Gaby).

Initially, the host of positive qualities ascribed to women characters suggests a strong feminist sentiment. At second glance, however, it is glaringly obvious that all the things that women apparently do well come from a more traditional discourse. Women are deemed better at relations and emotions, they are more human and more personal, but they are not as good as men when it comes to technical details or a complicated plot. Also, apart from Ellen, who says that she does not usually notice whether she is reading a book by a male or a female author, everybody feels that gender makes a huge difference. Surely it is an accomplishment of second-wave feminism to have made readers aware of gender difference. But, then, why is it just as ingrained in common-sense knowledge as it ever was? Women may be allowed more public careers, but they are still measured according to a separate set of personal rather than public standards. Second-wave feminism has also offered another insight: that women and men are not as different as traditional thinking would suggest; that gender difference is a construct particular to specific times, places, and contexts (Ang & Hermes 1991). The feminism in the interviews has no political bite: it is a depoliticized, domesticated conservative feminism; a feminism that does not wish to give up on ingrained notions of gender difference, but that has simply switched price tags. Only occasionally does the critical energy of feminist thought break through, without, however, breaking its everyday bounds – for instance, when Indra criticizes Henry for complimenting the protagonist in *Prime Suspect* for holding up so well in a male world:

Joke: What is it you like about *Prime Suspect*?
Henry: That men's world, how she holds up.
Indra: Yeah, when someone dies, she's there to ask for that job, she's . . .
Henry: Yes but, although I'm a man, I can identify with that. You see how these things work. You have to fight them off with your teeth or they'll walk all over you.
Elizabeth: Absolutely.
Indra: But that's what I have against that sort of emancipation. I mean you're emancipated when you're in the same pattern . . . You could also argue that

the idea of feminism is to feminize society. To introduce positive values, not to work with your elbows. Why would she be emancipated because of that sort of behavior . . . From time to time, I really don't like her.

Henry: I think they mean for her to be not nice.

Indra: But is that the only way to emancipate, to keep standing in a men's world? Well, not for me, thank you. I'll pass on emancipation in that case.

Henry: But it's very realistic. I mean, look around you! It's a men's world . . .

Indra: Yes, but . . .

Henry: If you don't open your mouth . . .

Indra: But you can also argue that those men should change, and be more open to . . . that would be good.

Henry: You know where I find that? In Hillerman [author of detectives featuring Indian–American culture]. The soft side wins; it isn't all that wise to go totally for a career . . .

[All start talking about other examples: "Wexford!" "Frost?!" (television detectives)]

Indra: Frost is the real feminist, when he says "75-year-old women don't belong in a cell. Make her a decent cup of tea!"

Everyday feminism is obviously not a totally lost cause, even though the celebration of Frost, a classic father figure, leaves something to be desired. It is a strange feminism, in which solidarity with women does not count and classic female traits are upheld as especially desirable regardless of their conservative connotation with all the things women supposedly cannot do. Feminism is thus about two highly different things: the conquest of male domains and the appropriation of male rules; and about feminization, and changing the codes of the public sphere. Despite my disappointment over how gender roles hardly merited the fighting and energy devoted to the negotiation of (middle-class) distinction for crime fiction reading in the interviews, both examples show how crime fiction engages us in debate about what would constitute a good society for all, the specific qualities that different groups may contribute, and what is to be appreciated in a person.

Cultural citizenship and crime fiction reading

The political knowledge mediated by the detective novel is particularly wayward in kind. Although there are, for instance, examples of more politicized feminist communities for whom crime fiction is a site of both pleasure and political contestation,[5] our readers preferred to go against any easy celebration of feminist achievement in women's crime fiction. Also, whereas (lesbian and straight) sex and romance are hot topics elsewhere, they were not for our interviewees.[6] Dutch readers would, however, use the yearly thriller and detective guide of a large public opinion weekly,[7] published every summer for two decades now, with a listing of mostly Anglo-American authors and their books still in print. This points to the institutionalization of a cultured, liberal left-wing, but unintended "middle-classness," for which the thriller and detective guide is the vacation alternative to the literary works reviewed throughout the year.

Critical, potentially political, energy generated by "being a crime fiction reader" turned predominantly against the remnants of the high–low culture dichotomy that readers identify as a thing of the past, but which nonetheless may still cast a worrying shadow over your social position, especially if you happen to enjoy a popular genre. It is infinitely preferable to be a member of an elite, if a wayward member, rather than to be seen as an undistinguished formula consumer. Strengthening the impression of waywardness are the two opinion journals that cater most to detective novel readers, the left-wing weekly mentioned above (*Vrij Nederland*) and a feminist monthly (*Opzij*). Both carry a majority of socio-political news and background, while a smaller part of the journal is devoted to culture. They embody what our crime readers want to be: liberal, self-styled, middle-class professionals with a leaning more to the left than to the right, who look for ways to distinguish themselves in their own right rather than trying to capture elite cultural bastions.

In terms of cultural citizenship, most obviously, crime reading concerns the mobilization of a (new) type of liberal middle-class identity. The many statements about the status of high versus low culture, however contradictory, point to a debate in progress and the search for a new vocabulary that will allow participants to overcome what, for now, remain uneasy bedfellows: every time popular culture is defended by using the criteria of high culture, or the equivalent of high cultural norms for nonfiction, the intrinsic value of the pleasures that popular culture offers is negated. It also becomes problematic to develop a feminist appreciation that would allow for a hybrid mix of politics and pleasure. From a liberal middle-class perspective, that would appear to be a particularly naïve move. Appreciation of the detective novel should capture both enthusiasm and proper critical distance: the recognizable and the exotic ("I'm like those women" and "This author offers an interesting portrait of . . .") should be mixed. Readers underline that novels are fiction and never entirely to be trusted or taken as gospel. High cultural appreciation of aesthetic merit forbids over-politicization of the genre. Reception of the feminist confessional autobiography and the consciousness-raising novel of the 1970s (Meijer 1996; Hogeland 1998), which were read as urgent texts that demanded immediate reaction, seems far away.

A pre-political agenda

While there is certainly no direct political link, surely more can be said about the political importance of this popular genre. Cultural citizenship as an activity of community formation and reflection, may well also be mobilizing a (pre-)political agenda of issues. The link between culture, status, and social position is such an issue, as is that of changing gender roles (notwithstanding the almost recalcitrant stand that readers took against what they may have seen as feminist dogma). All do underwrite the goal of feminist identity politics, to claim respect for difference under equal rights. How, in concrete terms, these rights (and presumably duties) should be upheld was less clear. Obviously, the pleasure of recognition in Fielding's characters (women whose trust in their husbands and their confidence that the men will support them is often gruesomely undermined) and the huge number of career women, especially in American women-authored thrillers and crime fiction, who are fighting for both their lives and their right to their jobs and incomes, can be read as appealing to women who experience a sense of confusion as a result of a conflict between everyday experience and an ideology of accomplished emancipation.

Confusion over whether popular culture is or is not "bon ton," and uncertainty over the state of change of gender roles, then, are the main items on a pre-political agenda, which in turn I would deem a most important part of the multi-level construction of citizenship that Allor and Gagnon (1994) have suggested we look for in domains of the cultural. According to them, cultural citizenship can be understood as a domain in which we may question how we belong in society, which is why, empirically, the politics and subjectivities involved all are built across "doubleness" and divisions.

As "consumer-citizens," detective readers are as much buyers in a capitalist system, who will keep that system going, as agents in rival economic (secondhand and exchange) circuits. Ideologically, the fascination with violence that undergirds detective novel reading (however much held in check) presents another kind of "doubleness." Readers are political citizens, who deeply believe that democratic governments should have a monopoly on violence. Yet they feel that they test their own resolve in the face of violence by reading about it (Diane), or they read novels in which the heroine or hero is often a loner who fights the fight that governments lose. Even police or other crime-fighting government officials are often shown to fight lonely and personal battles. As feminists, crime readers defend conventional femininity. In all cases, detective novel reading can be interpreted as a form of agency and (mild, nonradical) criticism of the system.

Ultimately, the interviews read like a manual on hegemony. In how readers are constructed as economic and political subjects, there is evidently enough space for them to find cracks in dominant culture to build sustaining identities and critical forms of empowerment, that paradoxically result in continuing allegiance to that system. Popular culture produces the consumer-citizen in a series of dialectical moves in which "empowerment" and the "energy to go on again" are rewards for marching in line. The "doing" of cultural citizenship may well be confusing and may involve navigating near-irresolvable dualities. But there is also a particular type of pleasure in reflection on those dualities and identities that will, in the case of detective fiction, by and large keep conservative and progressive forces in balance. Cultural elitism, cherished from the wrong perspective, may escape unscathed; it may also have unwittingly altered its plumage and acquired a new set of feathers – and have welcomed what according to some is "lightweight fiction" as literature.

Coming back to where I started from, I find that it is also possible to conclude from this material that feminism in popular culture is translated into a vision of fighting spirit, despite the strong stress on the middle-brow respectability of crime fiction. Changing gender roles are, after all, read as *opportunity* rather than a challenge. My initial idealism about popular culture may not be as misplaced as I felt it to be halfway through this project. To recognize yourself in feminist private eyes such as Kate Brannigan, or to like Paretsky's gutsy heroine, or to commiserate with and then applaud Joy Fielding's more tragic heroines – these are expressions of exhilaration. They show how popular representation may invite you into a vision of women's strength and resilience, which counteracts the pervasive sexism of everyday social life. Within the confines of capitalism, (radical) political investments can be made. Cultural citizenship, then, is an odd addendum to the citizenships (social, political, and so on) that we are familiar with. It is structured as a domain of pre-political consideration, of unease with states of being, rather than as a monument to specific rights, duties, or identities. It is this that makes popular culture worth defending, that makes it worthwhile over long periods of time, even if only as a favorite pastime. It is also what makes it very hard to channel the energy evoked by popular genres into other fields, be they cultural criticism or politics.

notes

1   I would like to thank Robert Adolfsson, Sara Platon, and Christel de Valk, who initially made contact with Indra Anderson, our central informant, and held individual and group interviews with seven respondents. I am especially grateful to Cindy Stello, who held individual interviews with nine informants, assisted with the group interview with Indra, Henry, and Elizabeth, and kept in touch with Indra.

2 Cf., Whitlock (1994) for discussion of the lesbian detective, and Zimmerman (1990) for a more general grounding of the lesbian detective novel in lesbian literature.

3 Crime fiction is widely read and available in the Netherlands in English and in translation. The majority of titles available are English and American. They outnumber local Dutch titles and translations from other language areas.

4 The group of readers consisted of a number of self-identified feminists (five), some men (four), and some gay respondents (four women, one man) and an assorted mix of readers who did not have outspoken (political) views (seven women). Two of the interviews were group interviews; 16 were individual interviews. The first group interview (Linda E., Linda B., Richard, Albert, and Indra – all names are pseudonyms) was followed up by individual interviews with the two women. Indra Anderson was our central informant. She runs a specialized thriller bookstore and half of our interviewees were her customers. She was present at both group interviews and we met with her several times at her shop. Other respondents were found via personal networks and the Internet (two specialized discussion lists).

5 The Australian Sisters in Crime network has chapters with regular meetings, newsletters, and a website, and wishes to further the career of women in the mystery/crime field, correct imbalances in the treatment of women writers, and promote recognition of their contribution to the field (*Sisters in Crime Newsletter* 12, Melbourne, spring 1996). The German feminist publisher Ariadne offers not only a strong list of crime fiction novels and a regular journal, but also organizes discussion evenings and events for readers.

6 Cf., *Ariadne Forum* 4, 1996, special issue on "Sex im Frauenkrimi"; or *Sisters in Crime Newsletter* 12, Melbourne, spring 1996, on "The great debate. Feminist crime fiction: lesbians do it better."

7 *Vrij Nederland*, or *The Free Netherlands*, a weekly started during the Second World War.

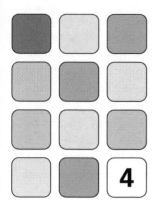

masculinity and the merits of textual analysis as part of an audience study

4

The merits of textual analysis as a provider of background material for an audience study are evident; and its uses for historical analysis undisputed (cf., Gray 2003, p. 127). But can it do more toward an understanding of popular culture in its everyday context? Needing to understand how my feminism was so different from that of my fellow thriller and detective novel readers, and why one of the thriller and detective group interviews was especially uncongenial in atmosphere and had felt very unproductive, I decided to investigate those books that were mentioned throughout the interviews that I had not read. Obviously, I had missed important clues along the road. Whereas before I had used my own (wide) reading in the genre, I turned to a symptomatic reading of the (small number of) authors that I was not familiar with. I will argue in this chapter that contemporary constructions of masculinity may well have been the bone of contention. The usefulness, and indeed attraction, of males for women who are so obviously capable of living their lives, solving crimes, and bringing criminals to justice suggests itself as an area of unresolved ideological struggle and unease. The chapter does more. It also focuses on the role of the researcher / author. Of course, as intellectuals, we like to understand ourselves to be mere translators or facilitators of nascent knowledges that are already out there. But we do have our own convictions and zeal to deal with, and this may be difficult when our offer of "translating" common sense into more radical, political knowledge may not be all that welcome.

This chapter deals with three related questions, then. How can incorporating textual analysis into audience research heighten its quality, and how does that improve our understanding of popular culture? Secondly, in the case of thriller and detective novel reading, does an improved reception- and text-based understanding produce a sharper notion of ideological struggle as it is going on? Masculinity – implicitly – is a concern to my detective novel readers. They favor novels that cynically reflect on it, or offer alternative scenarios to, old-fashioned patriarchal forms. Implicitly on the political agenda that is produced as part of cultural citizenship is the question what we should do with manhood and masculinity. The third question posed by this chapter has to do with the role of the intellectual in bringing these issues to the fore. Is it Gramsci's intellectual at work, who offers new insights to the people (who may not be waiting for them); or is it actually the other way around, informants bringing new insights to academics who wish to control processes of ideological and social change that others are happy to leave unresolved or solve themselves (cf., Gramsci 1972)? After a brief introduction to the debate about ethnographically inspired audience studies (such as the ones presented in this book), I will turn to the interview that caused me to rethink the place of textual research in cultural and media studies of popular culture. The study of books read by my informants then takes us to the disrepute into which masculinity has fallen. The chapter closes with a more formal rethinking of the role of intellectuals in broaching ideological debate and the legitimation of their (our) claims to be able to do so, both of which are political and methodological.

Ethnographic audience studies

Small ethnographic audience studies purport to provide insight into the cultural knowledges, called repertoires or vocabularies, that are available to users of popular culture, which they draw on to give meaning to, for example, popular cultural practices or texts. They try to convince their publics rhetorically by offering interpretations of and meaningful extracts from interviews or notes about participatory observation. By showing how the vocabularies and repertoires that readers use are structured, an exercise in theorizing the material, it can be shown how (popular) culture actually works. Such structures are, as it were, the backbone of culture-as-lived, rather than texts. Texts in the realm of popular culture are artistic creations that offer a plenitude of reading possibilities. The ones that are actually taken up, the idea is, reverberate with the deep logic of a given reader community or culture, at a given place and time. The validity of popular culture research might well benefit from a methodological strategy in which the audience study remains central but feeds and directs textual analysis (rather than the other, more usual, way round, which tends to obscure lived reality by privileging an author's perspective). As the discussion below will make clear, the question is what the dangers of such a strategy might be and what its value is for understanding popular culture.

The methodological pitfalls of qualitative audience research have generally been well documented by its critics as well as by methodologists. Qualitative audience researchers (including myself) are well aware that we often work with very small samples (as, indeed, is the case here) from which it is not really possible to generalize, but which we nonetheless often do (see Geragthy 1998). Nor is as much time spent with informants as probably would be beneficial, and as is implicitly promised in often-voiced allegiance to anthropological or ethnographic principles (Gillespie 1995, p. 55). Be that as it may, I am often impressed by work with audiences, and by how interaction between academics and those who are not leads to new impulses and insights, and generally forces us as intellectuals to broaden our scope and develop new visions of the (social) world. Whereas text-based work is often the more brilliant for the meanings that can be generated from small bits (or huge corpora) of writing or visual images, audience-based work is more moving and points to how, in text-based analysis, we tend to overrate the meaningfulness of any single text once it is part of an everyday setting.[1] Obviously, feminist audience studies (my own brand – the kind that focus on gender and related social power relations) are confronted with all of these issues. Reviewing the relation between the two most important starting points for (feminist) research in popular culture studies – audience-based and text-based research – leads me to powerful interviewees and the issue of irritation. It also brings back an old ghost from the feminist past: the ghost of paternalism and unequal power relations in audience research. I don't think it will want to be laid to rest unless confronted head on, which is planned for the next section.

Powerful informants

Anthropologists have documented how difficult it may be to gain access to, or elicit information from, powerful informants (Hammersley & Atkinson 1995, p. 139) and how gender is a highly important factor in negotiating relations with others (Warren 1985). For some reason, this type of anthropological reflection has not reached cultural studies, but then nor has the tradition of extended periods of fieldwork. We have preferred the series of long interviews, the textually oriented discussion of reflexivity, and ethnographic writing on the discursive power of the intellectual versus the described Other (cf., Clifford & Marcus 1986; Marcus & Fischer 1986) to form our view of what ethnography and qualitative work with audiences should be like (cf., Stanton 2000, 2004). This has merged well with how we, as feminist researchers, have trained ourselves to be sensitive to power relations, and it has strengthened our understanding of ourselves as representatives of the powerful academy (cf., McRobbie 1991 [1982]). Powerful informants, or men for that matter, have not been part of this at all. The net result has been that, although some highly interesting autobiographical accounts have been published by cultural studies scholars, reflecting on the position and perspectives of the researcher her- or himself, the issue of actual field relations has been almost totally elided.[2] Ellen Seiter's (1990) discussion of a difficult interview must stand as the exception to this rule. In "Making distinctions in TV audience research: case study of a troubling interview," she documents an interview with two middle-class, middle-aged men. Rather than cooperating and working with the two interviewers, as had other interviewees in the soap opera project, these two were especially interested, according to Seiter, in flaunting their knowledge of television and their superior taste. A transcript of the interview accompanies the article and offers a rare opportunity to compare the researcher's interpretation with the actual material.

From the transcript, it is obvious that Seiter's male co-interviewer was the one addressed by the two men. It is also obvious that they are not only trying to impress the two interviewers with their knowledge, of amongst other things, television technology, but that they are also trying to please them. In many ways, I was reminded of my own father, who would be at least as difficult a subject for research of this kind, and who would not really know how to listen to the questions and understand what was being asked of him. His eagerness to please in interactions with my partner and friends often managed to make me feel uncomfortable because of its misplacedness, and his misreading of what it was that others were asking of him. It may therefore be vicarious guilt over how I have, in a way, outclassed my father in terms of particular types of cultural knowledge and capital that leads me to think that Seiter is slightly too harsh in her assessment of the two men. At the same time, I can feel her irritation and anger mounting acutely, and I share her intuition that a certain type of arrogance is also at the root of what troubles her in the interview. In a similar manner, in one of the interviews in the crime fiction project, reported on in chapter 3, I was upset about how difficult it turned out to be to close the distance between myself and my co-interviewers on the one hand and our respondents on the other.

On irritation

As described in chapter 3, with an assistant and help from a group of students, 19 crime readers were interviewed at some length. They had replied to our postings on two specialized Internet websites, were clients of a thriller bookstore in Amsterdam or, in a few cases, were relations of our friends and acquaintances. Five were self-identified feminists, four were men, and five were gay (four women and one of the men). Although we had not particularly intended this to be the case, most of them had (professional) middle-class backgrounds. In general, they were a nice and cooperative group of people. For some of the time, however, their elaborate strategies to ward off any suggestion that they were not in full control of interpretations of their own reading and their positions as men and women, and also, in many cases, of the interview situation, baffled us – and, when we were analyzing the material, irritated us. In part, this was related to class and the management of social relations in a research context. But in retrospect it seems that it was also due to a more general lack of terms, or access to a repertoire via which important parts of what fascinates crime readers in the (sub)genres that they like can be expressed.

One of our two group interviews provides a case in point. My assistant, Cindy Stello, felt actively excluded by our three informants after she had failed to pick up on the title of a particular novel (which was what made me decide later that I needed to read as many of the books mentioned as possible). Cindy pointed out to me how I had been addressed throughout the rest of the interview, and how the interviewees had consistently used "we," "our group," or "our circle." My own frustration was with how they ridiculed some of my questions, as well as my opening statement, in which I tried to point to the difference between high and low culture and the difficult position of crime fiction in the middle. I had hoped to break the ice and relieve my guests (the interview was at my home address) of any feelings of unease. My question met with near-derision. The cultural status of the detective novel was totally unproblematic. To think otherwise was too old-fashioned for words. Time was when you had to hide or be ashamed of reading popular books, but this was considered to be in the dim and distant past.

Henry, one of the three interviewees, a few of whose remarks and observations I have singled out for this chapter (man, 48, public servant), held the view that detective novels are no longer seen as "low" culture (applause from the other two participants – and this was the first subject broached in the interview). I'll repeat his words here: "Detectives today are more an art form than they have ever been. Ten or twenty years ago, they may have been looked down upon but today . . ." This was enough to make me, as researcher and initiator of our conversation, feel guilty for forcing an apparently ridiculous and possibly insulting point of view on these readers. Irritation took over later. For all their vehement disagreement with me on the question of the social standing of thrillers and detective novels, our three informants did not so much argue that popular culture has become more accepted; rather, they were categorizing the popular books that they liked as Literature. They took pains to make it clear that they were collectors of a particular author, or subgenre, and also that they were Readers who were aware of the value of Good Books. We, the interviewers, were obviously the barbarians to whom such distinctions needed to be explained, or worse, who were trying to talk them into being readers of trash, with all its suspect pleasures. This group interview was not an exception – in the other group interview and in several of the individual interviews we came across the same type of "impression management" (cf., Goffman 1973 [1959]).

In the kind of audience research that cultural studies has invested in, irritation is the last thing you need. After all, our only material is what informants can and will tell us. As Dave Morley has famously suggested:

> In the case of my own research, I would accept that in the absence of any significant element of participant observation of actual behaviour beyond the interview situation, I am left only with the stories that respondents chose to tell me. These stories are, however, themselves both limited and indexical of the cultural and linguistic frames of references which respondents have available to them, through which to articulate their responses. (1989, p. 24)

If the words of our informants are all we have, then it will not do to allow irritation to cloud our ability to concentrate on what they say. For irritation not only threatens respect, and thus careful and unprejudiced attention to and representation of what respondents have to say, but it is hardly beneficial for what Gadamer called *Verstehen* (Gadamer 1986; Warnke 1987), or understanding, the very possibility of building a shared horizon across the divide of research and everyday life. This does not mean that it should be buried and forgotten and, like Seiter, I feel that it needs to be discussed, to be the subject of interpretation and theorization.

Respect

Having been trained in feminist research methods, I have been left with a particular legacy. Three deep convictions have remained with me over the years. The knowledge produced in research is not just of academic interest but always also of political importance. The power inherent in one's position as an academic needs to be wielded with care. And as a woman, I have a special obligation in terms of researching questions of gender and femininity. For me, feminist research is synonymous with showing respect. This is one of the reasons why I came to prefer the use of discourse analysis rather than more naturalistic and descriptive frameworks. After all, how are you to do justice to the complexities of another person's life, be it morally, methodologically, or theoretically? While it does seem possible to reconstruct funds of cultural knowledge, whether they be discourses, repertoires, or vocabularies, a discourse perspective allowed me to neatly circumvent that old ghost of paternalism: of knowing better than my respondents what moved them and how popular forms had meaning for them. In a sense, my irritation took me back in time, to what in my personal biography has come to be the cultural painfulness of upward mobility, and the need inspired by it to prove one's middle- or upper-class credentials. But my interviewees may have had totally different backgrounds – I can't say, because I don't know. So how could I interpret this and do myself the favor of finishing with this ghost of paternalism once and for all?

In the group interview, I was aiming for a form of subservience to the group process. As a well-meaning feminist researcher, I wished to enable the others to feel free to express themselves. I certainly did not want to impose my own frame of reference upon the group. My intentions misfired badly. I had neither correctly understood the position that our interviewees wanted to take up nor that they may have expected something totally different from an academic (we will never know what). I felt guilty and mad in equal measures. In retrospect, I can see how the dutiful feminist in me was out to get "the real story," as in naturalistic approaches to social reality, while knowing, of course, that there is no real story to be reconstructed. Rather, there are only fragments of stories that allow us, in audience research, to build a picture of the cultural knowledges that interviewees draw on in gaining pleasure from reading crime fiction, as well as in making it meaningful. This much becomes clear in light of the fact that the same defensive but also arrogant, middle-class way of talking was also part of the interviews conducted by my students. It was not aimed at me or the other interviewers personally. It is much more a matter of convention, of the discursive construction of talking about popular fiction. It could well be the case that my fears of having imposed myself or my own interpretive framework are preventing me from seeing how my "populist" defense was also a provocation to a reaction that is all the more interesting for its vehemence and at times arrogant insistence.

Games with ghosts are dangerous enough. Any positive effects of how the informants and I clashed in the group interview need at least to be consolidated by paying close attention to the bits and pieces of the cultural knowledge that they offered. The ghost would have me worrying over power and paternalism that would easily cloud the issue here, which is, stated in a perhaps somewhat functionalist manner: What goals are served by the particular way in which talk of crime fiction is organized? What else is there in the material that my irritation may help me to see? How can being trained as a feminist help me find more in the interviews, rather than lock me into methodological feelings of guilt?

Some issues were not problematic for our interviewees (if surprising and, in some regards, disappointing for me). Women's position in society is the example that was discussed in chapter 3. A majority of our informants stuck faithfully with a notion of women's emancipation as a taken-for-granted feature of today's world. With the exception of only some of the self-identified feminists, feminism was generally seen as over the top, too much, too aggressive, and not properly appreciative of women's qualities as women. Emancipation should be our goal. Issues of women, emancipation, and feminism had obviously been given a place on the maps of meaning that our informants employed. A ceasefire had been reached over women and femininity, in which a notion of natural differences between men and women continued to win out over more radical feminist suggestions that gender difference is constructed or a performance, rather than a given. My one solace remains this: that my readers were inspired by feisty heroines. The position of men was a different matter. This only became clear when I decided that a more "symptomatic" reading of the interview material was the best way to confront and lay to rest fears of paternalist mismanagement of interview relations, and to use my irritation to reconstruct and subsequently theorize a part of the material that we had mostly left alone: the books referred to in the interviews. To read up on, or familiarize oneself, with the material that one has been talking about is not a big step in an audience research project, but how to handle this material is another matter, which is at least as problematic, both politically and methodologically, as the management of interview relations.

Textual analysis

I feel strongly about the status of audience research versus the somewhat higher status (especially in terms of theory) of textual analysis. When the two are combined (as in older feminist work on popular culture), they jar. Textual analysis is the researcher's (superior) reading of a set of texts against the partial or nonpoliticized understanding of audience groups. Here comes the ghost of paternalism and condescension again. It blemished, for instance, Janice Radway's (1984) ground-breaking study on romance novels. Her conclusion (if not the research itself) that romance readers would be feminists if the world were to change, and that in the resultant ideal feminist world there would be no further need for romances, insults romance readers. It marks them as the lesser feminists, and feminists as the better women. It does not take pleasure itself, or the nature of the pleasure of reading a fictional formula text, seriously at all (Ang 1987). Likewise, in a study of the history of women's magazines, Ballaster et al. (1991) offer a last chapter based on interviews with readers and interpret what these readers have to say in an overly concerned vein. While they tell us that they share the pleasure these readers obviously take in the magazines, they counsel that (traditional) women's magazines should only be taken in small doses, because – like eating too much chocolate – they would otherwise make you ill.

Feminists have not had that good a track record of combining analysis of the texts with interpretation of audiences' uses of them. Nor have we always been very careful in our text-based work to make clear that without asking audiences, we cannot speak for them, which implicitly is exactly what we have done. The reason for and legitimation of work with popular media texts has too often kept to a modernist frame of reference, in which popular texts are always dangerous and possibly damaging for the less-tutored – paternalism at its worst, and out of line with the respect that feminism otherwise values so highly. More generally too, it is obvious that audience research is not easily combined with textual analysis. Apart from the different types of analytical tools that we have become accustomed to using, there remains a sense of drawing on knowledges that are too disparate. In addition to highly descriptive introductions of the material that the audience research is related to, many recent studies have therefore left the text for what it is and concentrated on the audience (Hagen 1994; Hermes 1995; McKinley 1997). We may have lost something in the process. It should be possible to talk about texts and interviews without talking about identities and personal choices in life. Both types of material are also indicative of shared social knowledges, of what issues we debate, and how we debate them, and the means we have available to do so. As Ann Gray puts it, it is the advantage of the interdisciplinary approach of cultural studies that the boundary between texts, and how they are used and interpreted, can be usurped (2003, pp. 144–5). The sometimes defensive, sometimes aggressive manner of defending "their" crime novels which we found in our interviews may not be a question of personal style so much as an indication of the constraints inherent in the mechanisms of "middle-class" discourse on popular culture.

Less systematic than Radway (1984), who had her informants give her lists of the best and the worst romances they had read, but inspired by her example, I followed the only clues left in the material; namely, the novels referred to in the discussions with which I was not familiar. This symptomatic reading cannot stand as more than a speculative undertaking. The texts studied do not answer questions about what the audience is really like, or why: ultimately they like crime fiction, but the books mentioned in the interviews may provide some idea of what the group of readers that we studied felt was important. They have, in Morley's words "indexical value" (1989, p. 24). In the light of my search for the links between popular culture, and especially popular fiction, and the public sphere, it is important to understand how there may be issues of public and political importance that can only be understood via a roundabout route. After reading them, I suspect that the position of men, and of what we understand and would like masculinity to be, is one such issue, which is only very partially addressed by existing vocabularies and repertoires. On then to recently published bestseller thrillers and what they can teach us about this.

Masculinity and the text

It was a long time since I had read a large number of titles by male authors (I know – I am a very parochial feminist) and I was amazed by what I found. Mixed in with recent work by feminist thriller writers, there is a strong suggestion that although gender studies may have put masculinity on the agenda, this has not reached everyday life. Men and in a sense masculinity are, of course, still mostly what detective and thriller fiction is about, notwithstanding the enormous and long-standing popularity of these genres for women as readers and writers (see also Coward & Semple 1989). The yearly authoritative *Vrij Nederland* guide for thriller and detective fiction writers and their work in print in the Netherlands consists mostly of Anglo-American authors and a small number of translated and Dutch authors. For 1999, it lists 266 male authors against 108 female authors. More female authors have male protagonists than male authors have female protagonists. Also, the standard for writing a particular type of detective (a private eye, a police officer) is set by older male-dominated genres (the mystery of the closed room, the "noir" or the classic private eye, the police procedural, and perhaps even the action and adventure thriller can be taken to be part of this group), against which the amateur spinsters of the Golden Age of detective fiction form a – wrongly endearing – contrast (huge numbers of corpses litter Agatha Christie's novels, for instance) (Nesaule Krouse & Peters 1975). Compounding the implicit male dominance in crime fiction is the fact that today's women crime writers have more often than not sought to create professional women as crime fighters, thereby (implicitly) referring to sets of standards that have historical ties to masculinity rather than femininity (cf., Tasker 1998). My claim, therefore, that masculinity may be more problematic than femininity in terms of the generic rules of interpretation for crime fiction developed by readers over time may strike an odd note. It is certainly the case that my own perception of this state of affairs is strongly slanted toward feminist issues, and masculinity has traditionally mostly been an issue because of its undesirability rather than anything else.

I did not (re-)read classic "noir" novels (such as Dashiell Hammett's *The Maltese Falcon*, 1934) that were also mentioned in the interviews, but chose instead to focus on more recently published novels that I had not read before. Amongst the authors I read are Kinky Friedman, David Baldacci, and Ken Follett. Friedman was great fun. The name Friedman is used by both the author and the protagonist of the novels, and this guarantees those readers who savor parody and irony a lot of reading pleasure. The same Henry who I quoted above referred to Friedman as an author who "tilts reality" and thus puts everything in a new perspective. This is according more literary merit to Friedman than I would think he is due. He is interesting, though, for the manner in which he satirizes masculinity (his own included) by operating on the cutting edge of cowardice and loyalty to friends. Women in the Kinky universe can best be characterized as the unknowable Other. Masculinity itself, though satirized, is secure in the thought of its enormous task in the world. It may be undoable, but it gets done.

Kinky's sympathetic version of traditional masculinity was complemented for Henry by Hillerman's native Indian thrillers, which show him the soft side of masculinity. Interestingly, these are novels about men who are not touched by a particular type of insecurity that has taken hold of the male protagonists in David Baldacci's *Total Control* (1997) or Follett's *The Third Twin* (1996, also a television mini-series), that were recommended to me by women as excellent thrillers. Baldacci and Follett join a not inconsiderable number of male authors who have broken with tradition (not many men have written female heroines in crime fiction; see Craig & Cadogan 1981) and present us with women as central figures in the narrative.[3] Both suggest that men have somehow lost the challenge posed by feminism, and by women's entry into professional fields that were formerly monopolized by men.

Baldacci's *Total Control* (deemed "excellent" in the group interview quoted in this chapter) introduces a well-off professional couple, Jason and Sydney Archer. (Her masculine name should immediately alert us.) Jason, though a brilliant computer technology executive, manages to get ensnared in what for him will be a deadly game. Although we are not told until halfway through the book that he did it all for the best reasons (a service to his country and money for his family), Archer gets himself abducted and ultimately killed, leaving Sydney to fight for his reputation and hers, and her own and their daughter's life, with all the acumen of her lawyer's professional knowledge and strength. Sydney is the real hero of this novel, wielding guns and intellect alike. In fact, she is only a heroine insofar as she becomes the romantic interest of FBI agent Lee Sawyer, who is trying to locate her husband. Sawyer is divorced, lonely, and overweight, and no match for how Jason Archer is described (athletic, beautiful, and intellectually gifted). Jason Archer's position is that of the prototypical female: good looks, lack of common sense, easily sacrificed for the sake of the story-line. In fact, we don't even know how or when he is killed; he more or less gets lost as the story unfolds. The modern male's predicament is that he is little more than an asset to a successful woman and no longer up to what was demanded of men traditionally. Of course, *Total Control* also offers us FBI agent Sawyer, the ordinary guy who – through divorce – loses his family because of his job (life is tough on men these days). Yet he may well win against muscle men and glamour boys, by ending up with Sydney Archer. The author leaves it to us to finish this particular scenario for ourselves. Meanwhile, Sydney is pregnant with dead Jason's child.

Traditional masculinity's lack of an answer to feminism, and women's "new" position in the world, is dramatized even further in Ken Follett's *The Third Twin*. Again, a professional woman is the central character in the novel. The men are mostly power-hungry, or raping beasts (with one exception of course, to provide the New Woman with a mate). The woman, Jeannie Ferrami, is the one who climbs on a white horse to battle injustice and crime. Hers is the classic male position, with the exception that she herself is, of course, also a victim of rape by one of the men, not something that, generally speaking, happens to men in crime fiction.[4] Follett offers us a succinct case against masculinity and its excesses. Socialization, he suggests, is the only solution. The only question is: By whom? The one man who has managed to curb his aggressive drive, the man who Ferrami falls in love with, was raised by a traditional housewife. Should she, the traditional "good" woman, be the one, or is it up to the professional woman, who is a better man for having breasts rather than anything else? Ferrami – who is, after all, a geneticist – is the one who, from early on in the novel, stresses that biology is never destiny, which enables her to believe in him.

Where to with masculinity?

The storylines in these novels and the positions in which male characters find themselves are exemplary for the confusion over masculinity that can also be found in other genres. Jackson et al. (1999) interviewed men about men's lifestyle magazines, and conclude that men tend to fall back on traditional and sexist repertoires of interpretation for lack of other ways in which to express a position more in line with the changes that feminism has wrought in society. In her entertaining study of horror film genres, Clover (1992) shows how, for instance, the rape–revenge subgenre (which was amazingly popular among young male audiences in the 1980s) presents a working-through of the changed gender power balance. Others too have underlined how men since the Second Feminist

Wave have been faced with the unpleasant task of giving up traditional privileges without any clear reward or evident means and strategies to do so
(Tolson 1978; Seidler 1991). Gender studies research makes clear how masculinity
has operated as the norm, thus making itself invisible and largely unspeakable
(Chapman & Rutherford 1988). Dudink therefore counsels the "outflanking
manoeuvre" rather than an attempt to deconstruct masculinity head on (1998,
pp. 430–1). Undeniably, here is a task for cultural critics, to show how the absent
presence of masculinity (as invisible norm and, concretely, as room for men to
do whatever they liked) has simply turned, in some fictional genres at least,
into an absence. There hardly seems a role left for them, neither ideologically
nor materially. Poor Jason Archer's death doesn't even merit narrative space. He
just gets lost.

Neither Jackson et al.'s male interviewees nor my mixed group of respondents had the means available to do more than hint at male identity as a possible site of trouble and strife. In general, the preference of the few men in my
research project was to read thrillers and detective novels that do not question
masculinity, but that deal with the burden of being a man either sarcastically
(the "noir" detective novel: whatever you do, it is never good enough – don't
ever trust a woman; she will betray you) or at great distance (women are absent,
or at the very least a source of eternal mystification). In some of the thrillers
that they mention, women are not in the story at all, having a walk-on part at
most (action and adventure thrillers). This is not to argue that the pleasures of
the text cannot be explored outside gendered terms – for example, in terms of
mood or description – but to point out how gender, and especially masculinity,
is invisible for the readers whom I interviewed. Henry reads the thrillers and
detective novels that his female partner likes, but he did not offer any comments
on them. He is also moved by the struggle of *Prime Suspect*'s Jane Tennyson.
For him, she occupies the position of an honorary male. He is not convinced
by comments from the two women in the group interview that her "male" strategy of coping with a woman-unfriendly workplace could be interpreted as a
loss for women, rather than a gain for them. This suggests that men may be
more comfortable with traditional models of masculinity even when applied to
individual women's struggle to achieve better positions. How this will ultimately
affect men's positions and their (remaining) privileges is conveniently left out,
even though this question haunts popular genres.

The women in our research were more open to dramatized criticism of masculinity (men as women's enemy, as rapist, as agent of violence), as portrayed
by women thriller writers. They also offered offhand suggestions about the type
of man and masculinity they preferred, for which television police detectives
Morse (*Inspector Morse*) and Frost (*A Touch of Frost*) were given as examples. It

strikes me that both Morse and Frost are older, and that although they obviously like to be with women, there is no regular woman in their lives. Morse is a hopeless romantic, who is unlucky in love; Frost a slightly more pragmatic widower, who will take on the cause of women and waifs if necessary. They are seen as gentlemen, and even despite their bullying of their sergeants, as basically gentle men. Neither needs to reconstruct their masculinity, nor, for that matter, appears to be threatened by feminism. As romantics, they both offer Man as a hardly sexual being, rather than as a menacing beast driven by lust. The men's preferences in novels and the women's preferences in television series suggest that romantic, individualist versions of (gentlemanly) masculinity are a preferred way out of the disreputable place in which masculinity has found itself in since 1970s feminist criticism, and its subsequent translation into popular fiction genres. This is the case whether these versions are of a more English type, personified by Frost and Morse, who are wayward members of a larger organization; or whether they are of a more American type, offering man as loner.

Methodology and understanding popular culture

Working across the division of textual analysis and audience experience, according to Richard Johnson, is the best we can hope to achieve in cultural studies (quoted in Gray 2003, p. 145). I tend to agree, but remain wary of including textual analysis on an equal basis. We know a lot about the structure and meanings of many popular forms, but little about what readers do with them. Audience-led re-reading of popular texts, it seems to me, is the most sensible way forward when and if warranted by the occasion. We do not need routine checks to see whether audiences have cottoned on to the central idea of a series, or whether they understand the ramifications of a certain type of star text correctly. That would be boring and a gross overstatement of the authority and the mission of popular culture studies. Academic legitimacy is grounded in argumentation and in convincing gown and town alike, not in ecclesiastical-type authority, laid down in paternalist missives akin to the encyclical letter. In other words, after reading Friedman, Follett, and the other male authors, I should have continued discussion with the obstinate group of readers. As it is, I can only conclude that the group interview helped me to focus on the thriller as text in a new way. This did result in a stronger understanding of how ideological change is embedded and mulled over in popular culture.

I may have overinterpreted what my informants had to say about men and masculinity. But I can't see how that would be especially wrong in this case, as my symptomatic reading was used to refocus on the text. My aim has not been to psychologically or intellectually test my informants, but to form a mental image of what might be going on in the folds of this particular genre. The interview material, as analyzed in chapter 3, shows that a self-confident, middle-brow sense of identity is produced by the reader community. It also makes clear that dealing with violence in a contained domain, as part of a process in book fiction, in which criminals are identified and brought to justice, is what fascinates – hence the clear injunction that a thriller or detective novel should never be too bloody. It is the process of solving the crime that is so reassuring, not the evil deeds that set the narrative process in motion. What this shows is how middle-class, middle-brow culture can only realize its sense of safety and legitimate its wish for gating its communities as long as there is an evil Other (cf., Morley 2000, ch. 6). The world of danger and violence out there makes you feel ever more secure in your own realm (cf., Boomkens 1996). Unfortunately, the evil other is partly in with "us." There is a bomb ticking away under the continually produced illusion of safety-amongst-our-own-kind, which can be labeled "man." Masculinity, after all, is still defined in relation to rationality, strength, and power. The tiniest abuse of the privilege claimed (a threat, an off joke) is the violence that should have been kept out of the safe haven. The thrillers of Fielding and other women authors deal with the double breach of contract implied in domestic violence: the home should have been safe and love should have conquered all. The highly ideological nature of this construct is shown in the fact that when women are perpetrators, this is attributed to individual psychopathology, which, apparently, is less and less easy to do in the case of men.

The older gentlemen mentioned above are difficult to see as rapists or as psychopaths who like to inflict pain just for fun, which is comforting. But how about younger men – the ones plagued by their hormones, who have more strength and less rational control? Or rather, how do we get beyond this loaded image, to reimagine what a younger attractive masculinity might be like? The tips for the books discussed here deal with exactly that problem. What I was given was a road map to navigate the enormous amount of available representations of masculinity and femininity in the domain of the popular. It is clear enough that popular culture offers resources and means to bond as well as to fight over the exact nature and contents of our collective imaginary – over what we wish for and what we fear – and that it does so by a range of means that include irony, suggestion, and prescriptive coding. It is only with reader-made maps in hand that we can navigate and come to be in a position from which we can evaluate popular culture's layered meanings, and determine what it has to offer society as a whole. Textual analysis can give more weight and deliver added focus, which is reason enough to include it. However, the burden of responsibility for the researcher increases with such dual strategies. Contrary to the Gramscian model, we are not in a direct relation to "the people" as translators, but we move in complex force fields when we express what we think matters, while the moments, the places, or the topics are not of our own choosing. This means that we have to carry a lot of baggage, most of which we will never be able to put to good use.

I cannot claim my tentative conclusion about the state of play regarding the ideological construction of masculinity to be a representation of the interview material; nor would I claim that the novels and characters that I have discussed do any more than point in the direction of this argument. To do so would be to take the paternalist route, the "I know what these readers are talking about, even if they don't realize this themselves." And I may have gone further down that road than I intended, unwittingly doing exactly what I criticized Radway and Ballaster et al. for. My goal, however, is simply to suggest that our cultural resources (those of critics and commoners alike) are highly limited when it comes to talking about masculinity and about violence. What was obvious from the interviews is that highly politicized feminist positions on masculinity, violence, and sexuality are much too radical to be palatable for a wide public, even though our readers felt involved in these issues. I found little evidence of crime fiction offering utopian hope, but I did find traces of how these texts offer a beginning of social criticism. That is what feminist work with audiences might realize: to trace what binds us to particular forms of culture, and to offer not so much explanation or description, but to work with fascination and to develop what can be said about such forms in relation to the social, cultural, and political state of affairs that we find around us; to clarify the reflection implicit in reading practices, to make it explicit, and to offer these practices for further discussion. Rather than simply using texts that we as academics find appealing or fascinating, thereby benefiting a cultural elite, we could extend common knowledge and offer repertoires to take up issues that are of everyday importance but that only find their way into public debate in too cryptic a shorthand to be of any use at all for our sense of well-being and our belief in democracy as a system.

notes

1 On the fallacy of meaningfulness in cultural studies work, see Hermes (1995, pp. 12–17).
2 Interesting examples are Fiske (1990b), who offers a discussion of his own living room; and Probyn's use of autobiographical details to structure her discussion of gender

and gendering in cultural studies (1993) and, more recently, of identity and (not) belonging (1996).

3 Another well-known example would be John Grisham's *The Pelican Brief* and *The Client*, featuring a woman law student and a female lawyer.

4 A notable exception is Val McDermid's *The Mermaids Singing*, and there are gay thriller writers who have taken up this theme.

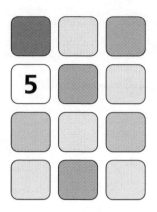

critical viewership

The self-transcribed audience is the dream of any interviewer in cultural research. By chance, I was directed to a website on which audiences can cast votes and debate the loss of merit of their favorite shows. Such material is a curiously disembodied but very concrete form of cultural citizenship as bonding over and reflection on the quality of popular television series. This chapter will take a closer look at the voting and debate related to two of the most-discussed series of the late 1990s: *Ally McBeal* (Fox, 1996–2002) and *Sex and the City* (HBO, 1998–2004), aired in syndicated reruns in the United States and broadcast over most of the globe. The shows themselves, which were key agents in establishing the era of quality popular programming, or "must see" television (Jancovich & Lyons 2003, Introduction), have recently ended. How do we fall out of love with television shows that used to be absolute favorites? What is it that they had to offer, but no longer provide? Is the mirror that the shows hold up for us to ponder on who we are, and how we are who we are, based on little more than a gimmick or a short-lived notion? Is it the case that although popular culture can and does have qualities that take the form of usable stories, or that help in the process of what Ellis calls "working through," these are highly time-bound and not of the lasting or fundamental kind? By focusing on the realism of the shows (according to viewers quoted in this chapter), and on their depiction and prescription of gender roles and body forms, and by looking at how television itself is discussed from the point of view of a critical viewership, I hope to come closer to an answer. First of all, I will say more about the shows, and about "Jump the Shark," the website that I raided for viewer comments; and then I will present some results of what might well be a new direction in audience research, now that we are in an age of more accessible multimedia platforms.

The drama series *Ally McBeal* featured very funny animated sequences, which – in a self-reflexive manner – observed the rules of male-to-female sexism and turned the tables on it. Ally's tongue is shown rolling out like a lizard's, ready to lick up Greg, love interest of the moment. Fighting her biological clock while kicking babies around also made Ally very funny. Some of the best sequences in the show feature interaction between the two central male characters: Richard Fish and John Cage, owners and managing directors of the law firm that also employs Ally. The relationship between the two men is intimate, and full of jokes about and criticism of traditional masculinity. When Cage lets Fish know that he loves him ("A kick in the head," aired in 2002), Fish jumps back and asks Cage whether he is gay, in which case, he would be happy to allow him the freedom to make this choice . . . Cage interrupts and assures him that, of course, he is not gay – but meanwhile he has (very nearly) kissed the other man in a loving gesture. This is unexplored territory in drama, and comedy usually turns it into a big routine in which abhorrence over the possibility of male gay intimacy is enough to fire up entire storylines. *Ally McBeal* goes much much further. Here, comedy is a guise in which to explore the issue of straight masculinity and the ban on male intimacy that goes unpunished (as in the action film, for instance, cf., Willis 1999; or in sports, cf., Poynton & Hartley 1990). The show is in fact much more than a comedy; it is a piece of satire on the basic assumptions regarding the construction of femininity and masculinity.

Of course, *Ally McBeal* never really crosses sensitive bridges. There is a short flirtation with lesbianism (Ally and Ling, another partner in the law firm, kiss in "Buried pleasures," aired in 1999), but this does not include sex. Male homosexuality is almost entirely ignored, but for a set of episodes that deal with a gorgeous transsexual woman, who still has a penis – much to Richard Fish's regret and abhorrence. It is also a very white show, with only a small number of African-American characters (Ally's roommate, Rene, and her ex-lover Greg, who is a doctor) and the one Chinese colleague. All nonwhite characters are racially stereotyped.

Until a short while ago, I would have defended this series for the fact that it at least attempts to put issues of the construction of gender on the agenda. I applaud its engagement with the tension between professionalism and femininity, for which women are usually punished (while men who are involved, caring professionals, are revered for such behavior). I loved it for being vanguard television in terms of style and the mixture of animation with realist drama and comedy routines. Why don't I any more? Falling out of love with television series is not well documented in television literature. Whereas there are a number of strong and interesting accounts of what fandom means to fans, and how they came to be fans, how one stops being a fan is a tale that is not often told.[1] To be sure, deception and disappointment are not as sexy as enthusiasm and involvement, but they are quite possibly the result of key moments at which a show stops being a means of reflecting on life, relationships, and so on. There is an intriguing website that chronicles fans' criticism and comments on television shows, which is called "Jump the Shark." This chapter will take a closer look at "Jump the Shark" comments on *Ally McBeal* and *Sex and the City* (the series that is so often named in tandem with it), and at the themes around which viewer appreciation and deception are structured, which allow for a closer look at how audience members feel that they belong to a viewer community, how these series are "theirs," and what the series allow them to do, think, and reflect on – or, in short, how they allow for a particular type of cultural citizenship.

Postfeminist television

Postfeminist television series such as *Ally McBeal* and *Sex and the City* no longer feature young women who earn their own living easily and enjoy autonomous love lives. They appear to be beyond being saved for heterosexual domesticity (cf., Bennett & Woollacott 1987, on the phenomenon of the Bond girl). The Carrie Bradshaws (*Sex and the City*) and Ally McBeals may from time to time yearn for such a life, but they never actually take it up. (That is to say, not as part of the ongoing series. *Ally McBeal* has just ended with McBeal choosing motherhood over her career and partnership in the law firm where she worked; while toward the end of the *Sex and the City* series, one of Bradshaw's friends, Miranda, initially a single parent, decides to move to Brooklyn with her partner and child.) In contrast to the classic soap opera, there is one lead character; all characters are middle or upper class; all main women characters, like the main male characters, provide for themselves; issues and themes are trendy; and popular psychology is often referenced between characters. Feminist concerns such as the right to work, the right to not be discriminated against, the integrity of the female body, and the right to a free sexuality mix with more traditional feminine concerns, such as how to make oneself attractive, and to get or hold onto a guy.

As a label, the term "postfeminism" has been in use since the mid-1980s. My favorite example comes from an article by Elspeth Probyn in *Screen* (Probyn 1988), in which she deconstructs then popular television drama in Canada that features well-educated women in their thirties, such as *Thirtysomething* (ABC, 1987–91). Probyn heartily disapproves of what goes under the term "postfeminist." Although it suggests that women now "have it all," she feels that the current "choiçoissie" (feminism as entailing the right to choose . . . motherhood) simply obfuscates the re-encoding of traditional gendered values.

Series such as *Sex and the City* and *Ally McBeal* are nowhere near as straightforward in their definition of postfeminism as *Thirtysomething*. For one thing, both are located in public or semi-public locations rather than in the home. In the case of *Ally McBeal*, this is mainly a Boston law firm (Cage and Fish; in the last season to become Cage, Fish, and McBeal), the club downstairs, and only occasionally Ally's home (although this too shifts in the last season). In *Sex and the City*, four friends meet in cafés. Their meetings and discussions, used by one of them – a sexual anthropologist – for her columns in a newspaper, are what the show revolves around. We do encounter all of them in their homes, but only as a backdrop for their continued conversation in the public world, whether cafes, bars, or party venues. Insofar as feminism has not only made the personal political (which both series undoubtedly do), but also put the public–private distinction up for discussion, these series have certainly followed suit. There is a distinct dearth of children, although in the last season Ally suddenly has a 10-year-old daughter, as a result of a donated and then misplaced egg; while Miranda, one of the four *Sex and the City* friends, gives birth to a son. Neither wishes to live with the (or a) father (although, in the last *Sex and the City* season, Miranda changes her mind), which leads at least in part to the outsourcing of care.

At face value then, a case can be made for these series to be associated with a more feminist postfeminism. Despite Ally's micro-skirts and the four friends' semi-obsession with their looks and their (mostly, though not exclusively, heterosexual) sex lives, their feminine foibles are painted against a backdrop that suggests more than simply the attainment of women's emancipation and equal rights. On the contrary, the right claimed would appear to be a right to difference and femininity as separate and not infringing on their professionalism. For many women, Colette Dowling's bestselling self-help book *The Cinderella Complex* (originally published in paperback in 1982) was an eye-opener: despite careers and high-placed positions, apparently a great many women executives still felt that they had mostly been lucky to get there, and also that on a bad day they might well be exposed as frauds. No such anxieties are to be found in these two series. The culture of shame described by Dowling – as long as no one finds out, I will be safe – has turned into a shameless economy in which feelings of satisfaction and pleasure hold equal sway with occasional feelings of guilt and self-doubt. All of the women talk about things that they have done right as well as wrong; and they have no qualms about publicly doubting decisions, either in their personal lives or in their professional lives.

Going by critical comments in the Press and on the Internet (about which, more in the next section), this may well produce, especially when watching Ally, vicarious embarrassment and irritation. As a viewer (and for quite some time a fan), while I enjoy the visual aids and animations used by the producers to express Ally's neuroses and strange behavior, I read them as her feminist claim to the right to be irritating and obnoxious. This is a right claimed by men that is long overdue in being granted to women. I expect, though, that Ally's knack of being irritating embarrasses those who feel that feminism itself is at stake in these representations of successful women.

My suggestion throughout the above has been that postfeminist television drama, and especially *Ally McBeal* and *Sex and the City*, are worth watching and discussing. There are at least four formal grounds for this claim. First of all, although television is much more a women's medium than film or radio, male characters still outnumber female ones, even in drama, which is the most equal domain in televisual representation of men and women. The coming into being of a new subgenre that foregrounds women, the narrative of which is organized via their experiences and views on life, is important. Secondly, the women in postfeminist television are hardly average females. They tend to be more independent, financially, sexually, and emotionally, than female television characters have been in, for example, soap opera. They have careers as well as strong views and they take a number of feminist viewpoints for granted. The narrative is centered on them. The large cast of characters around them is not organized from a more traditional concerned motherly perspective, as in soap opera (cf., Modleski 1984 [1982]). Thirdly, contrary to less recent women's genres such as the soap opera, they attract a more mixed audience. More men watch *and* talk about these series. Lastly, both series have used innovative techniques, especially in form, but also in their content. *Ally McBeal* introduced cleverly produced animated sequences to foreground her desires, hopes, and fears, especially toward the opposite sex. Its format has been dubbed "dramedy": a combination of drama and comedy. *Sex and the City* experimented with reality television type sequences in which "average New Yorkers" were interviewed in the street about the topic of the episode (which, of course, always had to do with sexual codes, conduct, and practices).

This mix of generic components points to a recoding of how television itself has meaning. As far as I am aware, women do not watch more television than men. Yet, the activity of watching television has – for a long time now – been coded feminine. Despite efforts to turn "couch potato" into an honorary label, watching television is understood to be a mindless, passive activity, whereby control of one's thoughts and feelings have been delegated to the set. In line with this cultural coding, entertainment programming, "easy" television, tends (or perhaps tended) to be seen as softer (and more dangerous for one's autonomy as an individual), while "serious" television, journalism, and the news tends to be seen as male television and the epitome of our public citizen duties. This is born out in part by viewer statistics and (older) qualitative research, such as that reported in David Morley's (1986) *Family Television*. Although there are usually some exceptions to the rule, the preferences of men (for hard news) and women (for soap opera) have tended to conform to some extent to the ideological coding of program categories (cf., Gray 1992).

Research conducted today would find it difficult to come to this conclusion. The past two decades have seen a more intense hybridization of television programming then ever before, as is witnessed by the new generic twists in postfeminist television. Reality television, as referenced by early episodes of *Sex and the City*, provides a case in point. Initially, reality television simply mixed the factual and the fictional (Bondebjerg 1999). Actors would replay scenes from everyday life that involved sensational moments. Gradually, more and more "real" footage was shown; for example, in series that showed videotapes from on-board video recorders in police patrol cars. A voice-over would explain what exactly was happening when the images were no more than a blur. For this kind of television there was no distinct gender imprint, nor were its reality-soap follow-ups, such as *Big Brother* (1999–present, Endemol, various countries) a gendered television hit. If anything, the new reality television introduced the multimedia format (by using online webcams on an Internet website; and using mobile phone text messaging systems for voting purposes) and separated younger from older audiences. The programs themselves have showcased caring masculinity in the Netherlands, as well as exhibitionist trans-sexuality (Meijer 2000). In feminist terms too, then, the generic reference in *Sex and the City* is at least noteworthy.

Web journalism and *Ally McBeal* and *Sex and the City*

The Internet is full of commentary on postfeminist television. Professional writers and journalists offer some of the commentaries. These professional viewers tend to introduce themselves as ordinary viewers and fans of the two series – and also of Helen Fielding's Bridget Jones novels (1996 and 1999), and films (2001, dir. Sharon Maguire; 2004, dir. Beeban Kidron) – by contrasting their own positions to those of "other feminists" or "other women" who are critical. On www.salon.com, Carina Chocano (2002) remarks that it is "unsettling to see how few, if any, farewell-to-Ally pieces have been written by women that do not emphatically put a disgusted distance between themselves and the skinny, nervous ditz in micro-minis." Ally, pioneer of what Chocano calls "the girl-in-the-city" genre, is bearing the brunt of a widespread feeling that these representations of women are all material for *Backlash II*, follow-up to Susan Faludi's shocking feminist deconstruction of the myths about women (single women, older women) propagated by American media (Faludi 1993). Chocano points out that a series such as *Ally McBeal* also gave us a number of highly neurotic (though lovable) male characters, including sexist Richard Fish ("bygones").

Another critic, Stine Jensen, opened her remarks about *Ally*, Bridget Jones's Diary, and *Sex and the City* in a Dutch quality newspaper (*NRC*, January 26, 2001, also published on the *NRC* web page) by stating, like Chocano, "that feminists are furious about the hunt for men in the TV series 'Ally McBeal' or the movie 'Bridget Jones's Diary.' " But Ally and Bridget are "heroines for our time" (opening paragraph). Jensen goes on to argue the qualities of these programs by pointing out how Ally's and Bridget's tendency to self-diminishment also indicates their willingness to accept their own insecurities and "loving yourself as you are." The cartoon self-descriptions in Bridget Jones and the animated sequences in *Ally McBeal*, which tend to focus on her uncouth feelings of lust (Ally's tongue rolling out like the proverbial red carpet when she first meets doctor Greg) or anger (kicking a small person while mistaking him for a fantasy baby conjured up by her biological clock), are both comical and critical of how we envision ideal femininity. Jensen mentions the Anti-Bridget Jones Brigade (a British feminist initiative) and Talented Women Malaise, as diagnosed by an American journalist: the theory being that intelligent women's thinking powers are self-reduced to zero when an attractive male (and potential father of as yet unborn children) enters the scene. Jensen herself concludes that this new trend in popular culture is emblematic of "lipstick feminism": feminism dressed up nicely and out to seduce men. She prefers *Sex and the City* over Bridget and *Ally* insofar as the series manages to strike a middle position between Madonna-macha-feminism and self-denigrating blundering about.

All in all, the journalistic critical response to this new wave of "liberated women's fiction" suggests that heterosexuality remains central to ideologies of femininity; that professionalism has – perhaps, hopefully – become less entwined with masculinity; and that male sexual codes (of looking at and hunting a desired object) have not led to happiness but to cynicism (cf., Shalit 1999; Erp 2002). On the positive side, women, feminist women even, have appropriated humor publicly. No matter that the jokes are still often at their own expense. But do note that in *Ally McBeal* the jokes are as much on the men, who are as neurotic, laughable, and lovable as the women.

"Jump the Shark"

I like that while Kim Cattral is older she is portrayed as the sexy one, which is so true. Older women can be sexy and guess what . . . we are all going to get old! (an appreciative viewer commenting on Sex and the City; posted on www.jumptheshark.com)

Television viewing involves viewers in dialogue about identity and selfhood. Television cannot dictate who or what we should be, but it can certainly put pressure on viewers by insistently showing certain body types, ethnicities, genders, sexual preferences, and ages rather than others. What do viewers themselves think of this? Over the last 10 years a multitude of fan websites for television series have been created on the Internet that provide ample examples, mostly from outspoken admirers.

There are different types of sites and newsgroups. Fans write their own fan fiction about characters (Jenkins 1991), discuss plots and characterization and, occasionally, use the net as an activist medium to save a favorite series (as in the case of *Nikita* or the American teen action series *Rosswell*). Sites that are tributes to a series, an actress or actor, or a character, can simply be viewed and quoted. Others are newsgroups. Participation in these groups is always by (Internet) name and e-mail address. Researchers such as Nancy Baym, who researched soap opera communities on the net (2000), and Luisa Stein (2002), who built her own websites and participated in others to reconstruct the meanings that teen television fiction has for viewers, have asked the other participants for permission to use material (quotes or artwork) and have used separate questionnaires in order to keep their fan/participant and researcher/onlooker identities apart. The site that I will use for my current purpose, of exploring how viewers make use of a particular type of television show by commenting on it on the Internet, is called "Jump the Shark."[2]

The website www.jumptheshark.com was pointed out to me when I was grumbling to a friend about how *Ally McBeal* was going downhill. She suggested that I log on to www.jumptheshark.com to share my misery with other viewers. Entirely unconvinced about the redeeming qualities of shared misery, I did visit "Jump the Shark." The site is a portal to lists of anonymous comments on hundreds of television shows, some of which have been discontinued, most of which still run. These comments have only one purpose, which is to decide whether or not a show has lost "it." Are its writers and producers still doing a good job? Or are they committing crimes against the show's audience by losing a particular character, or not writing good storylines for a show's lead? The aim of the lists is to find out when exactly a show stopped being rewarding and what caused it to flunk. Which scenes or episodes would have better remained untaped . . .?

I found little solace as a fan, but a goldmine of material for an audience researcher. Here was an incredibly rich source of material on not just one show, but a host of shows – and fully typed. Via the title of a particular show, a list of moments can be accessed at which a particular show jumped the shark. Most of the contributions are short, no longer than a few lines, and anonymous. It is also possible simply to vote for entries in a list supplied at the top of a show's page. Reading comments on "Jump the Shark," it is clear that the viewers who contribute are convinced that the television industry regularly checks what they are writing. In fact, the tone of the entries suggests that viewers consider television shows and their central characters as their property. Writers and producers should realize they are no more than guardians of a viewer's pleasure. They are delivery people rather than authors.

Throughout what turned out to be *Ally McBeal*'s last season (2001–2), I followed new entries on "Jump the Shark" for *Ally McBeal* and *Sex and the City* (which was also rumored to be coming to the end of its run). Both were screened in the Netherlands by the commercial network Net 5. Episodes followed closely, with less than a 2-month time lag on their original first showing in the United States, where they were made. Not many new entries appeared; nor did I offer any myself. I did become more and more familiar with the heated debate of the years before, which has been "archived" on line. Since I use the site's anonymous archived material, strictly speaking this is not "lurking" (visiting a website without contributing), although any comments on and debate about this issue would be most welcome. Research-politically too, I speak as a fan of women's television and as a (feminist) researcher.

Gender roles in postfeminist television elicit much comment (both positive and negative) from viewers, as will become clear below. What is most intriguing about the postings on www.jumptheshark.com about these series is that they disclose only incidentally, and usually contextually, whether the writer presents him- or herself as a man or a woman. Gender on the net may potentially be a much more open and flexible category than in real life. The computer screen may be less forbidding in this regard than the television has tended to be.

The "Jump the Shark" response to *Ally McBeal* and *Sex and the City*

By the beginning of June 2002 (just after the last episode of *Ally McBeal* had aired on American network television), *Ally McBeal* had amassed almost 600 votes; and *Sex and the City* (still running), half of that (some 300). *Ally McBeal* clearly always divided viewers into lovers or haters: 96 votes were given for "Jumped the shark when . . . Day one"; while 92 votes were cast for "Never jumped." *Sex and the City* has more camp followers: 69 votes for "Never jumped," and a mere 30 for "Day one." Furthermore, the opening statistics of the two pages show that for *Sex and the City* the controversial subjects were as follows: Miranda's choice to remain pregnant (65); Samantha's lesbian affair (41); and Carrie accepting Aidan's marriage proposal (27). All other categories have far fewer votes. With Ally, the two outstanding moments of "jumping" are her sudden elevation to motherhood (92 votes) and the death of Billy, Ally's boyfriend since youth, who marries someone else but remains interested in her as well (82 votes). Ally's weight loss, much remarked upon in the Press as well as in everyday talk among my friends, scores a mere 24, about the same as an especially melodramatic episode that has a neurotic client fly over a river, to his – happy – death (22).

The "Jump the Shark" count of listed votes (last seen in June 2002)

Ally McBeal jumped the shark when . . .	Percentage of votes (total number, 100% = 600)	Sex and the City jumped the shark when . . .	Percentage of votes (total number, 100% = 300)
Day one	16% (96)	Day one	10% (30)
Never jumped	15% (92)	Never jumped	23% (69)
Ally suddenly became a mother	15% (92)	Miranda chose to stay pregnant	22% (65)
Billy died	14% (82)	Samantha had a lesbian affair	14% (41)
		Carrie accepted Aidan's marriage proposal	9% (27)
Ally lost too much weight	4% (24)		
Ally's flying client died	3.6% (22)		

This collection of spontaneously offered comments is interestingly different from the journalistic comments. Three related qualities are appreciated: (1) the notion of the happy single woman as not a mother (the votes against Miranda's pregnancy and Ally becoming a mum); (2) the never-ending romance rather than marriage (cf., critique on the death of Billy as a focus for Ally's romantic longings; Carrie accepting a marriage proposal); as well as (3) heterosexuality

(Samantha's lesbian affair is voted down; as well as – though much less so – an episode in which Ally engages in kissing with Ling, a female colleague (nine votes against). The observations also sent in to the website, which follow the statistics, show more than a concern with the "ideal series," and contain arguments about television and gender as well. I have tried to reconstruct the discursive structure underlying these arguments by focusing on (a) realism and learning from (other people's/characters') experience, (b) content in terms of gender/feminism (including anorexia – the ideal of the slim body), and (c) critical viewership in terms of how viewers present themselves as knowable, self-reflexive viewers, and how, from such a position, they criticize generic convention and discuss innovation. This worked well for both series, even if the *Sex and the City* quotes had an altogether different focus and slant than the *Ally McBeal* comments. The *Sex and the City* quotes also included far more men, introducing themselves as such, and more interaction between the posters.

After downloading all comments, I used what Wetherell and Potter (1988) have termed repertoire analysis:

> Repertoires can be seen as the building blocks speakers use for constructing versions of actions, cognitive processes and other phenomena. Any particular repertoire is constructed out of a restricted range of terms used in a specific stylistic and grammatical fashion. Commonly these terms are derived from one or more key metaphors and the presence of a repertoire will often be signalled by certain tropes or figures of speech. (1988, p. 172)

After defining repertoire analysis as the search for recurring themes and tropes in order to reconstruct the logics that underlie them, Wetherell and Potter point out that quotations that are diametrically opposed to one another, which belong to different repertoires, may come from the same informant. In everyday life, language use needs to be functional. There is no great prize for consistency and shifts between repertoires will frequently occur. For that reason, it is inopportune to look for "positions" or "attitudes" (which are more common in psychological research). Strictly speaking, discourse analysts should focus on the language used. My disembodied arguments on when and why (or why not) these shows "jumped the shark" fit well with this requirement. I have no way of knowing whether a small group debated the development and qualities of these shows (and took up different speaking positions), or whether remarks come from different viewers; nor do I think this is at all important for my purposes. Last but not least, "Jump the Shark" has no fixed categories. The recurring arguments that it lists are, in the truest sense, members' categories.

Realism

Realism was fiercely debated in early (1970s) film and television studies. It has mainly been understood as a series of conventions that aim to depict a recognizable and truthful picture of reality. As such it is necessarily reactionary, because it "proposes a notion of the 'truth' that is seen as factual, not as a construct of culture and discourse" (MacCabe, quoted in Fiske 1987, p. 35). In cultural studies analyses of television audiences, conducted from the early to mid-1980s onward, realism is hardly ever used as a reference to textual properties. Rather, it is referenced as one of the qualities that audiences look for in television fiction. The audience use of the term can be related back to an earlier meaning, noted by Raymond Williams in *Keywords*, in which "realistic" is understood to denote the real, or deeper, truth and as the opposite of "appearances": inner reality against outward appearance (Williams 1976, p. 260). Ien Ang coined the term "emotional realism" for how her *Dallas* viewers (42 letter-writers who responded to an advertisement in the Dutch young women's magazine *Viva*) wrote about the program: although they were fully aware of the fact that *Dallas* was fiction – that "real life" millionaires might not be especially like these characters – they tended to recognize quintessential human characteristics in them. Watching *Dallas* provided a means of learning about human relations and life (Ang 1985). Given that television fiction is embedded in a medium that combines fiction with nonfiction and live programming (which easily translates as reality and realism), it is not too big a step to understand television fiction to be life-like as well.

Below the surface, *Ally McBeal* is easily read as "serious social commentary" and as a "sensitive portrayal of daily problems," while others expect to find this type of realism and fault the show for not providing it: "shallow social statement," "poorly depicting career women." What is interesting is the debate amongst those who feel that the show provides a poor role model (for young women) and those who then argue that this is "only a television show."

The *Sex and the City* comments are much more outspoken. They differ from the *Ally McBeal* comments in various ways: there are more men, who almost apologetically introduce themselves as such. Some boast that watching the show gives them an "in" with women; others have succumbed to the taste of girl-friends and wives. The tone is more aggressive and cynical, and there is an ongoing relay-race type of discussion between those who post messages. Those who comment on its realism usually criticize the show for its lack thereof, for which the writers are faulted. Others suggest that the show be seen as satire or comedy, which effectively moves discussion away from realism, and from the possibility of learning from the experiences of these four women. This is all the more remarkable because the series started out as a semi-reality program, with inserted quotes from "real New Yorkers." The category of "realism" in the sense of "what life is really like" is mostly used critically:

> I have tried to watch a couple of episodes since as a 25-year-old guy, every girl I know seems to treat this as their Bible to life today and I didn't want to be completely in the dark when it came to conversations with them. Having watched a few times now, I can only conclude this: no wonder so many girls are emotionally messed up. They watch these four completely unrealistic women in completely unrealistic situations, and then try to emulate what they see as if that would ever play in real life.

Interestingly, the speaker in such posts usually credits him- or herself with being able to distinguish televisual reality from real life, while others are not able to do so.

Gender

While coding posts about gender, I broadened the category to include feminism. The *Ally McBeal* "Jump the Shark" posts spend much time denouncing what is perceived to be the anorexia of the protagonist (Calista Flockhart, who plays Ally). Post 341 is exemplary – "Finally, can anybody give Calista Flockheart some food, the anorexic look is out babe." – as are the following: "She looks like death on a stick" and "I am tired of hearing about how Calista Flockheart is healthy, even though she is very obviously underweight. Making women and girls every-where thinking you not only can't be fat, but you have to be underweight to be pretty and acceptable."

Some are not only dismissive or upset, but use profanities to denounce Flockheart and call her names (e.g., "bag of bones"). This is also directed against her hair (her style of dressing it). Apparently, hair is a major concern, because Sarah Jessica Parker, lead actress in *Sex and the City* (as Carrie Bradshaw), is also continuously told to do something about her hair.

The role model theme is strong here. Ally is a "stereotype"; "she makes women look neurotic"; she is a "stupid anorectic who dresses like a prostitute"; "Ally is all that is dysfunctional about American women." Obviously, these series are read as presenting gender ideals. Not only are Ally and the other female characters taken to task for not living up to expectations (with a fan inter-vening from time to time saying that they are fantastic, or "hot"), but the men too are discussed in the *Ally McBeal* posts. The same mechanism is at work: there is a process going on through which "normality" is defined, as well as aberrations in relation to the norm. Billy (erstwhile lover, later colleague and married to someone else, but continuing love interest until his death at the end of the third season) is much discussed for two remarkable moves on the character's part. He dyes his brown hair white, and later takes up a pimp-like attitude and has himself chaperoned by a bunch of women clad in black latex (the Robert Palmer girls). He also propagates male machismo as an ideology of male self-respect that needs to be revived. The hair and the girls net him a lot of comments (though not as many as his death), which make clear that, although weird, this is seen as an interesting experiment in redefining masculinity in the context of a show that is clearly in favor of women having careers. His death puts an end to the possibility of continuing romance between him and Ally, which is bemoaned. His lapse into a conservative ideology of masculinity is not seen as despicable, but as an interesting taunt.

The *Sex and the City* posts also tend to be less forgiving to men showing sensitivity or weakness than to men acting out what they feel to be male prerogative. Carrie's ongoing feelings for Big, who treats her like dirt, are discussed in terms of her behavior but not his. When she introduces her then fiancée Aidan to Big, Aidan's friendliness counts against him:

> If I were Aidan, I would have more than a few choice words for "Princess Carrie" . . .

> She f*cks Big behind Aidan's back, tells Aidan and gets dumped, begs her way back to Aidan then invites the man she cheated on him with to HIS cabin! I know SATC isn't realistic on a lot of levels, but that episode was just ridiculous. It made Aidan look like a milquetoast . . .

And about Big:

> When Big showed up looking all broken and pathetic at Aidan's country house to cry over that movie star lady, that was pretty much it for me. I've always looked at Big like Mr. Macho, cool as a cucumber, and that episode made him look about as cool as a wet noodle.

When it comes to men versus women, there are quite a few posts by men who feel that it is women who get away with whatever. If there were to be a series about four men in an apartment talking about sex . . .

> I don't even watch, so maybe I shouldn't be commenting, but it kind of bugs me that if all the female characters on this were guys and vice-versa, it would've lasted about three episodes before someone shouted "SEXIST!" and it would be taken of the air. But because it's the other way around, it becomes a big hit.

Generally, people post against the extreme use of swearwords, and feel that the women behave like whores. This in turn inspired someone to post: "Who would've thought independent, free thinking women who like sex could still be so threatening to people?" Another adds: "I get the feeling that a lot of people are offended merely because the 4 women are sexually liberated & do what they want to do."

More threatening still, going by the later posts, is the fact that Miranda decides to keep the baby, while the three other women are in, or are contemplating, monogamous relationships – the end of the singles' dream of a fun, sex, and friendship-filled life:

> Season finale. Miranda is having a baby. Charlotte's already married. Then Carrie said yes to Aidan's marriage proposal. There won't be much Sex in the City if the women are tied down to husbands and babies. We've already been there & done that with Thirtysomething.

Or: "But now this formerly sharp, funny show about fabulous single chicks has weighed down 3/4 of its cast with domestic baggage." And: "Why ruin a fun, hip show? Parenthood is not sexy. Save it for the bland network sit-coms." And it goes on: "Why can't we just watch interesting women go out to eat and wear cool clothes and talk about sex with new people? Those of us who *are* married and *have* kids want to live vicariously." More complaints: "This was an awesome show; for once women were not represented as complicit broodmares. They dated men; they had sex; they had fun! Now what is it with !@£$% babies? I have no interest in babies, yet networks seem obsessed with them." A last one: "Babies? Cancer? Country houses? For God's sake – this show used to be about fun and frivolous things. Hot clothes, hot dates, hot sex and hot restaurants . . ." Of course, apart from the baby, the disaster is averted: Carrie breaks off with Aidan; Charlotte's marriage is over. And as for the baby, a lone soul suggests that maybe Steve (the father of the baby, with whom Miranda does not want to live) can take care of the baby. This was all resolved in the 2003–4 final season, quite possibly not to the delight of these viewers.

The criticism of the show does not always ring entirely true: "When will people realise this show just keeps women thinking they need men and they don't (though I admit I have one, but I also have a vibrator so could live on my own)." Is this just another guy who does not want to write about what he perceives as men-bashing by holding up a caricature of feminist sentiment? Or is this part of a slightly dated feminist sentiment that crops up here and there as well, as in the "broodmares" quote above? As regards feminism, there is mostly a strong sentiment against any form of right- or left-wing conservatism: both political correctness (the left-wing variety) and outdated ideas that women should not talk about sex are slighted. For example:

I have one question for some of the posters above: why do you feel that nudity on the part of SJP [actress Sarah Jessica Parker] or KD [Kristin Davies] would be good for the show, while having full frontal nudity on a man sign that this show has "jumped the shark"? I hate to break it to all you disillusioned males, but women do like to see naked men, women do enjoy having sex and women LOVE to talk to their girlfriends about it.

Clearer yet is a post on the *Ally McBeal* section of "Jump the Shark":

For once we have a thinking, feeling lead female, but she is not the "ideal" look-ing kind of female or the "normal" kind of pretty, and what do we all do? We bash her (jealous?) and any more talk of the show is gone. "Ally eat a burger," and we end it right there. Men can be neurotic and insecure, too, but god help you if you are a pretty, skinny girl, because THEN if you have any doubts, any longings, any visions of another life but you are not exactly sure of how to get there, admit you're not perfect (like I'm sure 90% of America feels) it means, well you can just chalk it up to the "female" stereotype of being whiny and wishy-washy. Men could act the same way and we would probably call them sensitive or thoughtful or funny. The stereotypes are just killing me.

Television

Clearly the posters are television-literate viewers, who have a strong sense of how fiction television is produced. Many posts directly address the writers. David Kelley, writer of *Ally McBeal*, is both praised and abused. The writers for *Sex and the City* are accused of not knowing what they are doing any longer, as well as of being gay and forgetting who they are writing about (because women don't sleep with everyone, gay men do). The role model discussion, the delight in television that is different, the references to other shows ("bland network com-edy" above, as well generic references, and references to other shows in which lead characters have had babies, such as *Murphy Brown* (CBS, 1988–96) and *Mad About You* (NBC, 1992–9), and the suggestions to the writers all imply more than familiarity and knowledge. There is a sense of proprietorship, even if a viewer's hold on a series is by definition tenuous. These viewers know that they are instru-mental to a show's success. It is hardly far-fetched to suggest that the posts discussed above are proof positive of how television is a means for a strong interpretive community to debate, in the case of these two series, issues of gendered identity (to be discussed at more length in the Conclusion).

Interestingly, there was little discussion of the aesthetics of these two shows, apart from discussion of the writing. *Sex and the City* is linked, for example, to the innovative series *Northern Exposure* (CBS, 1990–5, created by Joshua Brand) through the character of Aidan (John Corbett), who played Chris in the older series. *Northern Exposure* also delighted in fantasy sequences and emphasized strong women's rights sentiments. In the case of *Ally McBeal*, aesthetic references were mostly aimed at the dancing baby – the outward manifestation of one of Ally's neuroses, in this case her fear of getting too old to have a child for lack of not finding a suitable male partner. The earlier fantasy sequences were implicitly deemed acceptable and innovating, but the introduction of the baby took things too far. Whether this was disapproved of aesthetically or ideologically, in its suggestion that motherhood means all to women (or both), cannot be deduced from this material. In the case of *Sex and the City* (again apart from the writing), aesthetic qualifications are mostly directed against the over-the-top clothing style of Parker as Carrie Bradshaw. In addition, there is a clear divide in the adjectives used to describe the characters as well as the show. These are either: "weepy," "whining," "selfish," "egotistical," "consumerist," and "ugly"; or "sharp," "satirical," "edgy," "cynical," "witty," and "hot." "Whiny" is complemented by "neurotic" and "anorectic" in the case of *Ally McBeal*, and contrasted with "sexy." For both shows, the sizable airtime devoted to sex and sexuality is problematized, often by stating that the lead actresses are (or behave as) whores, "hos," prostitutes. I tend to read this as an aesthetic quality criterion too, although it may also point to unease in relation to the ongoing discussion of gender and gender relations.

At least one of the underlying repertoires, then, has to do with the codes of sexiness. These codes are not related to an older Platonic ideal of the coming together of the beautiful, the good, and the truthful; but to a Foucauldian disciplinary system that is structured around a central norm – women should be thin, but not too thin. Likewise, shows should break the mold, but not too much. Emancipated women can talk about sex, but not too much. Perhaps the pleasure is in always deeming whatever is on the show to be excessive. All comedy is structured around these moments of breaking social norms, and then coming back to the status quo (cf., Marc 1997). For some of the posters, these shows do all of the above, apart from returning to the status quo.

Going through the "Jump the Shark" comments, the bottom line is a discourse of self-distinction, both for the posters themselves as discerning viewers, and in what they expect of the characters. Ally is admired and berated for her neurotic behavior, but it is recognized as a highly specific and original style. As with Bridget Jones, there is admiration for a woman doing things her own way, even if she may sometimes show herself to be a buffoon or an idiot. Likewise, the four *Sex and the City* friends are judged and admired for "doing their own thing," whether in bed or out of it, and as regards their sense and style of dress. The anorexia comments usually understand the actresses to bow to an outdated norm of feminine beauty. Implicitly, this is replaced by a norm of "strength" (of character) for both the women and the men. Sensitivity is only acceptable if presented in a self-assertive manner (Ally); while it is never hip or sexy in a man (this is Aidan's predicament). Any reliance on received notions of what a woman, a man, or a feminist should be like meets with disapproval. Apparently, this "will to individuality and strength," to paraphrase Foucault's notion of the productivity of power/knowledge as engine of social and discursive relations and practices, is hard to transplant onto relationships or parenthood. Freedom, more than gender, is what this normative system revolves around.

Conclusion

We fall out of love with television shows that depart from the discursive framework that they helped to put in place. By the end of *Ally McBeal* and *Sex and the City*, the will to freedom and individuality within the context of self-built networks (friendship, workplace), and the negation of traditional roles in the relative safety of these networks, had given way to a new wish – to build new families, closer to traditional structures (without wholly reverting back to them). Moreover, while inventing new social structures and identities was fun, they too solidify and produce their own disciplinary effects. Popular culture generally proves ephemeral in that it may, as in the case of these two series, be at the vanguard of reinventing who we are. By its nature, reinvention (and the exhilaration accompanying it) has a short lifespan before changing to established new forms, and from there on to routine. The stories offered within the narrative frameworks of the series lose their usefulness; as viewers, we move on to choose anew from what the industry is offering us.

Meanwhile, something significant has happened, however time- and place-based. Gender relations have been rethought, as well as how the regulation of gender roles implies degrees of individual freedom and autonomy. Also, television itself, through practices of reception and discussion of what have also been called "the new comedies" (including, amongst other shows, *Friends* (NBC, 1994–2004) and *Will and Grace* (NBC, 1994–) as well), has changed. The staid gender regime underlying television's generic organization has been turned upside down, at least in this particular area. This is indicated by the sheer number of "male voices" that enter the discussion of these two "women's shows." Some may do so via comments that solely discuss the lead actresses as sexual objects: the posters tell us whom they'd want to have sex with. But there is also a category that engages with the shows and their topics as such. They may apologize for this (I'm just a guy but . . . I watch this show with my wife), but men do nonetheless feel addressed by the show's content and by its success. More men may have posted notes on "Jump the Shark" but remained pleasantly gender-anonymous. Likewise, some of the sexual posts may have come from women. Postfeminist television, then, may be a critical failure in feminist-textual terms (they offer women who have made careers but who revel in old-fashioned femininity, and depend on finding the right man for their happiness); in audience terms, they are successful in turning around the usual disdain for women's genres; while the method of virtual ethnography provides an opening to relativize gender, which would be much more difficult in non-virtual, material reality.

"Jump the Shark" discussion shows that the policing of television and its aesthetics is shifting away from older associations of, in particular, fiction television with passivity and femininity, to a more inclusive battlefield, a semi-public domain in which both the public role of television (role models) and its televisual qualities are discussed (innovation, good/bad writing and acting). Older structures that equate quality solely with aesthetics do not hold true here; nor does the old high–low culture divide. Television literacy is coming into its own; distinction can be earned in a number of fields that are not predicated on distance or reflection, but on debate and engagement. Identity is constructed in dialogue with the text and with other viewers. The television and the computer screen aid a more fluid sense of who we are. Of course, it remains to be seen whether men's genres too will shift in their coding of gender, and whether this will be the case in audience interpretation. Clearly, the rules of inclusion and exclusion set by the viewer community described here are very strict when it comes to a "softening" of masculinity. Billy is easily forgiven for his machismo, while Aidan and Big are criticized in no uncertain – and tellingly phallic – terms (in the wet noodle quote). Still, there is hope now that the mold of gender definition has been so thoroughly broken.

notes

1 Examples are Jenkins (1991), Lewis (1992), Stacey (1994), and Douglas (1995).
2 Apparently, the name of the site refers to an episode in the final season of *Happy Days* (ABC, 1974–84; the series is situated in 1950s USA). In it, central character Fonzie, who rents a room with the Cunningham family, literally jumps a shark during a beach visit. To the website builders, this was so inconceivable – and out of character for The Fonz, the master of Cool – that they felt that the show had signed its death warrant at that particular moment, obviously without realizing it (based on personal communication with Luisa Stein, New York, February 2002).

Chapter 5

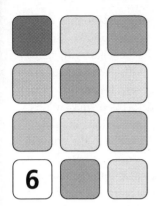

children and the media

6

Public debate idealizes children and childhood. It pictures them as naïve and in need of protection, which, says Ingegerd Rydin, conceals the fact that children use television the same way most adults do, and that they are quite competent in presenting their thoughts and views about the media (2003, p. 77). Children are active media users and social actors, "beings in their own right, rather than pre-adult becomings" (Holloway & Valentine 2000, pp. 5, 6). This chapter asks what uses children have for popular culture and how, for them, it is related to cultural citizenship. How do they feel they belong, and who is included and who is excluded from that feeling of belonging? How does popular culture, whether nonfiction or fiction, from the perspective of children themselves, allow them to think about who they are, and how they relate to others?

This chapter consists of two main sections. The first half is based on a case study of how children talk about the Third World. For most children living in the West, the Third World – or the South – is unknown territory. Their information and feelings about it stem mostly from how the South is represented in such popular culture as public service children's television, school television, children's news, and early evening family programming, which includes, for instance, fund-raising and travel advertisements. We can assume that by asking children about the Third World, they will give us a sense of how they define difference and identity based on their use of media content. Do they feel connected to other children, or do they build a more narrowly defined local or national sense of community? Are they encouraged by the media to participate in a humanitarian ideal, and the shared moral responsibility for the world that Nick Stevenson (2003) suggests is part of a cosmopolitan citizenship that would befit a globalizing world? Or is children's cultural citizenship of a different order?

The second half of the chapter takes a closer look at the intermedial field of children's entertainment, which they regard as their expertise: the computer games and popular television series that so often have parents and pedagogues up in arms. According to them, the violence and sexism that worried adults discover in children's favorite media fare will have detrimental effects. That remains to be seen. What is important is that these worries resonate with themes that have also surfaced in the other case studies. Abhorrence over and fascination with violence, and apprehension over constructions and lived forms of masculinity, are thought about and discussed in relation to football, crime fiction, and popular postfeminist television. Violence and constructions of gender in the context of children's media therefore deserve a closer look.

"Violence" has become an overused concept. It does not differentiate between choreographed and nonfrightening fighting and gruesome depictions of maiming and death. Of the last, there is not much in children's media diet. To build common ground before I present the views of the interviewed children, I will first discuss *Pokémon*, a much-merchandized hand-held computer game and animated television series. After that, I will turn to how the children talk about the games and series that they like, which includes their reflections on violence and the depiction of women. At the end of the chapter, I will return to questions of children's cultural citizenship. In both sections, children's preferences and examples of television programs and games have been taken as the point of departure for textual analysis. To illustrate the arguments made, some of the programs and games are described in more detail.

Good intentions

Public service television for children is commonly associated with education and cognitive learning effects.[1] It is taken for granted that public television might be less exciting but better for children; that it will help them learn worthwhile things and develop the right attitude to society and life in general; that, in short, it will teach them to be responsible "citizens" in a formal sense. But does it?

Anne Niewenhuys and Jessie Verbrugh interviewed 19 children, aged between 8 and 12 years old, about whether they were familiar with the term "Third World" and whether they knew anything at all about it. Had they, for instance, seen the Third World on television?[2] Their answers, and analysis of the television programs that they named, made clear that "Third World" is a term that children recognize and relate one-dimensionally to misery, poverty, and hardship. Items on *Children's News*, school TV, and the occasional fundraising commercial or show program convinced them that children in the Third World have to wear ill-fitting clothes (if they have any at all), have to eat grass because there is nothing else, and have nothing to play with. One boy said: "They just don't look healthy. And their clothes are all torn, and if you could smell them, with smell-television, I'd put a washing pin on my nose. They look filthy." My own daughter Sacha was one of our informants: "There was a pot with grass in it as if it were rice. It was perfectly clear that they could not get any food. And then they showed images of tents. Not real ones, like ours, but pieces of cloth, hanging from a stick in the ground."

The Third World is not so much a geographical place as an imagined space (cf., Soja 1989, 1996), a domain in which all that is fun when playing as a child living in the West becomes a harsh reality. Improvising a tent, make-believe cooking, and dressing up in old clothes are key elements in under-eight playing activity; but seeing them on television as everyday living conditions has a shock–horror effect that mostly has children distancing themselves as much as possible from all that misery. Much-watched public service television programs such as *Children's News* (*Jeugdjournaal*, 1981–) combine images with straightforward commentary to emphasize the civic and economic responsibility of the West for the Third World. The interviewed children, however, use a rote reply that the desperate situation of the Third World can only be remedied if we assume our responsibility as First World countries. That responsibility amounts to little more than donating money or old clothes. After all, they have learned to reason, the "poverty and misery" that they see are caused by war – not something that they can do much about.

Although this is a young age group, we did expect a more diverse set of answers and a wider range of images and associations to be available to these children concerning the Third World. We verified Nieuwenhuys and Verburgh's findings by visiting a multi-ethnic school class of 10-year-olds in Amsterdam. But when we showed them a tape with extracts from *Children's News* (among which was an item with Africans engaged in a silly contest for a worthy goal), part of a recent *School Television Week Overview* (*Schooltv Weekjournaal*) segment, and a commercial for a soft drink, set in Africa (savannah grass, a lion, and a dark-skinned boy), they only recognized the civil war item as set in the Third World. While racial characteristics and dress code are indeed multiply interpretable, natural setting hardly is. The advertisement's conventional African scenery was unrecognizable as another type of representation of that same Third World. The children paid attention to the storyline (a short adventure tale) rather than to the setting. Neither the beautiful scenery (a clear marker of the Third World for adult viewers) nor unfettered, free-moving exotic animals gave rise to such an interpretation. A tourist view of other parts of the world is clearly a perspective that develops later.

The 19 children who were interviewed at length all mentioned several channels and programs that they watched. In addition to public service and commercial television stations (such as FoxKids), Discovery and National Geographic were mentioned (as were regional television and stations from the country of origin of their parents, such as Moroccan television via satellite). Given their broad television menu, these children are offered much more than images of poverty and misery in the Third World. However, wildlife documentaries, anthropological series, and travel advertisements for faraway destinations hardly registered with them. There was also no notion that, in the South, there might also be people living under comfortable conditions, that there might be class differences and a range of lifestyles. Apart from the universal answer "war" as to what causes living conditions to be so dismal, there was no understanding of local social relations, or of the differences between all those far-flung countries around the globe that are grouped under the term "Third World."

Angola: a forgotten war

A closer look at the programs and items that the children refer to reveals that a singular logic is at work in interpreting these texts. Fund-raising spots, understandably, argue the case of extreme need. An example that the interviewed children named is a "People in Need" Angola advertisement, entitled "Angola: a forgotten war."[3] A blind Angolese father and son are introduced, walking along an unpaved road. A voice-over relates the father's story as a war victim and stresses that there is no future for this child unless we pay a mere 4 euros a month. The child (who is given a name) taking care of the father implies that they are basically good people, with a strong sense of family, who have been dealt an unfair hand by fate. We are to save them. While the voice-over stresses that, for them, there is only a future if we help them, we see father and son get into a car and then arrive at a school that has been shot to pieces (which refers back to earlier, gruesome war images in the spot). The voice-over suggests that Joachim's only wish is to learn and to get ahead in life – which is impossible in this ruin. While the voice-over gives us a phone number that we can use to enlist, we see Joachim eating in an improvised open-air space where some kind of teaching is going on. While we are invited to help change people in need into people with a future, we see Joachim and his father at work, rebuilding the school stone by stone. When the blind father feels a bullet hole he stops, and the boy grasps his hand. Thank you, says the voice-over, while Joachim is shown in a close-up, facing us directly.

In itself, this is a short story of people rebuilding their lives. They may need a little money but they are certainly not waiting for the next Western expert to stop by and tell them how to do it. With a little help, these people will be able to cope and leave the war behind. Looking at it from the perspective of the children who were interviewed, something completely different is going on. There is obvious poverty here. War is of course to blame. But, most importantly, there isn't even a school. The boy Joachim has to build his own school. He is not allowed to play; he has to work.

In the interviews the children describe it thus: "Some of those children do go to school, but not many of them do. And they had chicken wire instead of windows." "And then you saw one of those poor children. He was brown and he didn't have good clothes. You saw that on a photo and all these beds that were bad and then you give 5 euro per month and you really help one of those children" (Peter). Or Doris: "There was a school, but there were so many children in a huge area who had nowhere to go, or they would have to walk thousands of kilometers." Ruben: "They don't go to school." If David had to live in a Third World country: "I wouldn't be able to go to school." Or Sally: "Then, I'd have to take care of my parents." What stands out is the absolute divide between "us" and "them," and the conviction of the interviewed children that to be a child in the Third World means that you cannot go to school and that you have to work for food or money. The moving quality of the short story of Joachim and his father, and its appeal to the humanitarian values shared by the viewers and the story's characters, is lost in a host of semiotic markers of what an utterly desperate life would be like – from the dry, unpaved road to the school in ruins and their improvised clothes – which fits well with the children's preponderance to think in terms of True or False, with nothing much in between.

Children's news

Children's News (1981–) in the Netherlands is part of the public service regular news, broadcast as the last slot of public service children's programming from 6.45 p.m. to 7 p.m. We watch it daily, since our daughter was encouraged in fifth grade (8–9-year-olds) to follow the program. It always consists of a couple of longer items and three or four short items, and ends with a weather forecast. It follows the major news stories of the moment (global and national politics, disasters, war), and includes items that are directly relevant to children (a school burning down, children's poetry contests) and "funny" news (a man breaking the world record for eating ice cream – 4 liters within 2 hours, for a good cause), as well as showbiz and animal news (any friendly footage showing an animal is regularly included). The presenters are young, hip, and come from different ethnic backgrounds, while the setting is informal: a see-through desk and a curved, minimalist, multicolored couch. All in all, it compares favorably to the British and American programs (including *Newsround*, BBC,

1972–; *First Edition*, Channel 4, 1994–2002; and *Nick News*, Nickelodeon, 1999–) described and analyzed by David Buckingham in *The Making of Citizens: Young People, News and Politics* (2000).

As in *Newsround*, ecology and the environment are central concerns. Buckingham's impression of the kind of environmental discourse is that it "largely avoids questions of economics and politics" (2000, p. 45): "The threat to the environment here is not seen as systemic but as a result of individual villainy: it is at most, a result of the conflict between people and nature, and it can be solved by individual interventions, not least in the form of charity" (idem). What strikes me in *Children's News* is its direct appeal to children as responsible for the world in which they live. In the case of oil disasters, we see more than dead birds, dirty beaches, and experts: there are always also children living locally, who are angry and outraged and demand justice as well as more stringent rules (as in the case of the *Prestige* oil disaster on the Spanish coast in 2002). Ecology is clearly understood as one of the most direct routes to a strong notion of citizenship for children. After all, it consists equally of a sense of proprietorship (our future, our world), responsibility, and community (we have to make do with this world together). Nor does *Children's News* shirk a more political analysis. It explains how bad upkeep and profit motives may go hand in hand, turning innocent others into victims – while those innocent others may also benefit from the villainy at hand, because we all use oil and oil-based products. How we are implicated, however, in the misery of war refugees and people living in camps is a more difficult matter.

An Afghanistan item (aired shortly after the September 11, 2001, attack on the World Trade Center) is both critical of the United States and is a prime example of how the Third World is shown. A female voice-over states that the people in Afghanistan are very scared. Osama Bin Laden is assumed to be hiding in that country (inset of Bin Laden with a gun). According to America, he instigated the attack on the World Trade Center and other buildings, the voice-over continues. The people in Afghanistan are afraid that the Americans will now attack them. Meanwhile, what we see are open tents and a kind of hut. There is no privacy. Children are holding empty plates; women are sitting in the sand. There is hardly any water (shot of a rusty pipe coming out of a rock). The Red Cross is cited as saying that shortly there will be no food left. The item ends on what is intended to be an upbeat note, with a shot of a Unicef food, blankets, and medication transport. What we have seen is a completely passive group of people sitting in the sand, waiting for food. When they move, it is toward the structure from which the only Westerners (Red Cross volunteers) serve food.

Such items recur regularly over the years and are reflected directly in the repertoires of the interviewed children. There is the dominant image of poverty and misery; clearly, war is a cause that is easy to understand; and as rich people in the West we should do something, because these people cannot help themselves. Although the rhetorical structure of the Afghanistan item suggests that Osama Bin Laden is the villain of the piece, the voice-over also informs us that the Americans might attack and that Aghanistan is a very poor country. Poverty and war are connected as a matter of course. Vera: "They go to war with other countries; they don't spend money on these people. Money goes to bombs . . . in that war between America and Afghanistan." According to Peter, Osama Bin Laden cannot be blamed for all of this: "Well, maybe a little, but if that country was already so very poor, that can't be because of one person."

Black and white reasoning

There is little sense in the interviews that people might take their fate into their own hands, or try to act to change their worlds. For items to do with the North, however, including the (often happy) children's news items, the deployment of initiative is often the main constituent of an item's newsworthiness (a girl organizing a petition for traffic lights near her school; children producing artwork to raise money for new playthings in the park where they spend their free time). But such a logic does not apply to the South. As viewers, the children appear to be happy with a black and white scenario that connects what they would call the Third World with a place where people sit around being miserable, and where there is neither the time nor the means for children to play. The argumentative structure of the news items directly corresponds with their own one-dimensional logical and moral reasoning. It does not challenge them to take the structure or reality of the lives of others to heart and understand them contextually, and in shades of gray rather than as black or white, and governed by simple rules.

If the best-case scenario is that you get to build your own school (which will end up looking like all the other awful schools that have been shown), the situation of children in the Third World is not to be envied, period. As soon as the narrative of a news item or a commercial spot focuses on children who do have fun and are playing, the discursive structure of what the Third World is, and how we relate to it, forbids such a link, and the item becomes placeless and unrelated to the social reality that other people live. As a result, the motivational aspect to "Third World discourse" is always linked to the neediness of "them" far away, and the pleasantly enviable luxury and pleasure of our own lives. As soon as the media content can be interpreted away from poverty and misery, there is room to connect with children elsewhere and include them rather than exclude them.

The citizenship ideal promoted by well-meaning public service television implicitly congratulates those of us who are Westerners for being who we are. It lays the foundation for understanding the world as structured in tiers, rather than for a reflexive humanitarian ideal. In Maxim Gorki's words, this is the citizenship of cruel compassion, which fixates the other in victimhood, and silences him.[4] The challenge in making television for 8–12-year-old children, who clearly like to think in simple schemata and dichotomies, is to – quite forcefully – encourage them to step outside stereotypical definitions of right and wrong, and good and bad.

There is well-intended children's programming that goes beyond the logic of learning what is Right and what is Wrong; that entertains its audience *and* builds a positive sense of responsibility for a shared globe. But it is exceptional and, more importantly, it suffers from the dominance of "Orientalist" Third World thinking. The challenge to children's television is to build community and commitment across divides without moralizing and without referring to over-determined signifiers. From our small classroom experiment with the soft drink advertisement, we know that a strong storyline and the markers of action-adventure television can do so. In the class discussion that took place after the children had filled out short questionnaires and discussed their answers in small groups, Africa had clearly become a far more interesting continent than the children had imagined it to be at the beginning of our morning with them. Contrary to adult expectations, in documentary mode – a long-standing favorite in public service broadcasting – a more questioning and reflexive commitment is much harder to achieve.

From the perspective of cultural citizenship, lines of inclusion and exclusion may not be so much about specific places as about states of well-being. Fun images of the Third-World-as-place are immediately transferred to the much nicer imagined space of the West. This is clearly indicated by the lack, throughout the interviews, of much race-related observation. The interviewed children do notice that the Third World children are mostly "brown," but they do not use ethnicity in a racist sense at all – not even those of our informants who were a bit bored by the project and looked for ways to shock us and sabotage the interview. Nor was gender a significant category in the interviews, either in reference to "real people" or to the ways in which, for example, refugees are shown as powerless victims, "feminized" by circumstance.

Insofar as we can recognize specific forms of bonding and reflection on their own lives in how these children talk about the Third World, either implicitly or explicitly, this is mostly in the firm conviction that to be a child means that you have the right to play and to have fun. From that point of view, school might be a necessary evil; for this age group, it is clearly also coded as an acceptable domain that is not strictly about learning. After all, learning is perfectly possible with the simple means of the improvised African school that the children referred to. Learning in clean and nice surroundings, with the use of real books and art materials; clearly is that much more "fun." Bonding, in the interviews, is mostly bonding against misery and against the seriousness of adulthood. Children prefer not to exercise their imaginations too much in this adult domain. Responsibility remains abstract. It cannot follow "naturally" from a sense of bonding. It is a completely empty, decontextualized construct.

Just for fun

"Formal citizenship training" in serious children's television and fund raising shows a discrepancy between children's and adult notions of what media and popular culture are for. Children take for granted who they are and what they have (including a right to have fun), and their reflection consists mostly of knowing what they do not want to be, and who, therefore, does not belong in the imagined community of "children." They do not wonder much about the constructed nature of nonfiction television. In fact, they take the learned distinction between fiction and nonfiction very seriously. This is a pity, as I have argued throughout this book, because popular entertainment too has much to offer in terms of citizenship and reflection on life, whether as usable stories or as fictional rehearsal.

Concerning popular children's entertainment, there are even stronger discrepancies between children's and adults' views. However, in this case, the interview material affords a more embodied sense of how children reflect on the uses of their favorite media texts. This is far more their area of expertise. The material comes from a small exploratory project conducted by Sjoerd van der Helm, Eline Smith, and myself. Thirteen children from a broad age group (5–15 years old, seven girls and six boys) were interviewed, to map what programs they watched and liked and what games they played, and what arguments they had for doing so. I use this material here to answer two questions: First, how do children themselves talk about violence in the popular culture they like? And, secondly, how do they feel about gender and gender relations? To introduce the interview material and the subject matter at hand, I will first discuss *Pokémon*, the multimedia craze for children around the turn of the millennium and then move on to games and popular television series as discussed by our young informants.

Pokémon

Pokémon was first introduced by Nintendo as a game in 1998 and shortly after as a television serial. It became a mega-hit that clearly offered something for both boys and girls, across a wide age range. David Buckingham and Julian Sefton-Green analyzed *Pokémon*'s success across corporate strategy and marketing, textual analysis, and an understanding of children's culture as lived practice (2003). Their work has inspired much of the discussion in this chapter, and will be quoted at length below. As a parent, I always liked to watch *Pokémon* with my own children. They were avid fans of the television series and haphazard collectors of the paraphernalia. They made it their job to immediately recognize different kinds of *Pokémon*, a quiz element that is also part of the serial, and used their wide knowledge of names and characteristics in the games that they played.

The *Pokémon* television cartoon is regularly seen as instant proof of commercial television's threat to a healthy childhood. For many, the programs define the meaning of worthless and corrupt. By my reasoning, the television series can as easily be read (from a perspective of respect and sympathy for the martial arts) as instruction in loyalty and self-discipline. But those who regard it as the ultimate damaging TV fare only see that it will teach children that it is acceptable to train nonhuman creatures and use them to fight other such beasts. Of course, *Pokémon*'s enormous success with children marked it out for even greater suspicion in the eyes of educators and parents. However idealized a view our society might have of childhood, there is also deep distrust of the assumed instinctual drive of children toward all things sensational and bad. Scathing, negative evaluations of the television program, the cards, the game, and the merchandising are routinely made by adults who clearly have never bothered to watch the show, and have only heard of its success. This is a common phenomenon in the evaluation of children's television (cf., Seiter 1999, pp. 87–9). However, the friendship and loyalty between the key characters in *Pokémon* (Ash, a boy around 10 years old, Misty, a girl, and Brock, a teenager) is impressive; and the series' lack of sexism in depicting good and bad guys/girls is surely a redeeming quality.

What is most to *Pokémon*'s disadvantage, it seems, is simply that it is a cartoon series, and that it focuses on competition and (mostly choreographed) fighting – bad art and bad ethics, by the standards of critics such as Steve Kline (1993). The overarching storyline has Ash traveling with his friends and their Pokémon (which are fantasy creatures with different qualities and strengths in fighting; qualities that they are also encouraged to use in helping others outside the arena) to win enough badges to enter in a prestigious league tournament. Norwegian public television, for example, did not think the storyline strong enough to counter the reputation of the series that had resulted from its relentless merchandising (Hake 2003, p. 46), although its hero's quest is not much different from other successful storytelling for children. Remarkably enough, defense of the series in the Netherlands mostly came from individual parents, who remarked in "vox pop" segments in the Press upon the sheer playing pleasure afforded by the playing cards and the series. Affordable and easy to obtain, *Pokémon* cards and free plastic tossing coins ("flippos") were better value for money than most of the very expensive "good" toys that children also get.

David Buckingham and Julian Sefton-Green understand *Pokémon* as a practice rather than as a set of texts, which allows them to undertake a broader analysis of children's media culture. They suggest that the series' global success is a result of its ability "to 'speak' to shared aspects of childhood experience" (2003, p. 382). *Pokémon* in its many forms was uniquely successful in offering different kinds of appeal and levels of complexity across gender and across age groups (idem). Masculine and feminine qualities are incorporated: "Thus, the game is about nurturing and cooperating. In order to succeed, the game player has to capture all 151 Pokémon species; but s/he also has to look after them and 'train' them in special skills in order that they can 'evolve' (or grow up)" (2003, p. 383). After the 151 species have been collected, the game entails finding a fellow player with a Gameboy to hook up with, in order to have a final showdown. A last element that needs to be mentioned is that the Pokémon creatures involve the whole spectrum from cute to monstrous, their appearance often belying their vicious fighting powers (idem).

The textual pleasures of *Pokémon* are many. Buckingham and Sefton-Green identify Ash's quest as a starting point to discover what these pleasures might be. Ash needs to overcome his impulsiveness and emotional behavior; he needs to acquire self-control. These are familiar elements from the *Bildungsroman*, that return in role-playing games and fantasy literature for teenage boys, set in a world that children (or teenagers) themselves control (2003, p. 387). *Pokémon* is about acquiring knowledge by assuming adult character traits (self-control, care of the creatures). This knowledge, Buckingham and Sefton-Green argue, is portable between media (2003, p. 388): it also transports well to other areas of life. In metaphorical terms, the evolution of the Pokémon, and the training that mostly trains the trainer her- or himself, are all about transforming from a child into an adult in a space that is safe and under the child's control.[5] Lest this sounds like high drama, the many jokes and simple animé style of drawing also offer the easy pleasure of recognition of what is happening for younger children; and, for somewhat older children, the pleasurable predictability of laughing about a teenager who falls in love with each girl he sees. The true *aficionado* might even go so far as to recognize a camp element in Brock's infatuations, given that each township or island visited by Ash and company has an identical agent Jenny and a sister Joy to take care of sick or injured Pokémon, which will make his heart beat faster.

The *Pokémon* game is a good example of the type of game (and television) that the interviewed children like (or liked, when the *Pokémon* craze was at its height). It provides useful background for the discussion to follow of the children's remarks about violence and sexism in digital games and about the children's television that they like. The sections to follow will deal with games and violence, games and gender, and with violence and gender in television entertainment for children.

Games and violence

Children have a fairly balanced view of violence in computer games. They think it is cool when it signifies your skills as a fighter, and they think it is boring when it just signifies that you are a boy. It is not, as is implied in public debate, the opposite of self-restraint or discipline, virtues of the well-adjusted citizen. Nor does violence in games have much to do with anger, hate, or destructive passion in the real world. Games are, after all, in a domain of their own. Huizinga describes in his *Homo Ludens* (1955), how play is outside of everyday life, while "nevertheless capable of totally absorbing the player; an activity entirely lacking in material interest and in utility" (Huizinga, quoted in Ehrmann 1968, p. 34). Moreover, all play represents combat or a contest (idem). It is combat outside of daily life, a pretext for evading the responsibilities of the latter, acting "just because," "just for fun" (1968, p. 41). What is interesting is that play can confer prestige and power outside of the domain of seriousness; play is much more than luxury (Huizinga 1955, p. 50). Children's investment in their "right to fun" suggests that play might well be an important citizenship domain. Also, the very definition of play suggests that there might be more than true-or-false reasoning (as in the moral reasoning described in relation to nonfiction representation of the Third World); that strategy becomes important and thus the possibility of envisioning and reflecting on what has value. On Ehrmann's account, play is the utopian complement of "seriousness" (Ehrmann 1968, p. 47), which makes it next of kin to what I call cultural citizenship.

Stephan (five) stipulates that he likes fighting. Most of his examples of good fighting come from television series, but they all underscore how fighting for him has nothing to do with violence, but with the characters' supernatural control over any situation. Playing games feels the same to him: "Playing on the computer [is more fun than watching television]. Because you touch a button and then you can do something, make things happen." In fantasy, Stephan becomes

Action Man or Dr Z (Action Man's evil counterpart) and can do any of the impossible gymnastics and weapon handling that they engage in.

Robbie (10) has a Gameboy (a small hand-held computer) but dreams of having GTA (*Grand Theft Auto*, a very violent personal computer game that involves drug running and killing at the level of organized crime). "I'd love to have all the *GTA*s or the *Sims*. Because I really like fight games, unreal cool, that you have like 100 bullets and that you have to shoot down all sorts of things, that I'm on a machine with all those bullets. Dennis has a game, when you aim right, the head explodes and that is so cool. Blood gushing out. And baseball of course, I am totally hooked on it. And tennis and rugby." *Sims* is a game that you would not expect in this particular set. Roughly speaking, it is a game that has you building environments and characters, which you then have to "direct" through their lives. Although twice Stephan's age, Robbie describes a similar pleasure to that of the younger child, to be in control of the situation, with an array of tools on hand to help him do so.

Thomas and Mart, two brothers (12 and 15), name a number of violent games such as *Gangsters2* and *Renegade*, which they say they like for the challenge to excel strategically. For these older boys, control is based on learning and improving your skills. Moreover, they like their games to look good. THE MATRIX was their example of strategy and style come together:

Mart: The graphics are important and you shouldn't be able to play the whole game immediately.

Thomas: Yeah, it needs to look good, and it needs to be difficult. Not that you're playing and then after three hours you're done. That's really worthless.

What is striking in the interview is how the logic of game playing, organized into levels of difficulty, is echoed in how they talk about playing games on the Internet against countless others playing at the same time – "I'm not good enough to play on the net" – and television series: "nah, I'm too old for that."

Is violence a boy thing? Research suggests that it is (Nikken 2000; Feilitzen 2001, p. 20). When asked, two of the older girls, Lotte and Aysha (both 11, but a year ahead in school), describe boys' games as sleazy:

Lotte: I know one of those games – that's really a boys' game. You have to collect heroin, and dirty pictures.

Aysha: It's really sleazy.

Lotte: And these shooter games. When you ride a tank and you have to blow away all these guys and there's blood all over the place.

Aysha: I think they're meant a little for boys, but girls play them too.

They themselves don't: "Too boring, and drab and gray." "Or army green." "And it's always the same: you have to shoot people and there's blood." The gore of blood and brain splattering around, true enough, is more part of "boys' games." It is mostly liked by younger boys, and taken for granted by the older ones, who like games for their strategy elements, which they also find in non-violent games such as *FIFA 2004* (directing a football tournament). But some of the girls who we interviewed play these games as well, and all feel that they could if they wanted to.

Blood is hardly more than a style icon, a measure of how it "has to look real" while in fact it isn't. If it doesn't look real, it can only be saved by being funny (Joey, 10). While games do not represent reality, playing, as suggested by Huizinga, may confer status in everyday life: when you have access to really "cool" games (Robbie doesn't have the *GTA* or *Sims* games he would like to play); and when you are able to navigate all of the levels of a difficult game. The use that children and teenagers have for games as popular culture is clear: games give them a sense of control, either based on having a machine work for you or on improving your skills, which they experience as empowering.[6] There is also a direct link to cultural citizenship: gamers regard themselves as part of a community. The quality of a game is clearly related to what other gamers think of it. Even if you do not play on the Internet – which most, from a certain age upward do – you play games in the knowledge that countless of others do so too.

Games and gender

Gender is not of much importance in the gamer community. This is partly because players often play alone, or via the Internet, which makes gender less important as a direct marker of identity, and also partly because gender hardly interferes with playing itself. We can conclude that the visualized effects of violence are not a marker of much more than the graphics quality of the game and proof of the existence of a formal gender divide – visible, for example, in color coding (khaki is for boys) – that carries little weight. Fighting and shooting, like running and jumping, are what you do when you play a game, without much gender connotation. When Aysha suggests to Lotte that a game with a cute little turtle that they both play might be a boys' game, Lotte strongly disagrees:

> Lotte: That's no boys' game!
> Aysha: Isn't it a little though? You have to freeze them instead of shoot them, and then whoop, they're gone.

The argument is solved when they decide that it really is a game that you can play together, of which, they regret, there are not many. Gender is as relevant as gaming community members wish to make it – which for the teenagers was more important, as was age difference ("I'm too old for that"), while the younger children cared less about either distinction.

Gender is also a less distinctive marker than I would have expected when it comes to the characters in games. When asked, Robbie (10), who likes Action Man so much, says that he doesn't mind girl characters in games: "Unless they're Barbie. Better to throw those away." Like other gamers, he is very critical of the low quality of the Barbie games' graphics. For him, gender is really neither here nor there: "They can be women. As long as they have good weapons and fight well." Stiletto heels have impressed him positively in this regard. Joey (10), when asked whether he likes games with women in them, said: "It depends. As long as they don't dance. If the game's OK." Most of all, the immense popularity of the *Sims* series suggests that gender has low significance in assessing the quality and attractions of a game. It was mentioned by both boys and girls, and played by the older children. It has rightly been lauded for its power to inform and entertain (Jenkins 2003). *Zoo Tycoon* and *Rollercoaster Tycoon* are similar games.

In *Sims*, what I recognize as typical girl pleasures in dolls' houses are trans-ferred into a game that also requires tactical skills in developing the characters. They need certain talents and schooling to be able to do well in the job mar-ket, where they need to make money to put furniture in their houses and food in the fridge. The fun is not just in building, decorating, and amassing a healthy bank account, but also in experimental power play. Marloes (15) told us glee-fully that she had not provided food for her *Sims* characters for a while to see what would happen. To her satisfaction, without her help, they collapsed and died. Lotte and Aysha liked it too for the power that it confers onto the player:

Aysha: What I really like is that you can make people do things. For example, you can make them fall in love. Really funny when you have a woman fall in love with everybody, and then the guy gets really jealous. And you have a little voodoo doll, and two guys come onto the screen and then you have to stick them and then they hit one another.
Lotte: And I also like in *Animal business* that you can buy all these animals . . .
Aysha: . . . don't they eat one another?
Lotte: . . . no, and you can go to the city or on vacation.

Game playing – the skill training, the ability to decide (in *Sims*) on behalf of the characters, putting your strategic skills to the test, or simply the fun of "mak-ing things happen," as young Stephan said – is empowering. Neither violence nor gender are highly relevant points of entry for gamers – whereas a sense of power, playing with or against others, and the existence of a gamer community (to talk about games or to play on the Internet) are. This conclusion goes against the dominant view of games, which quotes as its evidence not just the outlaw storylines but also the shortage of women characters, and the way in which women and men are pictured: bulging muscle versus huge breasts and wasp waists. Research in other countries, however, comes up with comparable findings.

Over 10 years ago, Christine Ward-Gailey (1993) made an inventory of available games and interviewed children who played them. Sexism and violence are concerns that she too addresses. She finds but few female characters. In fantasy-odyssey games, "Females, if they exist are usually off-stage princesses and their handmaidens, who are rewards or goals for successfully negotiating the particular adventure or level" (1993, p. 86). In urban jungle games, women did appear sometimes in minority roles, "as dangerous gang members whom the hero must beat up or kill through the same martial arts techniques used on male enemies. Occasionally, a game will include a female ally as co-player. Usually, however, active females are portrayed as dangerous competitors who must be dealt with violently" (1993, p. 87). This state of affairs did not dissuade the five American girls interviewed by Ward-Gailey from playing,[7] although they tended (contrary to the seven boys who were interviewed) to find simple fighting games a bit boring, as did Lotte and Aysha in our interviews.

Ward-Gailey concludes her observations of gaming children, and her interviews with them and their parents, by stating that there is little or no evidence that gaming makes players more aggressive (1993, p. 91). She also expects, much like Buckingham and Sefton-Green, that games may offer children a positive sense of competence and safety in the predictable world of the games (1993, p. 92). Whether game playing was part of competitive dynamics or involved information sharing, excitement, and pleasure in the successes of others, just as much as shared disappointment in failure and notice of improved skills, was entirely dependent on existing forms of family interaction (idem): "The only consistent response children had to game playing was they attempted to empower themselves, individually and as a group through the process. In doing so, they redefined gender and other identities, or appropriated the dominant messages in ways that made sense to them and thereby altered their meaning" (1993, p. 93). Ten years later, Barbro Johansson (2003)[8] underwrites Ward-Gailey's conclusions. She concludes that we should accept "that children can joyfully and wholeheartedly play a horrible computer game, without necessarily having psychological problems or a future as criminals" (2003, p. 144). While children recognize violence in games, and its connection to dominant gender constructions, they are not much impressed by either.

Violence and femininity from the perspective of popular television series

The gender of characters in games was not felt by the children to be very important. Nor was the gender of television characters in itself a reason (not) to watch
programs. More interestingly, spontaneously offered suggestions of favorite
television series made clear that there is a new type of girl hero, liked by both
boys and girls. Stephan (five) feels that *Totally Spies!* is "really cool, because they
fight. I think that's really cool, and then they attack." Isabelle (seven) and Otje
(seven) think that the series is great fun because the spies never get caught and
they are tough. Robbie (10) feels that it is really funny when they fight over
a guy; or when Clover gets mad because someone has messed with her hair.
Imitating the character's voice, he says: "I warned you, one hair gets split and
you're done for!" According to him, the series is "in" for boys and girls. The
older children know of the series, but clearly feel a bit too old for it and mention soaps and other shows broadcast after 8.00 p.m.

Totally Spies! is reminiscent of *Charlie's Angels*. Sam, Alex, and Clover are three
high-school girls who, in each episode, "save the world in style." Lots of girl
jokes are combined with effective use of the martial arts, clever Bond-style gadgets designed in pink, and a little thinking. Whereas the surface text is all about
boys, fashion, and shopping, the girls are all about business in spy mode. They
save the world from psychopaths of various ilks, who often have old scores to
settle. Below the surface, the series offers tongue-in-cheek observations of plastic surgery ("Model Cityzens"); beauty contests (the continuing battle between
Clover and the Spies' arch enemy, Mandy), and cheerleading ("The Black
Widows"). Like the Angels, Sam, Clover, and Alex have a boss called Jerry, who
is immediately recognizable as a generic federal agent. He is also the provider
of gadgets and the jailer of the crooks when the girls return to Beverly Hills
High School to resume their everyday lives.

The *Spies* are heirs to a new tradition in animated television, which started
with the 1990s round-faced *Powerpuff Girls* (Cartoon Network), who found
themselves a camp following. Mostly, the increase in girls' half-hour drama (mainly
comedy, such as *Lizzy McGuire*, but also high-school soaps, such as *Sweet Valley
High*) and cartoons such as *Braceface*, continues a long-established tradition of
presenting Ideal Girls. They walk the fine line between the two polar opposites
for girls: boy-mad fashion victim or tomboy. The fact that this delicate balance
is thematized bodes well for the reflexive qualities of this type of fairly traditional television, and indicates, I hope, a change of policy in popular culture
production. Lizzy McGuire's worries over being a good footballer (Will all the
guys now see her as a guy-girl, a "dude"?) are eased after a talk with the school's
PE coach and weightlifter ("Just one of the guys," 2003). Built on stereotypical

1970s steroid-inflated Eastern European lines, coach Kelly is also a keen ballroom dancer. Girls, the message is, should definitely try to "have it all."

Children's cultural citizenship

We are used to defining children by age, and in opposition to being an adult.[9] In terms of media usership, this is hardly adequate. Children see much more than just children's programming on television; the game player community extends far into adulthood. By linking age to emotional and cognitive development, media scholarship excludes children from debate about what they like. Buckingham and Julian Sefton-Green suggest that:

> Broadly speaking, we are happy with *Pokémon* if it teaches children to be competent social beings, and if it enables them to develop cognitive skills; and we are unhappy if it teaches them to be greedy and acquisitive, and if it cheapens their appreciation of art. On the one hand, we appear to espouse what might be termed a pedagogy of "empowerment," which is concerned to develop children's competence and autonomy; while on the other, we implicitly adopt a protectionist pedagogy which seeks to segregate children from influences that are seen to have the power to harm them. (2003, p. 394)

When children are "harmed" in the vocabulary of concern, it means that our investment in human capital is devalued. Despite the tearjerker rhetoric of those who use it, there is above all grave apprehension for the future of society. Concern is a lead-in for a functionalist perspective on media consumption that entirely misses the connection with children's life worlds.

In their evaluation of European public service children's television, for instance, Blumler and Biltereyst (1997) insist on the rights of children to quality television. This is a noble goal that I share, but their reasoning is dodgy: children are vulnerable (p. 10, item 11), and prone to damage (p. 35; item 100) when their television menu lacks diversity, they say. In psychological and policy research, as a term to describe the effects of television on children, "vulnerable" has great implicit rhetorical power. The Latin for "woundable," it suggests that children are breakable puppets – harmless, defenseless creatures. But it really means that children are clean slates, easy to manipulate, and susceptible to the logic of commercialism that will teach them egocentric materialism and lack of consideration for others. In this vocabulary, children are potential monsters. Fed on an early television diet of commercials that suggest a happy life on the condition you have any number of toys or sweets; to be followed by a large intake of crudely sensationalist, sexist, and violent content for tweens and teenagers, youthful television viewers will turn into the beasts that commit atrocities against the social and moral order.

Although it stems from a deep and real concern, the protectionist point of view ignores the pleasure that children and adults take in popular television, and it ignores the fact that, unfortunately, the serious children's television that it cherishes strengthens children in black-and-white moral reasoning, rather than encouraging them to think more flexibly and creatively. In any case, children tend to keep such energy for the games and entertainment programming that they like. Holding their accounts to the light, what we see are the outlines of a sense of community that is akin to the cultural citizenship of adults. What is included is the right to have fun, the joy of empowerment through play, and a highly flexible manner of dealing with differences. Gender is sometimes important; at other times, it is not. Age, likewise, may have considerable meaning as a hurdle to be jumped; whereas, at other times, children enjoy "not acting their age" or just like "to have a laugh" (cf., Davies, Buckingham & Kelley 2000). Race and ethnicity did not matter much at all in either case study.

In their media use, children exercise and experience forms of power that they do not otherwise have; part of that power is to be members of interpretive communities that mock adult taste (Davies et al. 2000, p. 22), and that use little-appreciated cultural forms and texts, such as Pokémon or Totally Spies!, for a children's grammar of exchange. In themselves, learning to distinguish between 151 species of Pokémon, or practicing to "get the jokes," are processes of competence building that children like. This mirrors the pleasure of gaming, of becoming adept and moving up levels, and then on to other games. The violence and crude depictions of gender difference, and the sleazy storylines, are really immaterial to that pleasure, but they are, of course, an excellent means of subverting adult investment in propriety and restraint. In their uncouthness, they can be "owned" by youngsters as badges of player merit, as the ultimate in "cool." Like camp, children's appreciation of commercial entertainment culture is a means of resisting dominant (adult) culture, in order to bond with other children and to train themselves in the cultural survival skills of being able to distinguish between good and bad, and between appropriate and inappropriate behavior as circumstances require.

notes

1   Commercial television, if seen as providing a positive learning experience at all, is at best credited with forms of social and affective learning. Soaps inform audiences about relationships, for instance. Cartoons, on the other hand, are usually seen as producing negative social learning effects.

2   See Niewenhuys and Verbrugh (2003). I have their gracious approval to quote from their material at length and offer my own interpretations and conclusions. My involvement was that of supervisor and partly that of a co-researcher.

3   Televised throughout 2001, and exemplary for more recent material as well.

4   Gorki quoted in Wit (2000, p. 16).

5   Seiter (1992, pp. 57–8) remarks on a similar logic in *Teenage Mutant Ninja Turtles*, who have been taught by Splinter to be Ninja Teens, but draws out the overcoming of structural boundaries in children's culture; that is, animal/human, nature/culture, and so on. Still, the Turtles "seem to reinterpret the nature/culture split as freewheeling, nonconformist American adolescence (nature) versus strict, conformist Japanese adulthood (culture)" (1992, p. 58).

6   The joy of playing itself is what motivates gamers. Von Feilitzen, in a wide-ranging overview of children and media research, also names the challenge of advancing in a game, overcoming difficult situations, solving problems and competing (2001, p. 20).

7   Cf., www.gamegirlz.com, with many contributions by gaming mums about their gaming daughters – and sons.

8   She observed and talked with four Swedish boys (9–11 years old), who like to play a game called *Bonkheads* and interviewed three of their eight-year-old classmates.

9   Cf., Davies, Buckingham, and Kelley (2000) who, when looking for distinctive children's taste cultures, found that the social construction of childhood as opposed to adulthood is far more important.

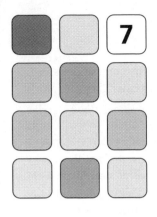

7

popular culture: a modern and a postmodern genealogy

Whether or not I have succeeded in "revaluing" popular culture throughout these chapters is, of course, up to the reader. It depends on whether we can agree that my examples show that popular culture produces bonding and reflection on that bonding, and whether we agree that reflection on how we live our lives is of key social importance. The value of popular culture does not, for me, depend on whether the kind of bonding that popular cultural texts allow for can always be valued positively, or on the inherent qualities of popular cultural texts – although those too are of interest and need to be part of any analysis of popular culture's attractions. After all, if popular culture did not "seduce" us, it would not offer itself as a domain for social reflection; if it did not offer "usable stories," or troubling images that address what needs "working through," in the words of John Mepham and John Ellis, there would not, for us, be any incentive to ponder who we are, what life is about, and how we relate to others.

If this makes perfect sense, there may be little need to read the remainder of this chapter. If it does not, the two-pronged genealogy of views on popular culture outlined in this chapter should prove to be useful. It explains some of the difficulties in accepting popular culture as the domain of debate that it is. I have named the two prongs the "modernist" and the "postmodernist" perspective. After a brief outline, the modernist project is interrogated for how its horror of the feminine has heavily influenced the (current) reputation of popular culture. Although the postmodernist project has questioned constructions of gender, much work remains to be done in relation to masculinity. Overall, it is the gendered circular logic that defines feminine popular culture versus male public debate as a fixed and gendered opposition that needs to be dismantled. The chapter will close with suggestions for a new understanding of popular culture.

Modernism, popular culture, and gender

Modernist views on popular culture are mostly held by communications schol-ars, who keep their distance from its actual, textual attractions. They are joined by others who also dread that popular culture (in the form of key media genres and as a global commodity capitalist money maker) threatens civilization as we know it. Rightly famous and good reads are such classics as Jerry Mander's *Four Arguments for the Elimination of Television* (1998 [1978]), or Neil Postman's *Amusing Ourselves to Death* (1986) and *The Disappearance of Childhood* (1994 [1982]). Underlying their work is a dark vision of popular culture. Average tele-vision viewers or magazine browsers will be lost to reason, debate, and, in fact, citizenship in a traditional sense. Lazy, creature-comfort oriented beasts is what we will become if we don't uphold the rigors of learning, reading, and thinking as they used to be more or less before electronic media re-oralized our culture, and before women and the lower classes invaded public culture. Taking our leave of oral culture, after all, was what helped us leave the dark Middle Ages behind, to enter the age of Enlightenment and progress. No matter that progress came at a terrific cost, and that modernism was not all blessings, sunshine, and roses (Jensen 1990; Miller 1998).

Three related key aspects of the modernist perspective on popular culture stand out. First, modernist thinking cherishes art, rational debate, and citizen-ship, and tends to be wary of popular culture. It does not feel a great need to investigate it in detail. By implication, the whole domain is declared as being of no possible interest. Secondly, popular culture is – often implicitly – placed outside the realm of value and quality, by suggesting its dire influence on citizenship and democracy. Where there is popular culture, citizenship cannot thrive. Thirdly, the associative logic that relegates popular culture to the realm of the abject in modernist thought is also gendered. Popular culture is the domain of the feminine, of consumption and passivity (Cronin 2000, p. 2). Nothing could be more threatening to a healthy, robust nation, the building of which is claimed by those who understand themselves to be vigorous, straight-thinking . . . men.

Crucial to modernism, or to Enlightenment discourse, is its dual structure. It holds an optimistic view of history, the rationality of human beings, and our capacity to know and recognize truth. This is set off against a dark vision of the irrationality and dangerous emotionalism of the masses, which may turn progress and history against itself. Modern masculinity is constructed as a defense against these "dark forces" and their feminine connotations.[1] Women (no capital) may cope and even make careers in male domains (as "honorary men"), but "Woman," according to Andreas Huyssen (1986), should be seen as modernism's Other.[2] This isn't to say that male modernist authors have not flirted with femininity. Indeed, Huyssen quotes Flaubert's famous claim, "Madame Bovary, c'est moi," to show how the imaginary femininity of these authors was a way of excluding women from the literary enterprise and a token of the misogyny of bourgeois patriarchy (1986, p. 45).

"Woman," or "the feminine," is not entirely absent from modern thought, but she is no more than a place of inscription, a blankness, a void. In the mass culture debate she has been inscribed, Huyssen (1986) continues, "as reader of inferior literature –subjective, emotional and passive – while man (Flaubert) emerges as writer of genuine, authentic literature – objective, ironic, and in control of his aesthetic means" (1986, p. 46). The aesthetic means of modernism can be read as a warding off – a protection against – popular culture and the banalities of everyday life, and the domain of women, which is the private sphere. According to Huyssen, from the second half of the nineteenth century there is a "chain effect of signification: from the obsessively argued inferiority of woman as artist . . . to the association of woman with mass culture . . . to the identification of woman with the masses as political threat" (1986, p. 50). A historical reconstruction of the place of woman and the feminine in modernist ideology presents us with an intricate web of meanings, which is no longer in place in its entirety but remains "on call" in the shadows of accepted knowledge.

The gendering of mass culture and of consumption and emotion exist as part of an implicit, naturalized consensus, which slows down the dismantling of what Tania Modleski has called "the masculinist bias" in criticism (1986, p. 42). By adopting metaphors of production and integrity as opposed to shallowness and consumption in order to differentiate between progressive and regressive, the gender divide and the low esteem of popular culture hold each other in place. This complicates the finding of common ground on which a sensitive criticism of popular culture could be based that would be meaningful in modernist terms, while employing a more postmodern, constructivist notion of femininity and masculinity.

The result of this standoff is that, on the one hand, citizenship and popular culture would seem to be each other's opposites, while on the other it is clear that they mutually, if partially, construct one another. While the citizen can be defined as a partaker in public debate, as the bearer of educational qualifications, or the addressee of "serious" television, it needs to be recognized that some of that public debate is about popular practices and popular culture. Moreover, serious television can be so defined because the same citizens know about other, nonserious, types of television (presumably because they – perhaps only occasionally? – watch it). A second interesting characteristic of the citizen is that although s/he is formally defined as belonging to a nation/state, this belonging remains abstract and carries little connotation of community or actual bonding. The citizen, I would argue, appears as a lonely figure and as one who has to operate within highly constricting rules. Despite the modernist rhetoric of production, initiative, and vigor around citizenship, the citizen is governed by repressive means.

The modernist understanding of citizenship is constructed in diametrical opposition to the popular and hence to the realm of the feminine. This means that (naïve and girly) enthusiasm is a disqualification, because seriousness is required to participate in debate. Seriousness is ultimately grounded in formal educational qualifications. Those who lack such education, and occupy the balcony seats reserved for middle-brow wannabees, have to compensate by showing a near overdose of concern for the nation, for Culture, for the future, or for all those others led astray by commerce and corruption. That means that anxiety, fear, and concern function as entry fees for participation in public debate and hence citizenship. This state of affairs overshadows the fact that community and allegiance are (also) built across and in the domain of popular culture. All citizenship is implicated in "cultural citizenship." This is recognized and abhorred in discussions of public service broadcasting. What used to be the pride and joy of Western European democracies is now seen as falling from grace under the onslaught of commercial television. This particular debate also makes clear how the assumptions that organize hegemonic modernist discourse about popular culture still hold sway today.

Popular culture as threat

A collection edited by Jay Blumler exactly illustrates my argument. His *Television and the Public Interest: Vulnerable Values in Western European Broadcasting* appeared in 1992. Its main theme is that the break-up of the old public service monopoly in many European countries (which took place at the end of the 1980s and into the early 1990s) is coterminous with the loss of consensus over the purposes that broadcasting should serve (Blumler 1992, p. 2). This is not good; a "commercial deluge" awaits those of us who live in Europe. Producers will only focus on ratings, and in his conclusion Blumler forewarns that broadcasting will no longer be able to fulfill its role in encouraging "reasoned argument in civic and electoral choice" (1992, p. 203). Quality, innovation, professionalism, standards, social relevance, serving a variety of interests, and cultural self-determination are all at risk (1992, p. 206).

In the realm of television, commercial television is synonymous with popular culture and with purchasing power (Blumler 1992, p. 32). Although Blumler does not argue this point, there is an underlying logic that the "many"-ness of the masses provides them with their purchasing power, in exchange for which standards of taste and intellectual challenge are lowered. The result will be a "bland and homogeneous international media culture" (1992, p. 34) – international rather than national, for popular culture is controlled by transnational global capitalism. This will threaten no less than the integrity of civic communication. Providers and viewers alike will shift their priorities from information to entertainment. Current affairs programs will cater more for viewers' spectator interests than their citizen roles. Blumler speaks of a horse race model, of sound bites over substance, information, and dialogue (1992, p. 36). Responsibility for citizenship is apparently something that is only cared about by a small professional elite, while the multitudes, helped by irresponsible and unscrupulous capitalists, neither care nor seem to know what is good for them in the long term. That these very multitudes may not feel addressed by the repressive and judgmental qualities of good citizenship is irrelevant. In its alignment with education and an ethical professionalism, modernist citizenship logic is repressive and paternalistic. Blumler's recognition that the public broadcasting system that he reveres did tend to neglect the audience, in that it was based on the bond that broadcasters felt with their audiences, which they could *imagine* to be reciprocated, underscores the point (1992, p. 17).

If we distinguish between viewers' spectator interests and their citizen roles (Blumler 1992, p. 36), a particular "truth" is constructed. Spectating and consuming are defined as forces outside of citizenship that threaten to colonize its ethical spirit, its industriousness, and its sense of responsibility. Nick Stevenson sums up that "[t]he language and duties of citizenship, in this context, become overrun by the seductive rather than the disciplinary logics of consumer society" (2003, p. 129). Of course, Stevenson points out, the very notion of citizenship that is upheld here is closely tied to early capitalism (self-discipline, hard work), which a century ago was opposed by the then avant-garde modernist movements. Their agenda of lifestyle experimentation and innovation clashed with the restrictive nature of the common culture of capitalist mass-production (2003, pp. 127–8). Ironically then, it is modernism's elitist nature that is salvaged through a century of commercialization and the popularization of culture, rather than its free spirit.

Following modernist logic a bit longer, the question arises as to whether something has been corrupted by popular culture; or whether popular (or mass) culture has prevented a civilization campaign from taking off. In general, I would hold to Waites, Bennett, and Martin's argument that "cultural relationships were fundamentally transformed with the working out of capitalist industrialisation during the second and third quarters of the nineteenth century" (1982, p. 15). The urbanization and literacy of new social groups resulted in entirely new cultural experiences (cf., Williams 1961; Thompson 1963). How the world was imagined, and which groups one might feel that one belonged to, changed unrecognizably. A qualitatively different and new social formation came into being. One of its characteristics was undoubtedly that authenticity and inauthenticity became issues, as described by Walther Benjamin. Another was that directness and liveness became electronically mediated by radio, and later television, as mass media (Gripsrud 1998), which arguably led to "realness" as a criterion for television in the early twenty-first century. Apparently, "real" is not defined by material presence but by the absence of what might be seen as skills and professionalism (acting skills, for instance), and by a redrawing of codes of ethics (what can be shown) and aesthetics (ordinariness comes to be a quality in addition to beauty or expressiveness). A greater contrast with eighteenth-century blood sports and other popular pastimes is hard to imagine. Real-time killing (of animals) and other forms of excessive violence have been relegated to the domain of the perverse and the sick. Although contemporary popular culture is fascinated by such aberrations, "enjoying" them is restricted by the codes of crime fiction and crime reconstruction novels and, in the case of serial killers, by the codes of news reporting (cf., Seltzer 2001).

Contemporary popular culture, then, is fundamentally different from older forms of folk culture in that it is mediated. The (media) literacy needed to partake in contemporary popular culture underscores this. Although popular culture is in many regards closely related to older forms of oral culture (Ong 1982; Postman 1994 [1982]), it doesn't make sense to disregard the skills and knowledges involved in understanding and enjoying it. This is exactly the point at which modern authors and postmodern adepts such as myself part ways. There is a difference of opinion regarding class-based forms of literacy and reverence for a canon of great works that excludes newer cultural forms. There is also a difference of opinion regarding the uses and values of orality in culture. For one thing, oral culture (which is close to the heart of any reception researcher) has a much stronger sense of community than written culture, which is predicated on distance. Respect for orality, then, provides a way of linking popular culture to older, folk culture. Moreover, orality is not the opposite of literacy, insofar as both are relevant to and implied in narrativity and storytelling, and both are needed in the project of recognizing the variety of pleasures afforded by popular culture. Such pleasures are directly relevant to the community-building capacities of popular culture.

Cultural citizenship: last time round

In their study of the coming into being of an independent Quebec public culture since the early 1960s, Martin Allor and Michelle Gagnon (1994) remain close to older and formal notions of citizenship.[3] Quebec never became an independent state, but in its wish to become one we can follow the "production of the field of *la citoyenneté culturelle*; a field of distinction of the citizen as both the social subject, the sovereign subject of a nation, and as the object of new forms of political power linking the distinctive traits of the citizen with those of the cultural producer and consumer" (1994, p. 26). To define the citizen as both subject and object of state power, and as both consumer and producer, is to merge older modernist discussions and preoccupations with the more recently established agenda of cultural studies. When citizenship is a field of *distinction*, an opening is created for a redrawing of boundaries. When culture is a field of multiple in- and exclusions (and distinction understood as multi-axial), there is room to rebrand citizenship in a more cosmopolitan communitarian sense, as advocated by Nick Stevenson (2003), and to reinclude the domain of the popular. If, however, distinction takes us back to class difference, described by Bourdieu (1984) as cultural capital, escape from the modernist, elitist notion of citizenship is more difficult.

In this respect, John Hartley suggests that we think along lines of "democratainment." In the same way that learning (informal, with little organization and no tests, and opportunity- and interest-driven) is different from education, we should understand use of the media as a primary emancipatory force for groups with little social status: the working classes, women, ethnic minorities (1999, p. 169). Hartley describes how marginalized groups maximize the uses of television (versus those of schooling); and how the inclusive "we" of television entertainment offered a sense of identity and cultural rights for those not belonging to the elite (1999, pp. 171–2). Such identities are not necessarily shared with entire populations, but the right to identity is implicitly present in what the media show and thus attains a right of existence (1999, p. 181). Difference becomes a fact of media life, which opens the door to respect as a central category. For disempowered citizens – the young, the feminine, the working class – television opens up a wide vista of possibilities. By using the possibilities of semiotic self-determination as well as new means of communication, they build communities across the borders of nation and physical location (1999, pp. 184–5, 210). The consumption of popular culture always also entails the production of hopes, fantasies, and utopias, which – to my mind – should therefore be part of politics and of citizenship in its (ideal) sense as deliberation about what, for most of us, would be the best kind of life. Such a renewed political debate would not, as is the case now, recognize only rational argumentation as valid. Cultural citizenship entails that rational and moral argumentation needs to be extended to encompass aesthetic and emotional claims.

It is in this regard that we can well use part of Habermas's theory of communicative action, a key modern critical work. The three types of claims that we make in communicative action relate to three different kinds of rationality. Some of our claims are cognitive-instrumental, others are normative, and a third set are aesthetic and practical (Habermas 1981, vol. 1, p. 326). The third set of claims in Habermas's writing is the most problematical. It relates to the inner world (as opposed to "the objective world" and "the social world") and its claims are elsewhere described as claims of authenticity and integrity (Habermas 1984, pp. 439–40). In the normal course of events, these claims are not disputed. The theory of communicative action presupposes, however, that all claims are open to dispute in specialized discourses. Both political theory and practice should therefore, in an ideal world, have to be opened up to such specialized discourses. For the time being, modernist media studies should recognize that its own jargon is based on the exclusion of the feminine, which entails a far too narrow conception of (public) knowledge and politics and a much too judgmental stance concerning all that is deemed feminine. What exactly is it that makes enjoying popular literature, a tabloid newspaper, or commercial television programs so bad for democracy? And how can anyone guarantee that "serious" news media are not secretly consumed as if they were the equivalent of a sports match? How can what Habermas calls the forces of colonization be countered, and what exactly are they?

Peter Dahlgren and Colin Sparks edited two collections – *Communication and Citizenship: Journalism and the Public Sphere* (1991) and *Journalism and Popular Culture* (1992) – in which questions such as these are entertained. Most interesting are those contributions that not only signal the interwovenness of public and private life but try to make theoretical sense of it. From such a perspective, the media can be seen as a starting point that may prove to be the lever that is needed to pry open the public sphere and citizenship debate. Such a rewriting could start, for example, from the conclusions that Ann Crigler and Klaus Bruhn Jensen (in *Communication and Citizenship*, 1991) draw from two audience studies about how people make sense of politics. They state that "the interesting common feature of the samples is the nature of the themes, which are at once generalized yet concrete, practice-based concepts that appear to derive from everyday experience" (1991, p. 180). They also conclude that the "fictional genres of mass communication and the stories and jokes of interpersonal communication may have been under-researched as aspects of political communication and understanding" (1991, p. 191). Through audience studies, then, the everyday domain of the feminine may yet find its place in political theory other than in a paternalist derogatory sense of a domain in which the people need to be educated, disciplined, and controlled.

Other theorists concur that citizenship can and should be written out of the binary distinction between reason and affect (Young 1987), between the West and the Rest (Hall 1992), between self and Other (Said 1987), between Quality and trash (Jancovich & Lyons 2003), and between information and entertainment. Inscribing popular culture and pleasure in the domain of Quality and Citizenship, however, can only be successful when it slays – read "demythologizes" – the monster of the feminine disguised as the popular, which is what motivates the grim holding onto neutrality, impartiality, and noncommercialism. Presumably theoreticians of popular culture have fared better in this regard, although, as will become clear, citizenship and politics have been paid too little attention. We turn to postmodernists, then, in the next section.

Postmodernism and gender in the popular culture project

The uses and values of popular culture as texts and practices are tainted, from a modernist perspective, by the economic logic that rules most of its production. Corporate capitalism is motivated by profit rather than by improving the world. More money is made of children (the huge turnover in the merchandising market; the use of children in advertising imagery) than is spent on, for example, television for them (Feilitzen 2001, pp. 8–9). This is true – and important to know in order not to idolize the economic and cultural order. But it is hardly an argument against the meanings and pleasures that children do derive from their choice of what is available for them. There is, however, a need to clarify how the postmodernist critique of popular culture has defined its own politics. Given its roots in modernist early second-wave feminism and subsequent development toward a postmodern critique in the field of popular culture, feminist politics and gender are an obvious starting point.

Basically, the modern "public knowledge project" (Corner 1991) doesn't recognize how it demonizes popular culture by linking it to the feminine. In postmodern popular culture research, gender (like ethnicity) is often thematized. But putting women and constructions of femininity on the agenda is not enough to dislodge the modernist "truth" of popular culture's seductiveness, as that which turns you into a guy with no balls, a victim of the leisure industries. If we want to understand media consumption – the crossroads of the victimization of viewers and the semiotic and narrative inscription of gender – we need theoretically sensitive tools that were not at hand a mere decade ago (cf., Ang & Hermes 1991). Debate in popular culture studies has been about women and the construction of femininity rather than, for example, about how women and men take up temporary gender identities that don't necessarily correspond to their sex; or about the gendering of practices. A short overview will chart how a postmodern understanding of popular culture and of gender (produced in tandem by the then upcoming second wave of feminism) developed out of a critical modernist agenda.

Early 1970s feminist media criticism tended to focus on what was felt to be media texts' unrealistic and dangerous depiction of women. What sustained these accounts were the twin assumptions that media images carry transparent, straightforward meanings, and that women as viewers passively absorbed these messages and would act accordingly.[4] These modernist accounts were countered by feminist scholars who used structuralist, semiotic, and psychoanalytic frameworks. They stressed that the media construct meanings and identities that serve as subject positions from which texts become meaningful and pleasurable.[5] However, the focus on femininity and its dominant meanings remained: not much transgression was identified until studies such as Kathleen Rowe's *The Unruly Woman: Gender and the Genres of Laughter* (1995). Slightly before Rowe's book appeared, a third generation of postmodern-feminist critics began to criticize the textual determinism of the structuralist second generation of feminist critics. This third generation of postmodern-feminist media researchers argued that texts become meaningful in particular, local contexts, and that ethnography or in-depth interviewing were essential to reconstruction of the meanings of these texts. Examples from the accounts of all three generations can still be found. One discursive moment may be preceded by another; it rarely wipes it off the chart. Here, however, I will focus on the ideas of the third generation, of which my own audience research and theoretical work is part, and which, I believe, offers the best hope for a constructive cultural politics.

This briefest of overviews of debate in what John Corner (1991) dubbed "the popular culture project" exemplifies three characteristics of how gender was discussed in the early 1990s, just before the high point of postmodern feminism. It is feminist debate and women researchers who have predominantly taken up issues of gender. Secondly, they don't so much discuss gender (femininity and masculinity), as women and femininity. Men and masculinity are conspicuously absent. Insofar as gender presented a problem, it was a problem of women, the defined sex, rather than of men. Masculinity, after all, is the norm (Coward 1983). The third point is the development in feminist/popular culture research toward poststructuralist and postmodern points of view. The ongoing predominance of a postmodern perspective in feminist popular culture research has much to do with the near incompatibility of a strict modernism with feminism. This becomes clear when one takes a closer look at classic feminist texts on popular culture.

Friedan's (1974 [1963]) concern in *The Feminine Mystique* over women's magazine readers, with whom she strongly identifies, and Greer's (1971) cynical evocation of her herself as a young girl swooning over romances in *The Female Eunuch*, show how the feminist author was always too close to "ordinary women" to argue the case of the false consciousness of all those women reading women's magazines and romances convincingly. Psychoanalytic conceptualization of the subject as split provided a welcome way out of the untenable position that feminism's modernist/Marxist inheritance had wrought. The fault line between modernist and postmodernist thought in feminism is therefore marked by the confession. I am a feminist, but I also happen to love reading . . . romances, lesbian pulps, or *The Thorn Birds*, or watching soap opera.[6] Identity, from a feminist perspective, one can understand Millett, Kaplan, and Ang as saying, is more productively seen as partial and constructed, involving fantasy scenarios, political criticism, and dealing with oppression, hardship, and disappointment as well as with building a sense of mattering to the world at large and so on. If that is the case for feminist intellectuals, then why should it not be the case for feminism's (potential) constituency, "ordinary women"?

Therefore, for many feminist cultural critics and media theorists, postmodernism was a logical choice. While the term "postmodernism" was claimed by theoreticians such as Lyotard (1979) and Jameson (1983), who effectively declared the bankruptcy of "Grand Narratives" and introduced radical relativist epistemology, feminist popular culture research fuelled a political line of reasoning within postmodernism (Flax 1990; Fraser & Nicholson 1990). Feminists' involvement in questions of how the media could provide women viewers and readers so much pleasure, while they offered such patently distorted representations of women, was a strong incentive to theorize gender in relation to particular (groups of) women, and to distrust the universalism of (modernist) Grand Theory. Feminism's own "grand narrative" of women's emancipation, based on the presumed universality of women's oppression and the idea that essentially there was something uniquely feminine that all women shared, broke into pieces over the contradictory feelings that theorists themselves had over specific media genres. Nor was it tenable to see one locus of power producing what was soon seen as a wide range of feminine consciousnesses. Discourse analysis, inspired especially by the work of Michel Foucault (1979, 1980), reconstructed different and competing constructions of femininity. Meanwhile, black feminists and lesbian feminists wrecked havoc with any unitary feminist program politically, claiming it to be white, middle-class, and "heterosexist."[7] As a result, insofar as one can speak of a feminist program, singular, since the late 1980s it needs to be seen as a poststructuralist program that advocates respect for difference and diversity.

Though initially not deliberately postmodern, feminist poststructuralism started to merge with and enrich the political strand of postmodernism, as opposed to its textual twin.[8] It is formulated as a critique of Enlightenment values (Flax 1990) or as a blueprint for a politics of difference, particularity, locality, and respect.[9] Although feminist postmodernism does not consist of a concrete program and never completely breaks its link with a modernist metanarrative of (personal) emancipation (McNay 1992, p. 123), it is a useful label to denote feminism's investment in social relations at the micro-level, as well as on a more abstract level, and its investigation of the personal as (part of) the political. Regrettably, the fact that the politics of the personal or the micro-analysis of everyday life are just as political as macro-analysis escapes many critics. Drotner (1993) chastises Corner (1991) for letting the distinction between macro- and micro-levels analysis, distinctive of the public knowledge project and the popular culture project, respectively, slide into a discussion of political hierarchies in which "macro-analysis per definition seems to be more political in nature" (1993, p. 34). Drotner counters that the analysis of viewing relations is not less political, but that it may involve a different kind of politics.

Politics in the popular culture project

Drotner's reply to Corner urges the question what kind of politics is involved in popular culture research. In general, popular culture research has come to focus more and more on media reception, as part of the postmodern-feminist interest in the local and the everyday, and in how women and men "actively and creatively make their own meanings and create their own culture" (Ang 1990, p. 242). Because of its open research structure, its lengthy contact with media users, and its interest in how culture is actually made, this type of reception analysis has been given the label "media ethnography." Chapter 4 has traced how the type of ethnography used is inspired by interpretive ethnography (Clifford & Marcus 1986; Marcus & Fischer 1986), and its political involvement in research practice in general and with informants in particular. Marcus and Fischer (1986) understand ethnography to be a critical practice in itself, which should be aimed at giving a voice to other groups and other cultures. Fieldwork accounts should ideally take the form of dialogues or even polylogues (see also Clifford 1988). A first political aspect, then, is giving voice to those who are usually silenced by dominant culture. Secondly, interpretive ethnography questions the position and authority of the researcher her- or himself, and urges her or him to be self-reflective to a much higher degree than mainstream social research would ask for. How, for example, does one's ethnicity, gender, or age matter (see Warren 1985)? But also, as Probyn puts it, ". . . in acknowledging our own particularities, we are forced to approach those of others with care and always remember that our stories and our bodies, can displace others, that as we speak we may be perpetuating the conditions that silence the subaltern . . ." (1992, p. 96).

The third form that politics takes in the popular culture project is the politics of (everyday) resistance as given form in and through media consumption. John Fiske (1987) is probably the best-known spokesperson for the theoretical position that our pleasure in popular culture, and especially in popular television, comes not only from recognition and identification but, in particular, from playing with and exploring the rules and limits of popular television texts. He argues that television in a way "delegates" the production of meaning and pleasure to its viewers, which makes television a "semiotic democracy" (1987, p. 236). Popular pleasure, like carnival, is based on a refusal of control, of the social identities proposed by the dominant ideology (1987, pp. 240–1). Discussing quiz shows, for example, Fiske points out two forms of liberation involved in viewing these programs, contrary to the dominant view that watching quiz shows is a form of incorporation in dominant capitalist or patriarchal norms. "[T]he first is to give public, noisy acclaim to skills that are ordinarily silenced; the second is simply to be 'noisy' in public, to escape from demure respectability, from the confines of good sense that patriarchy has constructed as necessary qualities for 'the feminine'" (1990a, p. 136).

Fiske's position, which is based on de Certeau's view of everyday resistance as the tactics of the subordinate versus the strategies, the rules, and the marked places of the powerful (Certeau 1988), is suggestive. However, de Certeau is rather a romantic about everyday life, and tends to understand the tactics of everyday life solely as a means of escape from obligations and the dominant order, whereas many forms of escape are in line with, rather than opposed to, the overarching structure of people's lives (Radway 1988, p. 366). De Certeau's romanticism is reflected in Fiske's work, which has been criticized on the same grounds for its exaggeration of the resisting qualities of the pleasures of media consumption.[10] Despite the sometimes critical reception of his work, Fiske's views are a strong example of the politics of media ethnography (see also Fiske 1990b).

In earlier work on how women's magazines are read, like Fiske I invoke the concept of "empowerment" to show how reading magazines may, from time to time, strengthen readers' identities in the form of fantasies of ideal selves. However, especially in the case of a mundane, everyday medium such as women's magazines, which tend to take second place to other media and other (daily) activities, empowerment needs to be seen in combination with the criticism of and disappointment in the magazines that readers voiced much more strongly (Hermes 1995, pp. 48–51). I suspect that for most media it is the balance between empowerment and criticism (or disappointment) that is important to understanding their appeal and resistive qualities. Such a starting point would be more in line with what Ien Ang has called "a more thoroughly *cultural* approach to reception" (1990b, p. 244) which would not stop at the "pseudo-intimate moment of the media/audience encounter, but should address the differentiated meaning and significance of specific reception patterns in articulating more general social relations of power" (idem). Although the politics of popular culture research centrally address issues of pleasure, they are more than a liberal defense of these pleasures. Rather, ideally, they constitute a cultural critique from the point of view of active audiences that recognizes the local and contradictory nature of everyday meaning-making. Such a critique is born theoretically out of the strength of poststructuralist thought and its recognition that discipline and seduction work in tandem, and produce agency (however limited) and structures of control as a package deal.

Masculinity

What might such a critique look like? How can dominant metadiscussion of popular culture as bad and as a force of feminization be restructured concretely? One route would surely be to re-understand how we define masculinity. Although a far-less researched topic than femininity, strictly speaking it is not true that masculinity has been totally neglected in the popular culture project (cf., Easthope 1990). Bennett and Woollacott's (1987) intertextual analysis of James Bond, for example, perpetuates a tradition of literary analysis of male genres and male heroes (cf., Cawelti 1976; Berger 1992). However, the male heroes are usually not analyzed from a gender perspective – until recently, that has been reserved for women and femininity. Analyses of genres that foreground male heroes focus on their professional identities and on how the text works against homoerotic identification. After all, work, or a profession, is what makes a man a man (Tolson 1978; Seidler 1989; Segal 1989). And a real man cannot be gay (cf., Wernick's 1991 analysis of advertising aimed at men).

The call to analyze masculinity in terms of gender is recent, but not unproblematic. Often, there is a suggestion that it is time for a simple redressing of the balance: we have concentrated so much on women; let's now take a closer look at men. Implicitly, it is stated that femininity and masculinity are on a par and that the same set of tools would enable the critic to deconstruct either or both. In fact, this amounts to a perpetuation of an essentialist view of gender, which not only suggests a symmetry between masculinity and femininity (and between women and men) but also a more or less direct relationship between men and masculinity, and women and femininity. In order to recalibrate discussion of popular culture, but also to address the concerns of the readers interviewed for this book, I will turn to studies of masculinity in popular media to see what use can be made of them.

Exceptional and groundbreaking are those studies that deconstruct masculinity as an object for the female gaze. Heroes in action and adventure series such as *Magnum P.I.* (Flitterman 1985) and *Miami Vice* (King 1990), or in the DIE HARD films (Willis 1997) are on display. One may wonder with Fiske (1987, p. 257) whether the masculine is becoming both the object and the subject of the look, which exscribes the feminine from the narrative. Arguably, in the case of *Miami Vice*, the designer wardrobe of Crockett and Tubbs can be seen as a masculine appropriation of a feminine language and pleasure (idem). The masculinity of both detectives is not in question, however, according to Fiske. He reads the style of both men, as well as their possessions (the Ferrari), as markers of the masculine popular hero (1987, pp. 258–9). King (1990) disagrees: "Sonny is 'feminized' by his objectification; the cultural gender confusion over the prominence of a *male* model manifests itself physically in Sonny's trademark stubble, which serves to remind us that this pretty displayed human is, counter to our expectations, a man" (1990, p. 283). King goes on to argue that it is not just the homoerotic implications of the male model as object of the male and the female gaze that is unsettling about *Miami Vice*, but also the "feminine" position of the male character. Sonny Crockett is a consumer, surrounded by consumer goods (even though, remarks King, there has yet to be an episode in which Sonny shops; see King 1990, p. 285); it happens that he is unable to do his job.

The postmodern gender confusion that *Miami Vice* gives rise to is directly a result of its play with fundamental gendered categories: to consume is no longer exclusively associated with femininity; to produce or to work no longer with masculinity. The deep divide in modernism is visited upon its postmodern stepchild. King's argument runs along lines similar to my critique of the modernist public knowledge project. He is convinced that "[g]ender still remains obscured as an explicit issue within the postmodern debate, a structuring absence that can only be implicitly read into the masculine and feminine assignments given to categories of postmodernism like surface, consumption and work" (1990, p. 290). Textual or aesthetic postmodernism has little in common in this regard with feminist postmodernism.

In the Craig collection *Men, Masculinity and the Media* (1992), most of the articles reiterate the points of view referred to above, such as the identification of maleness with work (Strate 1992); or the warding off of homoerotic implications when the male body is on display (Steinman 1992, p. 203). What this collection adds is that masculinity should not be thought of in binary terms (Fiske 1987, p. 203), elucidating though that may be, but as the uniform norm for all (see Root 1984, p. 16; Fiske 1987, pp. 200–1). Just as women may participate in the public sphere as long as they assent to being "one of the boys," maleness can actually incorporate the feminine and the spectacular to an extent that is not usually obvious. Denski and Sholle's case study of 1980s "heavy metal" bands makes this quite clear. They wonder how "young, heterosexual, white boys come to identify with performers who border on transvestism?" (1992, p. 53). The feminized appearance of the band is analyzed as an attempt at flamboyance and rebellion against societal and parental rules. But it is also a response to feminine power: "By taking the feminine into itself, heavy metal disavows the need for women, thus overcoming the fear of exercising desire" (1992, p. 55). Two male informants weren't too impressed by the long hair and make-up, and saw it as a sign of individuality and as a marketing ploy – not surprisingly, because the aggressive heterosexuality of heavy metal assures the fan that all the gender bending is under control, and is simply one more form of outrageousness.

Masculinity (with a capital M), then, remains the norm for both men and women and can incorporate femininity in a myriad ways. According to some, postmodern culture can be recognized by its gender bending at a textual level, which should not be misread as a reaching out to feminism or to women. Boscagli (1992) argues that the display of emotion on television by men, including the tears of army general Schwartzkopf in Desert Storm (1991), the first Iraq war, is no more than a ploy by patriarchy to control both ends of the gender spectrum. Just as femininity is related to – but not identical with Woman – modernism's Other, Masculinity is the norm, not identical with but related to almost all imaginable categories, encompassing femininity, ethnicity, age, and so on under the icon of the all-powerful Male. In the modernist public knowledge project, it is usual for masculinity-as-norm to be displaced onto other categories (rational discussion and debate, citizenship), whereas it would seem to be less veiled in the postmodern popular culture project. But there too Man (i.e., heterosexual, white, middle-class, healthy masculinity) is like a fun-house mirror – although there isn't much to laugh about – in which others (women, blacks, gays, the physically disabled) see themselves reflected as deviant and lacking.

Individual men do not control Man-as-mirror, just as individual women are not a real blankness or void in the public sphere. The distance between social subjects, producers of culture/producers of meaning, and discursive identities cannot be stressed enough if we are to understand how gender works in media research, and if we are to concretely formulate a new agenda for making sense of popular culture. The new agenda for discussing popular culture can only be successful if reference to concrete bodies is radically resituated – if it starts from a discussion of practices and activities rather than assuming that these follow from having a particular type of sexed body. Judith Halberstam's writing on the topic of female masculinity provides an excellent example of understanding practices as producing identities, rather than the other way around. Her drag kings provide living proof that masculinity is entirely thinkable and doable without men (Halberstam 1997). Gender is performed, in Judith Butler's words (1990, 1993). Likewise, the quality of citizenship is in how it is performed. Unfortunately, there has only been one standard for such performance: the postmodern popular culture research agenda suggests that it is high time there were more. That access is a key political issue, not so much for specific groups, but as allowance for different styles and types of argumentation, is what we can learn by respecting how popular culture is used.

Toward a new understanding of popular culture

Masculinity-as-norm values reason and control above all. Strength is mere animal violence if not harnessed for higher goals; emotion denotes lack of perspective and direction and muddies the clear waters of rational discussion and progress. It is along these lines that the talk show is seen as messy and chaotic by those who don't like the genre (Livingstone 1994). Citizenship has been cast in the mold of male rationality. The lynchpin of theories of the public sphere is reason. If anything, popular culture research (guided by postmodern and feminist theory) has argued that emotion and feeling are just as important to our (everyday) lives. If democracy can be said to be deliberation among the many about how to attain the best life possible for as many as possible, then it makes no sense to set such exclusive store by reasoned argument in our theorization of it. To rethink citizenship as cultural citizenship means accepting that those who inhabit mass democracies use many different logics to shape their lives and to deliberate what for them, personally or as a group, is the best life possible. These different logics all have their different accents regarding emotion, experiential knowledge, and rational thought.

I have therefore re-read popular (media) culture in terms of practices (of inclusion and exclusion and of meaning-making) rather than in terms of, for example, identities to allow for as wide a variety possible of experiential knowledges and styles of reasoning. I have used "cultural citizenship" as a means of exploring where the public and the private spheres meet ("brush up against each other," as Miller says) and produce notions of taste, style, or national identity; and I have taken "experience," "bonding," and "community" as hallmarks to discuss the value(s) of popular culture. In so doing, it becomes clear that although gender may well be understood as a privileged category in identity formation (and in the (negative) valuation of popular culture), dimensions other than gender are often more important in understanding how popular media are used. Class formations of taste may be related to definitions of gender – they are certainly not identical with them. Likewise, ethnicity is more important than gender for male football fans' sense of nationalism. A personal favorite example comes from Ingunn Hagen's interviews with viewers of the Norwegian news program *Dagsrevyen*. Hagen (1994) found that the dominant opposition in which *Dagsrevyen* became meaningful was between one's duty as a citizen versus boredom; feminine and masculine viewing styles had nothing much to do with it.

Then, there is the multiforum structure of cultural citizenship, another resource in re-reading popular culture. Here is a means of mixing issues of pleasure with issues of politics (by strategically crossing between the pleasurable and the political or by mixing terms and claims), which can help to further redefine the boundaries of the public and the private. Cultural citizenship is a way of insisting on how politics and pleasure are both articulated at the level of the everyday and are reciprocally involved in how we constitute ourselves in relation to society. The public knowledge project has, of course, tended to keep the public and the private too far apart (while fearing the intrusion of the one upon the other); whereas the popular culture project has tended to conflate the two too easily. Neither project has focused on how public and private influence each other; on how popular and public culture are deeply implied by each other. Ideal versions of the public sphere often entail visions of a range of many different spheres, or debates (Murdock 1993, p. 523) alongside each other, that have a plural and decentered rather than a privileged character (McLaughlin 1993, p. 606). The relation between these different debates, practices, and discussions, by my reckoning, is provided by the cultural; by shared, common frames of reference – by watching national football, or by reading or watching popular genres. In that sense, politics – painted with a broad brush – cannot do without the cultural, and popular culture would be an excellent place to start.

My third and last point to further a new understanding of popular culture, after a call to rebalance the value of ratio and emotion in citizenship; and to start from practices rather than (given, anatomically based) identities; is to stress that community experience must be understood as mediated. Community, or bonding, is what is produced by popular culture, whether in the form of new alliances and coalitions or in the rewriting or renewing of older, existing connections, affinities, and group loyalties. This is, by the argument of this book, how popular culture has value. It offers a means of bonding and of reflecting on it, sometimes critically and inventively, sometimes uncritically or by discriminating against those perceived as belonging to other groups. If we are willing to understand the centrality of practices in which identity, subjectivity, and community are constructed, and after we recognize the interwovenness of the public and the popular, we can, if we so wish, contemplate a new *Öffentlichkeit* in all its constructedness. Such a new, ideal public space would provide room for what Negt and Kluge (1993 [1972]) called "counterpublics." Counterpublics are communities that understand themselves, in the words of Miriam Hansen (1993, p. 207): "as rhetoric, as a trope of impossible authenticity." Community is at best a promise of belonging, which admits to "difference and differentiation within its own borders (and) is capable of accepting multiply determined sexual-social identities and identifications" (idem). The uses to which popular culture is put by football fans and middle-class detective novel readers make clear that it suggests ways and means of belonging that imply the existence of cultural citizenship. Proof of that, for example, is the agenda of concerns that contains such issues as the restructuring of everyday practices of constructing and performing masculinity.

Much depends in the end on whether we, as intellectuals, choose to work with rather than against popular culture, and use its potential, as well as its often implicit forms of community building and reflection, to further the goal of more equal, more open and more reflexive societies. If anything, this book has made it clear that popular culture is neither solely a progressive nor always a conservative or regressive force. Popular culture cannot be reduced to commercial exploitation, capitalist junk, or resistance against the powers that be. Of its nature, popular culture engages with what interests us and what binds us. At times, this includes critique of social power relations or its own production logic. But, more importantly, it is related to what is of value to audiences, which deserves our recognition and reinterpretation, counter to the widespread misunderstanding that popular culture follows singular and unitary logics. Objectification of the body – for instance, in the case of male footballers – can be considered a good thing, since it counters the common logics of sexism and racism; while to have female officers planted precariously in high-ranking functions in police series may be a bad thing in its misrepresentation of socioeconomic relations, even if it does counter stereotypical imaging of women. And this is without even mentioning the more hidden worries that we have over postfeminist masculinities; and our misunderstanding of children's preference for and sense of security in straightforward right/wrong reasoning, which makes violence in a game absolutely acceptable, and the results of violence in Third World countries too horrible to contemplate. We need to make more and better use of popular culture.

notes

1 For a fascinating account, see Theweleit (1980).
2 See also Bowlby (1985).
3 As in the work of Marshall (1994 [1964]); cf., Steenbergen (1994), Stevenson (2001), and Turner (1994).
4 For example, Brownmiller (1984), Friedan (1974 [1963]), and Greer (1971).
5 For example, Kuhn (1982), Modleski (1984 [1982]), Doane (1987), and Gamman and Marshment (1988).
6 See, e.g., Millett in Koski and Tilchen (1979); and also Kaplan (1986) and Ang (1985, 1990a).
7 For early examples, see hooks (1989) and Echols (1984).
8 Baudrillard (1983, 1988), see also Best and Kellner (1991) and Kellner (1995).
9 Haraway (1988), Young (1987, 1990), and Fraser and Nicholson (1990).
10 See Ang (1990a), Gitlin (1991), and Morris (1988).

concluding remarks

This book has suggested that re-reading popular culture is a worthwhile project. More than other forms of culture (whether the Arts or political culture), popular texts allow us to bond and build communities. They do so because they are of use to us; they allow us to reflect on our lives by providing "usable stories" (John Mepham), occasions for fictional rehearsal and a domain for what John Ellis calls "working through." Many of the usable stories that readers and viewers referred to throughout the chapters are centered around heroes, stars, and celebrities – whether created in fiction or in real life. The strong women in detective fiction, footballers such as Ruud Gullit, and the three spies in the children's animated series *Totally Spies!* inspire audiences. As viewers, we try on their qualities and achievements for size; or use them to compare ourselves to. We may also use them as negative examples (poor Third World children; ruthless Detective Tennyson, who cannot count as a feminist; Kluivert, when he was involved in killing a man accidentally and later in an alleged gang rape). They figure as central characters in stories that make clear what life is and should be about; what we want to bond over with others, with whom we want to belong and why. Shared pleasures may refer to a shared sense of class, or worthwhile skills or standards for feminine and masculine behavior and style. Using popular culture has all the hallmarks of – cultural – citizenship. I will briefly review what that means and then wrap up this conclusion by tackling that last important question: If popular culture has such obvious value, why is it not held in higher regard?

Popular culture and cultural citizenship

If the use of popular culture produces cultural citizenship, what rights and responsibilities are involved? How do its mechanisms of inclusion and exclusion work? Responsibilities are located at the level of practice: to make sure you watch the game; that you collect books by a favorite author; that you improve your skills by working your way up through the levels of a game; that you suggest good reads or games to others. Because of these responsibilities, as a member of a particular interpretive community (whether of sports, of animated children's television, or of Internet discussion of television series), you can take pride in your knowledge, in what you collect materially or virtually. Rights too are easy to pinpoint: as a gamer, you know that you are entitled to change games every six months or so (sooner if a game doesn't offer a real challenge any longer); as a child, you know that you are entitled to a fun life; as a viewer, you know that without you, a television series could not be a lucrative enterprise and that you therefore are at the very least a shareholder in favorite programs. Without viewers, the commercial media industry would not exist.

Based on what are in themselves small examples, I conclude that the pleasures of popular culture do not only have material effects in the organization of social life, but that they can be valued for their contribution to citizenship, understood as the reflexive belonging to communities that contribute to and include the nation-state. My re-reading of popular culture along lines of use is, above all, meant to plead that it be held in more regard. The problem is not so much that old "high versus low culture" divide, although it does rear its head from time to time. The examples in this book underwrite the point of view that in practices of use, the distinction between high and low culture is no longer important. For instance, in answering questions about what makes a good thriller, literary titles are named as well as titles that are part of long series (not, in the twentieth century, seen as a mark of cultural quality). The talent of top sportsmen has never been a cultural issue, but the question of who may enjoy popular sports has. The mixed class background of our viewers indicates that this is no longer an issue either. The *Ally McBeal* and *Sex and the City* television series (about which I followed discussion on the Internet) belong with a cluster of texts that are currently denominated as "quality popular television" (Jancovich & Lyons 2003). Even behind the simple animé style of *Pokémon*, David Buckingham and Julian Sefton-Green find classic literary merit. From the perspective of how such texts are used, this means just as much that literary merit can be saved by accessible style as, putting it the other way around, that a lowly valued style of drawing may be saved by quality in narrative.

156 Concluding remarks

Popular culture and civic disengagement

The problem with popular culture is not so much in the distinction between high and low itself, but in the double genealogy of debate about it. In *Bowling Alone: The Collapse and Revival of American Community*, Robert Putnam's (2000) impressive study of social cohesion in the USA, he is highly concerned with the decline of civic engagement. Very briefly summarized, Putnam shows that Americans belong to fewer organizations, and spend less of their time on community affairs. A number of factors contribute to such a development. The decline of the traditional, extended family is one, as is suburbanization. "Big government," the welfare state, and capitalism might be factors. White flight from organizations after the success of the civil rights movements is not, but television viewing is (Putnam 2000, pp. 277–84). In itself, this correlates directly with John Hartley's (1999, p. 100) historical argument that the policing of populations meant a push for the one-family home, a development that was sealed with the invention of the fridge (no need to go to the market or the pub every day for food) and the television set (or to go out for entertainment). It is the way in which Putnam questions the role of the mass media and television in particular in furthering the decline of community activity that I want to point out. I will follow his argumentation in somewhat more detail.

Putnam correlates reader and viewer statistics with attending club meetings and so on, which makes clear that newspaper readers are easily the most civic-minded, with television news viewers in second place. Then, Putnam moves on to entertainment, which is the major part of what we call "popular culture," even though popular culture includes many nonfiction and news formats: "Most of the time, energy and creativity of the electronic media, however, is devoted not to news, but to entertainment. Watching the news is not harmful to your civic health. What about television entertainment?" (2000, p. 221). This is strong and suggestive rhetoric, and there is more to come. He goes on to convincingly argue the immense social change wrought by television's incredibly rapid success in binding viewers. By correlating different types of civic activity with the increasing number of hours spent watching television, he concludes that "television . . . is particularly toxic for activities we do together" (2000, p. 229). I object strongly to the phrasing of this conclusion. To mark television viewing as toxic produces much more than a new fact (television viewers engage in less volunteer work and donate less blood than those who say that television viewing is not their primary form of entertainment): it produces a particular truth about television and by implication popular culture. All television viewing, including the television viewed by the more civic-minded, is now labeled as a hazardous activity. The counter-argument that (an average dosage of) television viewing might also be productive of other or newer forms of bonding cannot even be contemplated under such discursive outlawing. Television, and popular culture in general, is cut off from what makes it worthwhile from the perspective of its users, other than offering the opportunity to play hooky.

I agree with Putnam that it is a grave matter that we socialize less, and that we find it less important to contribute to social and political life. I firmly underwrite his admonition that we should try to ensure that more people participate in the public life of our communities (2000, p. 412). But why not work *with* rather than *against* what is so high on the agendas of the citizens? Why not understand what they find in popular culture that not only amuses them but is a means of understanding society and social relations; to reflect on such issues as violence and the construction of masculinity, in the case of the detective novel readers; or what it means to be a Western child today, in the case of the children who were asked about their views on the Third World?

The art of listening to others

The answer is simple. The double genealogy of thinking about popular culture (modern and postmodern) makes it nearly impossible to both appreciate and be critical of popular culture. John Hartley is utterly serious when he suggests "democratainment" as the result of television's use by all of those with little access to formal schooling, resulting in an entirely new way of understanding differences. The fact that a multicultural ideal may become hegemonic (as in the 1980s in the Netherlands), as a result of the televised successes of a national football team with a small number of (extraordinarily gifted) black players, should tell us that to miss the connection to the popular is definitely the loss of the civic-minded.

Civic-mindedness would seem to be indelibly written into the jargon of modernism, which perhaps is best defined by its double allergy to all that can be associated with the feminine and all that has to do with postmodern irony and relativism. What a shame. Our young gamers and television viewers were more open-minded, and listening to them suggests that we pay attention to how they define the good life today – the core of all democratic practice. For one thing, they did not distinguish greatly between forms of gaming: they liked playing games on their PCs, and with others on the Internet, as much as they liked playing board and card games. "It is more companionable," said 15-year-old

Marloes. Let's play more games. Mostly, the detective novel readers liked to talk about their favorite books. Clearly, most of them did not often find a listening ear, except when in the company of those with whom they exchanged books. Let's ask each other more about what we like and why we like it. Even more than the detective novel readers, the football fans enjoyed talking about the game and all of those involved. More used to talking about football (quite a few participated in amateur-after-the-Saturday-afternoon-match-canteen philosophizing), they were thrilled to be able to try to convert a new soul to the joys of football. In general, the interviews that my students and I held suggest that neither popular culture generally nor television specifically should be blamed for civic disengagement, but that we need to bone up on our listening qualities. That includes respect for what others like. I therefore have to insist that popular culture is re-read, if only because a wide popular cultural literacy can be extraordinarily useful in engaging with other people (the civic ideal); but mostly because the success of popular culture is a direct result of what it teaches us about ourselves. And it is a democratic imperative to understand what that is.

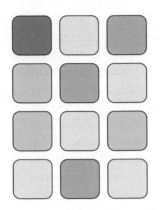

references

Allor, M. and Gagnon, M. 1994: *L'etat de culture: généalogie discursive des politiques culturelles Québécoises*. Montreal: Grecc (Concordia University / Université de Montréal).

Amerongen, M. van and Leistra, G. 1990: *Gullit*. Amsterdam: de Arbeiderspers.

Anderson, B. 1983: *Imagined Communities: Reflections on the Origin and Spread of Nationalism*. London: Verso.

Ang, I. 1985: *Watching Dallas: Soap Opera and the Melodramatic Identification*. London: Methuen.

—— 1987: Popular fiction and feminist cultural politics. *Theory, Culture and Society*, 4, 651–8.

—— 1990a: Melodramatic identifications. Television fiction and women's fantasy. In M. E. Brown (ed.), *Television and Women's Culture: The Politics of the Popular*. London: Sage, 75–88.

—— 1990b: Culture and communication. Towards an ethnographic critique of media consumption in the transnational media system. *European Journal of Communication*, 5(2/3), 239–60.

—— and Hermes, J. 1991: Gender and/in media consumption. In J. Curran and M. Gurevitch (eds.), *Mass Media and Society*. London: Edward Arnold, 307–28.

Ballaster, R., Beetham, M., Frazer, E. and Hebron, S. 1991: *Women's Worlds: Ideology, Femininity and the Women's Magazine*. Basingstoke: Macmillan.

Baudrillard, J. 1983: *Simulations*. New York: Semiotext(e).

—— 1988: *The Ecstasy of Communication*. New York: Semiotext(e).

Baym, N. K. 2000: *Tune in, Log on. Soaps, Fandom, and Online Community*. London: Sage.

Bennett, T. and Woollacott, J. 1987: *Bond and Beyond: The Political Career of a Popular Hero*. Basingstoke: Macmillan.

Berger, A. A. 1992: *Popular Culture Genres*. London: Sage.

Best, S. and Kellner, D. 1991: *Postmodern Theory: Critical Interrogations*. London: Macmillan.

Bianculli, D. 1997: *Dictionary of Teleliteracy: Television's 500 Biggest Hits, Misses, and Events*. New York: Syracuse University Press.

Billingham, P. 2000: *Sensing the City through Television*. Bristol: Intellect.

Blumler, J. 1992: Introduction and Conclusion. In J. Blumler (ed.), *Television and the Public Interest: Vulnerable Values in Western European Broadcasting*. London: Sage.

—— and Biltereyst, D. 1997: *The Integrity and Erosion of Public Television for Children: A Pan-European Survey*. Monograph of research sponsored by the Centre for Media Education (Washington, DC), the Broadcasting Standards Commission (UK), the European Institute for the Media (Düsseldorf, Germany), and the European Broadcasting Union.

Bondebjerg, I. 1999: Public discourse/private fascinations: hybridization in "true-life-story" genres. In H. Newcomb (ed.), *Television, the Critical View*. Oxford: Oxford University Press, 383–400.

Bordo, S. 1993: *Unbearable Weight: Feminism, Western Culture and the Body*. Berkeley: University of California Press.

Boomkens, R. 1996: *De angstmachine: over geweld in films, literatuur en popmuziek*. Amsterdam: De Balie.

Boscagli, M. 1992: A moving story. Masculine tears and the humanity of televised emotions. *Discourse*, 15(2) (Winter 92/3), 64–79.

Bourdieu, P. 1984: *Distinction: A Social Critique of the Judgement of Taste*. Cambridge, MA: Harvard University Press.

Bowlby, R. 1985: *Just Looking: Consumer Culture in Dreiser, Gissing and Zola*. London: Methuen.

Brownmiller, S. 1984: *Femininity*. New York: Fawcett Columbine.

Brunsdon, C. 1998: Structures of anxiety. *Screen*, 39(3), 223–43.

Buckingham, D. 2000: *The Making of Citizens: Young People, News and Politics*. London: Routledge.

—— and Sefton-Green, J. 2003: Gotta catch 'em all. Structure, agency and pedagogy in children's media culture. *Media, Culture, and Society*, 25, 379–99.

Butler, J. 1990: *Gender Trouble: Feminism and the Subversion of Identity*. London: Routledge.

—— 1993: *Bodies that Matter: On the Discursive Limits of "Sex."* London: Routledge.

Caldwell, J. T. 1987: *Televisuality: Style, Crisis and Authority in American Television*. New Brunswick, NJ: Rutgers University Press.

Cawelti, J. 1976: *Adventure, Mystery and Romance: Formula Stories as Art and Popular Culture*. Chicago: University of Chicago Press.

Certeau, M. de 1988: *The Practice of Everyday Life*, trans. S. Randall. Berkeley: University of California Press.

Chapman, J. 2000: *Licence to Thrill: A Cultural History of the James Bond Films*. New York: Columbia University Press.

Chapman, R. and Rutherford, J. 1988: *Male Order: Unwrapping Masculinity*. London: Lawrence and Wishart.

Chocano, C. 2002: Bye-bye, dancing baby. Uploaded May 2, 2002 on www.salon.com Arts and Entertainment; last accessed June 11, 2002.

Clifford, J. 1988: *The Predicament of Culture: Twentieth Century Ethnography, Literature and Art*. Cambridge, MA: Harvard University Press.

References $\boxed{161}$

—— and Marcus, G. E. 1986: *Writing Culture: The Poetics and Politics of Ethnography*. Berkeley: University of California Press.

Clover, C. J. 1992: *Men, Women and Chain Saws: Gender in the Modern Horror Film*. London: British Film Institute.

Cobley, P. 2000: *The American Thriller: Generic Innovation and Social Change in the 1970s*. Basingstoke: Palgrave.

—— 2001: "Who loves ya, baby?": *Kojak*, action and the great society. In B. Osgerby and A. Gough-Yates (eds.), *Action TV: Tough Guys, Smooth Operators and Foxy Chicks*. London: Routledge, 53–68.

Corner, J. 1991: Meaning, genre and context: the problematics of "public knowledge" in the new audience studies. In J. Curran and M. Gurevitch (eds.), *Mass Media and Society*. London: Edward Arnold, 267–84.

Coward, R. 1983: *Patriarchal Precedents: Sexuality and Social Relations*. London: Routledge and Kegan Paul.

—— and Semple, L. 1989: Tracking down the past. Women and detective fiction. In H. Carr (ed.), *From My Guy to Sci-Fi: Genre and Women's Writing in the Postmodern World*. London: Pandora, 39–57.

Craig, P. and Cadogan, M. 1981: *The Lady Investigates: Women Detectives and Spies in Fiction*. London: Victor Gollancz.

Craig, S. (ed.) 1992: *Men, Masculinity and the Media*. Newbury Park: Sage.

Cranny-Francis, A. 1990: *Feminist Fiction: Feminist Uses of Generic Fiction*. Cambridge: Polity Press.

Crigler, A. N. and Jensen, K. B. 1991: Discourses on politics: talking about public issues in the United States and Denmark. In P. Dahlgren and C. Sparks (eds.), *Communication and Citizenship: Journalism and the Public Sphere*. London: Routledge, 176–92.

Cronin, A. 2000: *Advertising and Consumer Citizenship. Gender, Images and Rights*. London: Routledge.

Cuklanz, L. M. 2000: *Rape on Prime Time: Television, Masculinity, and Sexual Violence*. Philadelphia: University of Pennsylvania Press.

Curran, J. 1990: The new revisionism in mass communication research: a reappraisal. *European Journal of Communication*, 5(2/3), 135–64.

d'Acci, J. 1987: *Defining Women: Television and the Case of Cagney and Lacey*. Chapel Hill: The University of North Carolina Press.

Dahlgren, P. and Sparks, C. (eds.) 1991: *Communication and Citizenship: Journalism and the Public Sphere*. London: Routledge.

—— and —— (eds.) 1992: *Journalism and Popular Culture*. London: Sage.

Davies, H., Buckingham, D. and Kelley, P. 2000: In the worst possible taste. Children, television and cultural value. *European Journal of Cultural Studies*, 3(1), 5–25.

Davis, H. 2001: *Inspector Morse* and the business of crime. *Television and New Media*, 2(2), 133–48.

Décuré, N. 1994: Friendless orphans: family relationships in women's crime fiction. *Phoebe*, 6(1), 27–41.

Denski, S. and Sholle, D. 1992: Metal man and glamour boys: gender performance in heavy metal. In S. Craig (ed.), *Men, Masculinity and the Media*. Newbury Park: Sage, 41–60.

Doane, M. A. 1987: *The Desire to Desire: The Woman's Film of the 1940s*. London: Macmillan.

Douglas, S. J. 1995: *Where the Girls are: Growing up Female with the Mass Media*. New York: Times Books.

Dowling, C. 1982: *The Cinderella Complex: Women's Hidden Fear of Independence*. New York: Pocket Books.

Drotner, K. 1993: Media ethnography: an Other story? In U. Carlsson (ed.), *Nordisk forskning om kvinnor och medier*. Göteborg: Nordicom, 25–40.

Dudink, S. 1998: The trouble with men. Problems in the history of "masculinity." *European Journal of Cultural Studies*, 1(3), 419–31.

Dyer, R. 1992: *Only Entertainment*. London: Routledge.

—— 1998: *Stars*. London: BFI.

Easthope, A. 1990: *What a Man's Gotta do: The Masculine Myth in Popular Culture*. London: Paladin.

Echols, A. 1984: The taming of the id: feminist sexual politics, 1968–83. in C. S. Vance (ed.), *Pleasure and Danger: Exploring Female Sexuality*, Boston: Routledge and Kegan Paul, 50–72.

Ellis, J. 2000: *Seeing Things: Television in the Age of Uncertainty*. London: I. B. Tauris.

Ehrmann, J. 1968: *Homo Ludens* revisited (trans. C. Lewis and P. Lewis). *Yale French Studies*, no. 41, pp. 31–57.

Elsaesser, T. 2000: *Weimar's Cinema and After: Germany's Historical Imaginary*. London: Routledge.

Erp, B. van 2002: Dertiger, hip, vrouw en ongelukkig. *Vrij Nederland*, 30 maart 2002.

Faludi, S. 1993: *Backlash: The Undeclared War against American Women*. New York: Vintage.

Feilitzen, C. von 2001: The new media landscape and its consequences for children and young people. Speech for the EU expert seminar "Children and young people in the new media landscape," Stockholm, February 12–13, 2001.

Fish, S. 1980: *Is there a Text in this Class?* Cambridge, MA: Harvard University Press.

Fiske, J. 1987: *Television Culture*. London: Methuen.

—— 1990a: Women and quiz shows: consumerism, patriarchy and resisting pleasures. In M. E. Brown (ed.), *Television and Women's Culture: The Politics of the Popular*. London: Sage, 134–43.

—— 1990b: Ethnosemiotics: some personal and theoretical reflections. *Cultural Studies*, 4(1), 85–99.

—— and Hartley, J. 1978: *Reading Television*. London: Methuen.

Flax, J. 1990: Postmodernism and gender relations in feminist theory. In L. J. Nicholson (ed.), *Feminism/Postmodernism*. New York: Routledge, 39–62.

Flitterman, S. 1985: Thighs and whiskers, the fascination of *Magnum P.I. Screen*, 26(2), 42–58.

References

Foucault, M. 1979: *Discipline and Punish: The Birth of the Prison*, trans. A. Sheridan. New York: Vintage Books/Random House.

—— 1980: *The History of Sexuality*, vol. I: *An Introduction*, trans. R. Hurley. New York: Vintage Books/Random House.

Fraser, N. and Nicholson, L. 1990: Social criticism without philosophy. An encounter between feminism and postmodernism. In L. J. Nicholson (ed.), *Feminism/ Postmodernism*. New York: Routledge, 19–38.

FrauenFilmInitiative 1992: *Mörderinnen im Film*. Berlin: Elefanten Press.

Friedan, B. 1974 [1963]: *The Feminine Mystique*. New York: Dell.

Gadamer, H.-G. 1986 [1960]: *Wahrheit und Methode: Grundzuege einer philosophischen Hermeneutik*. Tübingen: J. C. B. Mohr.

Gamman, L. 1988: Watching the detectives. The enigma of the female gaze. In L. Gamman and M. Marshment (eds.), *The Female Gaze: Women as Viewers of Popular Culture*. London: The Women's Press, 8–26.

—— and Marshment, M. (eds.) 1988: *The Female Gaze: Women as Viewers of Popular Culture*. London: The Women's Press.

Geragthy, C. 1998: Audiences and "ethnography": questions of practice. In C. Geragthy and D. Lusted (eds.), *The Television Studies Book*. London: Edward Arnold, 141–57.

Gillespie, M. 1995: *Television, Ethnicity and Cultural Change*. London: Routledge.

Gitlin, T. 1991: The politics of communication and the communication of politics. In J. Curran and M. Gurevitch (eds.), *Mass Media and Society*. London: Edward Arnold, 329–41.

Guilianotti, R. 1999: *Football: A Sociology of the Global Game*. Cambridge: Polity Press.

Glaser, B. G. and Strauss, A. L. 1967: *The Discovery of Grounded Theory*. Chicago: Aldine.

Goffman, I. 1973 [1959]: *The Presentation of Self in Everyday Life*. New York: Doubleday.

Gough-Yates, A. 2001: Angels in chains? Feminism, femininity and consumer culture in *Charlie's Angels*. In B. Osgerby and A. Gough-Yates (eds.), *Action TV: Tough Guys, Smooth Operators and Foxy Chicks*. London: Routledge, 83–99.

—— 2002: *Understanding Women's Magazines: Publishing, Markets and Readerships*. London: Routledge.

Gramsci, A. 1972: *The Prison Notebooks*. New York: The Free Press.

Gray, A. 1992: *Video Playtime: The Gendering of a Leisure Technology*. London: Comedia/ Routledge.

—— 2003: *Research Practice for Cultural studies: Ethnographic Methods and Lived Cultures*. London: Sage.

Greer, G. 1971: *The Female Eunuch*. London: Paladin.

Gripsrud, J. 1995: *The Dynasty Years: Hollywood Television and Critical Media Studies*. London: Routledge.

—— 1998: Television, broadcasting, flow. In C. Geragthy and D. Lusted (eds.), *The Television Studies Book*. London: Edward Arnold, 17–32.

—— (ed.) 1999: *Television and Common Knowledge*. London: Routledge.

Habermas, J. 1981: *Theorie des kommunikativen Handelns*, two vols. Frankfurt a. M.: Suhrkamp Verlag.

References

—— 1984: *Vorstudien und Ergänzungen zur Theorie des kommunikativen Handelns.* Frankfurt a. M.: Suhrkamp Verlag.

Hagen, I. 1994: The ambivalences of TV news viewing: between ideals and everyday practices. *European Journal of Communication*, 9, 193–220.

Hake, K. 2003: Five-year-olds' fascination for television. A comparative study. In I. Rydin (ed.), *Media Fascinations: Perspectives on Young People's Meaning Making.* Goteborg: Nordicom, 31–49.

Halberstam, J. 1997: Mackdaddy, Superfly, Rapper. Gender, race and masculinity in the drag king scene. *Social Text 52/3*, 15(3/4), 104–31.

Hall, S. 1980: Encoding/decoding. In S. Hall, D. Hobson, A. Lowe and P. Willis (eds.), *Media, Culture, Language.* London: Hutchinson, 128–38.

—— 1992: The question of cultural identity. In S. Hall, D. Held and T. McGrew (eds.), *Modernity and its Futures.* Cambridge: Polity Press, 273–325.

——, Critcher, C., Jefferson, T., Clarke, J. and Roberts, B. (eds.) 1978: *Policing the Crisis: Mugging, the State, and Law and Order.* London: Macmillan.

Hammersley, M. and Atkinson, P. 1995: *Ethnography: Principles in Practice*, 2nd edn. London: Routledge.

Hansen, M. 1993: Unstable mixtures, dilated spheres: Negt and Kluge's *The Public Sphere and Experience,* twenty years later. *Public Culture*, 5(2), 179–212.

Haraway, D. 1988: Situated knowledges: the science question in feminism and the privilege of partial perspective. *Feminist Studies*, 14(3), 575–99.

Hartley, J. 1996: *Popular Reality.* London: Edward Arnold.

—— 1999: *The Uses of Television.* London: Routledge.

Hermes, J. 1995: *Reading Women's Magazine: An Analysis of Everyday Media Use.* Cambridge: Polity Press.

—— 1998: Popular culture and cultural citizenship. In K. Brants, J. Hermes and L. van Zoonen (eds.), *The Media in Question: Popular Cultures and Public Interests.* London: Sage, 157–67.

—— 1999: Media figures in identity construction. In P. Alasuutari (ed.), *Rethinking the Media Audience: The New Agenda.* London: Sage, 69–85.

—— 2001: *The Persuaders!* A girl's best friends. In B. Osgerby and A. Gough-Yates (eds.), *Action TV: Tough Guys, Smooth Operators and Foxy Chicks.* London: Routledge, 159–68.

—— and Bruin, J. de 2003: Red herrings. Ethnicity, multiculturalism and gender in new Dutch television crime fiction. Paper presented at Screen conference, Glasgow, UK.

Hogeland, L. M. 1998: *Feminism and its Fictions: The Consciousness-Raising Novel and the Women's Liberation Movement.* Philadelphia: University of Pennsylvania Press.

Holloway, S. L. and Valentine, G. 2000: Children's geographies and the new social studies of childhood. In S. L. Holloway and G. Valentine (eds.), *Children's Geographies: Playing, Living, Learning.* London: Routledge, 1–26.

hooks, b. 1989: *Feminist Theory: From Margin to Center.* Boston, MA: South End Press.

Howley, K. 2001: Spooks, spies and control. Technologies in the *X-files. Television and New Media*, 2(3), 357–80.

Huizinga, J. 1955: *Homo Ludens: A Study of the Play Element in Culture*. Boston: Beacon Press.

Huyssen, A. 1986: Mass culture as woman. Modernism's Other. In *After the Great Divide: Modernism, Mass Culture, Postmodernism*. Bloomington: Indiana University Press, 44–62.

Innes, S. 1999: *Tough Girls: Women Warriors and Wonder Women in Popular Culture*. Philadelphia: University of Pennsylvania Press.

Irons, G. (ed.) 1995: *Feminism in Women's Detective Fiction*. Toronto: University of Toronto Press.

Jackson, P., Brookes, K. and Stevenson, N. 1999: Making sense of men's lifestyle magazines. *Society and Space*, 17, 353–68.

Jameson, F. 1983: Postmodernism and consumer society. In H. Foster (ed.), *The Anti-Aesthetic. Essays on Postmodern Culture*. Port Townsend, WA: Bay Press, 111–25.

Jancovich, M. and Lyons, J. 2003: Introduction. In M. Jancovich and J. Lyons (eds.), *Quality Popular Television*. London: BFI, 1–8.

Jenkins, H. 1991: *Textual Poachers: Television Fans and Participatory Culture*. London: Routledge.

—— 2003: To inform AND entertain. The Ivory Tower, www.igda.com; accessed on April 11, 2003.

Jensen, J. 1990: *Redeeming Modernity: Contradictions in Media Criticism*. Newbury Park: Sage.

Jensen, S. 2001: Lippenstift feminisme. De neuroses van Bridget Jones en Ally McBeal. *NRC Handelsblad*, January 26, 2001; accessed at www.nrc.nl/cultuur/, November 2001.

Johansson, B. 2003: Good friends, merry fighters. In I. Rydin (ed.), *Media Fascinations: Perspectives on Young People's Meaning Making*. Goteborg: Nordicom, 131–45.

Kaplan, C. 1986: *The Thorn Birds*: fiction, fantasy, femininity. In *Sea Changes*. London: Verso, 117–46.

Katz, E. and Liebes, T. 1990: *The Export of Meaning: Cross-Cultural Readings of "Dallas."* New York: Oxford University Press.

Kellner, D. 1995: *Media Culture: Cultural Studies, Identity and Politics between the Modern and the Postmodern*. London: Routledge.

King, B. S. 1990: Sonny's virtues: the gender negotiations of *Miami Vice*. *Screen*, 31(3), 281–95.

Klein, K. G. 1988: *The Woman Detective: Gender and Genre*. Urbana: University of Illinois Press.

Kline, S. 1993: *Out of the Garden: Toys and Children's Culture in the Age of TV Marketing*. London: Verso.

Koski, F. and Tilchen, M. 1979: Some pulp sappho. In K. Jay and A. Young (eds.), *Lavender Culture*. New York: Jove/HBJ, 262–74.

Kuhn, A. 1982: *Women's Pictures: Feminism and Cinema*. London: Routledge and Kegan Paul.

Leeuw, S. de 1995: *Televisiedrama: podium voor identiteit*. Amsterdam: Otto Cramwinckel.

Lenning, A. van, Meijer, I. C., Tonkens, E. and Volman, M. 1996: *Wel feministisch, niet geemancipeerd: feminisme als nieuwe uitdaging* [*Feminism Yes, Emancipation, No Thanks: Feminism as a New Challenge*]. Amsterdam: Contact.

Lewis, L. (ed.) 1992: *The Adoring Audience: Fan Culture and Popular Media*. London: Routledge.

Lijphart, A. 1968: *The Politics of Accommodation: Pluralism and Democracy in the Netherlands*. Berkeley: University of California Press.

Lindlof, T. R. 1988: Media and audiences as interpretive communities. In J. Anderson (ed.), *Communication Yearbook 11*. Newbury Park: Sage, for the International Communication Association, 81–107.

Livingstone, S. 1994: Watching talk: gender and engagement in the viewing of audience discussion programmes. *Media, Culture and Society*, 16, 429–47.

Lusted, D. 1998: The popular culture debate and light entertainment on television. In C. Geragthy and D. Lusted (eds.), *The Television Studies Book*. London: Edward Arnold, 175–90.

Lyotard, J.-F. 1979: *La condition post-moderne: rapport sur le savoir*. Paris: Editions de Minuit.

Mander, J. 1998 [1978]: *Four Arguments for the Elimination of Television*. Mapusa, Goa, India: The Other India Press.

Marc, D. 1997: *Comic Visions: Television Comedy and American Culture*. Oxford: Blackwell.

Marcus, G. E. and Fischer, M. M. J. (eds.) 1986: *Anthropology as Cultural Critique: An Experimental Moment in the Human Sciences*. Chicago: University of Chicago Press.

Marshall, T. H. 1994 [1964]: Citizenship and social class. In B. Turner and P. Hamilton (eds.), *Citizenship: Critical Concepts*. London: Routledge, 5–44.

McKinley, E. G. 1997: *Beverly Hills, 90210: Television, Gender and Identity*. Philadelphia: University of Pennsylvania Press.

McLaughlin, L. 1993: Feminism, the public sphere, media and democracy. *Media, Culture and Society*, 15(4), 599–620.

McNay, L. 1992: *Foucault and Feminism, Power, Gender and the Self*. Cambridge: Polity Press.

McRobbie, A. 1991 [1982]: The politics of feminist research. Between talk, text and action. In *Feminism and Youth Culture: From* Jackie *to* Just Seventeen. Basingstoke: Macmillan, 61–80.

Meijer, I. C. 1996: *Het persoonlijke wordt politiek: feministische bewustwording in Nederland 1965–1980*. Amsterdam: Het Spinhuis.

—— 2000: Vriendschap, vaderschap en zwangerschap. In I. C. Meijer and M. Reesink (eds.), *Reality Soap! Big Brother en de opkomst van het multimedia concept*. Amsterdam: Boom, 65–73.

Mepham, J. 1990: The ethics of quality in television. In G. Mulgan (ed.), *The Question of Quality*. London: BFI, 56–72.

Miller, T. 1993: *The Well-Tempered Self: Citizenship, Culture, and the Postmodern Subject*. Baltimore: Johns Hopkins University Press.

—— 1998: *Technologies of Truth: Cultural Citizenship and the Popular Media*. Minneapolis: University of Minnesota Press.

—— 2001: *Sportsex*. Philadelphia: Temple University Press.

Mittell, J. 2001: A cultural approach to television genre theory. *Cinema Journal*, 40(3), 3–24.

Modleski, T. 1984 [1982]: *Loving with a Vengeance: Mass-Produced Fantasies for Women*. New York: Methuen.

—— 1986: Femininity as Mas(s)querade. A feminist approach to mass culture. In C. MacCabe (ed.), *High Theory, Low Culture*. Manchester: Manchester University Press, 37–52.

Moran, A. 1998: *Copycat TV: Globalisation, Program Formats and Cultural Identity*. Luton: University of Luton Press.

Morley, D. 1980: *The Nationwide Audience*. London: BFI.

—— 1986: *Family Television: Cultural Power and Domestic Leisure*. London: Comedia.

—— 1989: Changing paradigms in audience studies. In E. Seiter, H. Borchers, E. Warth and G. Kreutzner (eds.), *Remote Control*. London: Routledge, 16–43.

—— 2000: *Home Territories: Media, Mobility and Identity*. London: Routledge.

Morris, M. 1988: Banality in cultural studies. *Block*, 14, 15–26.

Munt, S. 1994: *Murder by the Book? Feminism and the Crime Novel*. London: Routledge.

Murdock, G. 1993: Communications and the constitution of modernity. *Media, Culture and Society*, 15(4), 521–39.

Negt, O. and Kluge, A. 1993 [1972]: *The Public Sphere and Experience*, trans. P. Labanyi, J. Daniel, and A. Oksiloff. Minneapolis: University of Minnesota Press, published originally in 1972.

Nesaule Krouse, A. and Peters, M. 1975: Why women kill. *Journal of Communication*, 25, 98–105.

Nieuwenhuys, A. and Verbrugh, J. 2003: "Soms lachen ze op tv, maar in het echt doen ze dat nooit." De kijk van kinderen op de Derde Wereld. Unpublished MA thesis, University of Amsterdam.

Nikken, P. 2000: Voor Elk wat Wils. Inventarisatie van het aanbod van jeugdprogramma's in 1999 [Something for everyone. Inventory of the supply of youth programs in 1999]. Utrecht, Netherlands: Stichting Jeugdinformatie Nederland.

O'Donnell, H. 1999: *Good Times, Bad Times. Soap Operas and Society in Western Europe*. London: Leicester University Press.

Ong, W. 1982: *Orality and Literacy: The Technologizing of the Word*. London: Methuen.

Oswell, D. 2002: *Television, Childhood and the Home*. Oxford: Oxford University Press.

Postman, N. 1986: *Amusing Ourselves to Death: Public Discourse in the Age of Showbusiness*, New York: Penguin.

—— 1994 [1982]: *The Disappearance of Childhood*. New York: Penguin.

Poynton, B. and Hartley, J. 1990: Male viewing. In M. E. Brown (ed.), *Television and Women's Culture: The Politics of the Popular*. London: Sage, 144–57.

Probyn, E. 1988: New traditionalism and post-feminism. Television does the home. *Screen*, 31, 147–59.

—— 1992: Theorizing through the body. In L. Rakow (ed.), *Women Making Meaning: New Feminist Directions in Communication*. New York: Routledge, 83–99.

—— 1993: *Sexing the Self*. London: Routledge.

References

—— 1996: *Outside Belongings*. London: Routledge.

Putnam, R. D. 2000: *Bowling Alone: The Collapse and Revival of American Community*. New York: Touchstone book by Simon and Schuster.

Radway, J. 1984: *Reading the Romance: Women, Patriarchy and Popular Literature*. Chapel Hill, NC: University of North Carolina Press.

—— 1985: Variable literacies and interpretive communities. The functions of romance reading. In M. Gurevitch and M. R. Levy (eds.), *Mass Communication Review Yearbook*, vol. 5. Beverley Hills: Sage, 337–61.

—— 1988: Reception study. Ethnography and the problems of dispersed audiences and nomadic subjects. *Cultural Studies*, 2(3), 359–76.

Root, J. 1984: *Pictures of Women: Sexuality*. London: Pandora Press.

Rosaldo, R. 1999: Cultural citizenship, inequality and multiculturalism, In R. D. Torres, L. Miron and J. X. Inda (eds.), *Race, Identity and Citizenship: A Reader*. Oxford: Blackwell, 253–61.

Rowe, K. 1995: *The Unruly Woman: Gender and the Genres of Laughter*. Austin: University of Texas Press.

Rydin, I. 2003: Children's television reception. Perspectives on media literacy, identification and gender. In I. Rydin (ed.), *Media Fascinations: Perspectives on Young People's Meaning Making*. Goteborg: Nordicom, 77–93.

Said, E. W. 1987: *Orientalism*. New York: Random House/Vintage Books.

Segal, L. 1990: *Slow Motion: Changing Men, Changing Masculinities*. London: Virago.

Seidler, V. 1989: *Rediscovering Masculinity: Reason, Language and Sexuality*. London: Routledge.

—— 1991: *Recreating Sexual Politics: Men, Feminism and Politics*. London: Routledge.

Seiter, E. 1990: Making distinctions in TV audience research: case study of a troubling interview. *Cultural Studies*, 4(1), 61–84.

—— 1992: Semiotics, structuralism and television. In R. Allen (ed.), *Channels of Discourse, Reassembled: Television and Contemporary Criticism*, 2nd edn. London: Routledge, 31–66.

—— 1999: *Television and New Media Audiences*. Oxford: Oxford University Press.

Seltzer, M. 2001: *Serial Killers*. London: Routledge.

Shalit, W. 1999: Sex, sadness and the city. *Urbanities*, 4(4); accessed at www.city-journal.org, November 27, 2001.

Shklar, J. 1984: *Ordinary Vices*. Cambridge, MA: The Belknap Press of Harvard University Press.

Shohat, E. and Stam, R. 1994: *Unthinking Eurocentrism: Multiculturalism and the Media*. London: Routledge.

Soja, E. 1989: *Postmodern Geographies: The Reassertion of Space in Critical Social Theory*. London: Verso.

—— 1996: *Thirdspace: Journeys to Los Angeles and Other Real-and-Imagined Places*. Oxford: Blackwell.

Spangler, L. C. 1992: Buddies and pals. A history of male friendships on prime-time television. In S. Craig (ed.), *Men, Masculinity and the Media*. Newbury Park: Sage, 93–110.

Sparks, R. 1993: Inspector Morse: the last enemy. In G. Brandt (ed.), *British Television Drama in the 1980s*. Cambridge: Cambridge University Press.

Stacey, J. 1994: *Star Gazing: Hollywood Cinema and Female Spectatorship*. London: Routledge.

Stanton, G. 2000: The way of the body. Paul Stoller's search for sensuous ethnography. *European Journal of Cultural Studies*, 3(2), 259–77.

—— 2004: Writing culture in the 21st century. *European Journal of Cultural Studies*, 7(2), 155–65.

Steenbergen, B. van 1994: The condition of citizenship. An introduction. In B. van Steenbergen (ed.), *The Condition of Citizenship*. London: Sage, 1–9.

Stein, L. 2002: "Subject: Off-topic: Oh my God U.S. terrorism!" *Rosswell* fans respond to September 11th. *European Journal of Cultural Studies*, 5(4), 471–91.

Steinman, C. 1992: Gaze out of bounds: men watching men on television. In S. Craig (ed.), *Men, Masculinity and the Media*. Newbury Park: Sage, 199–214.

Stevenson, N. (ed.) 2001: *Culture and Citizenship*. London: Sage.

—— 2003: *Cultural Citizenship: Cosmopolitan Questions*. Maidenhead, Berkshire: Open University Press.

Storey, J. 1997: *An Introduction to Cultural Theory and Popular Culture*, 2nd edn. Harlow, Essex: Pearson.

Strate, L. 1992: Beer commercials: a manual on masculinity. In S. Craig (ed.), *Men, Masculinity and the Media*. Newbury Park: Sage, 78–92.

Street, J. 1997: *Politics and Popular Culture*. Cambridge: Polity Press.

Swanson, J. and James, D. 1996 *By a Woman's Hand: A Guide to Mystery Fiction by Women*. New York: Berkley Prime Crime.

Symons, J. 1985: *Dashiell Hammett*. San Diego: Harcourt Brace Jovanovich.

Tan, U. 2000: *Het Surinaamse legioen: Surinaamse voetballers in de eredividie 1954–2000*. Schoorl: Conserve.

Tasker, Y. 1998: *Working Girls: Gender and Sexuality in Popular Cinema*. London: Routledge.

Taylor, E. 1989: *Prime-Time Families: Television Culture in Postwar America*. Berkeley: University of California Press.

Tetzlaff, D. 1991: Divide and conquer: popular culture and social control in late capitalism. *Media, Culture and Society*, 13, 9–33.

Theweleit, K. 1980: *Männerphantasien*. Reinbek bei Hamburg: Rowohlt.

Thomas, L. 1995: In love with *Inspector Morse*. *Feminist Review*, 51, 1–25.

Thompson, E. 1963: *The Making of the English Working Class*. London: Victor Gollancz.

Tolson, A. 1978: *The Limits of Masculinity*. London: Tavistock.

Turner, B. S. (ed.) 1993: *Citizenship and Social Theory*. London: Sage.

—— 1994: Postmodern culture/modern citizens. In B. van Steenbergen (ed.), *The Condition of Citizenship*. London: Sage, 153–68.

—— 2001: Outline of a general theory of cultural citizenship. In N. Stevenson (ed.), *Culture and Citizenship*. London: Sage, 11–32.

Waites, B., Bennett, T. and Martin, G. (eds.) 1982: *Popular Culture: Past and Present*. London: Croom Helm, in association with the Open University Press.

Ward-Gailey, C. 1993: Mediated messages. Gender, class and cosmos in home video games. *Journal of Popular Culture*, 27(1), 81–97.

Warnke, G. 1987: *Gadamer: Hermeneutics, Tradition and Reason*. Cambridge: Polity Press.

Warren, C. A. B. 1985: *Gender Issues in Field Research*. Newbury Park: Sage.

Wernick, A. 1991: *Promotional Culture: Advertising, Ideology and Symbolic Expression*. London: Sage.

Wetherell, M. and Potter, J. 1988: Discourse analysis and the identification of interpretive repertoires. In C. Antaki (ed.), *Analysing Everyday Explanation: A Casebook of Methods*. London: Sage, 168–83.

Whannel, G. 1992: *Fields in Vision: Television Sport and Cultural Transformation*. London: Routledge.

—— 2001: *Media Sport Stars*. London: Routledge.

Whitlock, G. 1994: "Cop it sweet": lesbian crime fiction. In D. Hamer and B. Budge (eds.), *The Good, the Bad, the Gorgeous: Popular Culture's Romance with Lesbianism*. London: Pandora Press, 96–118.

Wilcox, R. and Williams, J. P. 1996: "What do you think?" The *X-files*, liminality, and gender pleasure. In D. Lavery, A. Hague and M. Cartwright (eds.), *Deny all Knowledge. Reading the X-files*. London: Faber and Faber, 99–119.

Williams, R. 1961: *The Long Revolution*. London: Chatto and Windus.

—— 1976: *Keywords*. London: Flamingo.

Willis, S. 1997: *High Contrast: Race and Gender in Contemporary Hollywood Film*. Durham, NC: Duke University Press.

Winner, D. 2001 [2000]: *Brilliant Orange: The Neurotic Genius of Dutch Football*. London: Bloomsbury.

Wit, T. de 2000: Gevoel zonder grenzen. Een onsentimentele inleiding. In T. de Wit (ed.), *Gevoel zonder grenzen: authentiek leven, medelijden en sentimentaliteit*. Nijmegen: Thomas More Academie, 7–31.

Young, I. M. 1987: Impartiality and the civic public. Some implications of feminist critiques of moral and political theory. In S. Benhabib and D. Cornell (eds.), *Feminism as Critique: Essays on the Politics of Gender in Late-Capitalist Societies*. Cambridge: Polity Press, 56–76.

—— 1990: The ideal of community and the politics of difference. In L. J. Nicholson (ed.), *Feminism/Postmodernism*. London: Routledge, 300–23.

Zimmerman, B. 1990: *The Safe Sea of Women: Lesbian Fiction 1969–1989*. Boston: Beacon Press.

Zoonen, L. van 2004: *Entertaining the Citizen: When Politics and Popular Culture Converge*. Lanham, MD: Rowman and Littlefield.

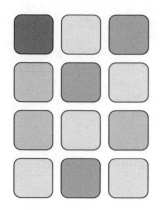

index